Blockchain and Cryptocurrency

A Blockchain and Cryptocurrency Guidebook for Everyone

By Dr. Liew

Copyright ® 2019 Liew Voon Kiong

All rights reserved. No part of this e-book may be reproduced in any form or by any means, without permission in writing from the author.

About the Author

Dr. Liew Voon Kiong holds a bachelor's degree in Mathematics, a master's degree in Management and a doctorate in Business Administration.

Dr. Liew is a sought-after **Blockchain Architect** by companies in the blockchain industry. He has played a lead role in designing and developing the native cryptocurrency of an incubation hub in Southeast Asia, as well as successfully getting it listed on a renowned exchange via an IEO campaign. He is also the Chief Strategy Officer of an Australian blockchain company that manages a crypto hedge fund.

Dr. Liew is also a blockchain researcher and has developed several use cases such as blockchain-powered supply chain management for the automotive and textile industries, building a blockchain-powered digital government, event and ticketing DApps, and more. He is skilled in setting up blockchain networks such as private Ethereum networks, as well as writing smart contracts using Solidity and creating DApps. He has also created a blockchain blog titled Blockchain Guide for Everyone (http://www.blockchainguide.biz/).

He is the head of the education subcommittee of the Access Blockchain Association of Malaysia, as well as a regular speaker in regional blockchain events and workshops.

Preface

Blockchain has been the most hyped technology in the last decade. Though blockchain technology is being overhyped somewhat, it has the potential to disrupt many existing industries. Many start-ups, MNCs, governments, non-profit organizations and individuals have developed and implemented blockchain-based applications.

Blockchain has crept into our daily life as we are bombarded with news from social media, web portals and advertisements. As a result, nearly everyone is talking about cryptocurrency today. However, most people still do not understand blockchain, the technology that powers cryptocurrencies. Therefore, I have written this book with the hope to help everyone understand blockchain technology and cryptocurrencies better.

This book is a comprehensive guide covering fundamental and advanced topics such as:

- Storing your cryptocurrencies securely in crypto wallets
- Smart contracts
- dApps

- Enterprise blockchain frameworks like Hyperledger and Corda
- How to conduct ICO and IEO
- DeFi
- Blockchain for financial services
- Blockchain for supply chain management
- Building a digital government with blockchain
- HR transformation powered by blockchain

The book also covers technical topics such as:

- Improving scalability with Plasma
- Storing blockchain data on IPFS
- Writing smart contracts with Solidity
- Developing DApps
- Developing ERC-20 tokens
- Setting up a private Ethereum blockchain
- Creating a multisig wallet
- Creating an automotive supply chain management blockchain platform with Hyperledger Fabric

I have also authored two books on DeFi, please check them out using the following links:

"DeFi Handbook: A Comprehensive Guide to Decentralized Finance" using the following links:

Paperback: https://www.amazon.com/dp/B08P4SPHGX
Kindle Version: https://www.amazon.com/dp/B08P9S9K68

"DEFI Investment Made Easy: A Beginner's Guide to Investing in Decentralized Finance" using the following links:

Paperback: https://www.amazon.com/dp/B08S2Y5GRS
Kindle Edition: https://www.amazon.com/dp/B08RZCYBX1

Table of Contents

Preface 3

Chapter 1 26

Introduction to Blockchain 26

    1.1 A Short History of Blockchain 27

    1.2 Blockchain in a Nutshell 28

    1.3 The Blockchain Network 30

    1.4 The Composition of Blockchain 33

    1.5 The Block Structure 35

    1.6 Block Height 36

    1.7 Nonce 36

    1.8 Difficulty 37

    1.9 Timestamp 37

    1.10 Hash 39

    1.11 Merkle Tree 40

Chapter 2 43

Bitcoin- The First Application of Blockchain 43

   2.1 A Brief History of Bitcoin 43

   2.2 What is a Digital Signature? 47

   2.3 What is Mining? 51

   2.4 The Purpose of Mining 51

   2.5 How Does Mining Work? 52

   2.6 Technical Explanation of Mining 53

   2.7 How to achieve Proof of Work? 57

Chapter 3 60

Ethereum - The Programmable Blockchain and DApps Platform 60

   3.1 A Brief History of Ethereum 60

      3.1.1 What is Ethereum? 61

      3.1.2 Gas, Gas Price and Gas Limit 62

      3.1.3 What is Gas? 62

      3.1.4 What is Gas Price? 62

      3.1.5 Gas Limit 64

3.2 Smart Contracts 65

    3.2.1 Solidity 67

    3.2.2 Writing and Deploying the Smart Contract 67

    3.2.3 The Smart Contract Code 68

    3.2.4 Understanding the Code 69

    3.2.5 Decentralized Applications (DApps) 70

Chapter 4 71

Storing your Cryptocurrencies 71

    4.1 Crypto Wallet 72

    4.2 Types of Crypto Wallets 73

        4.2.1 Full Node Wallet 73

        4.2.2 Hot Wallet 73

        4.2.3 Centralized Wallet 75

        4.2.4 Cold Wallet 75

    4.3 How Should You Store your Cryptocurrencies? 78

Chapter 5 - Crypto Fundraising 80

5.1 Initial Coin Offering (ICO) 81

5.2 Initial Exchange Offering (IEO) 83

    5.2.1 What is IEO? 84

    5.2.2 Advantages and Disadvantages of IEO 85

    Advantages 85

        Increased Investor Confidence 85

        Win-Win for The Project Owner and The Exchange 85

    Disadvantages of IEO 86

        Ambiguous Regulations and Restrictions 86

        All Investors Subjected to Stringent AML/KYC 86

        Limited Number of Tokens 86

        Botting Concerns 86

    5.2.2 How to Conduct an IEO? 87

        Step 1 Design the Business Model 87

        Step 2 Assemble a Formidable Team 87

Step 3 Preparing the Whitepaper and Other Documents.88

Step 4 Develop the Token 89

Step 5 Marketing 89

Step 6 Engage a Crypto Exchange 90

5.3 Security Token Offering (STO) 90

Chapter 6 94

Hyperledger - A Framework for Enterprise Blockchain 94

6.1 The Mission of Hyperledger 95

6.2 The Hyperledger Greenhouse 96

6.3 Open Source and Open Governance 97

6.4 Hyperledger Fabric 98

6.5 The Hyperledger Fabric Architecture 99

6.6 Consensus Protocol 100

6.7 Hyperledger Fabric Network 101

6.7.1 Peers 102

6.7.2 Ordering Service 102

  6.7.3 The Transaction Workflow 103

    Phase 1 Transaction Endorsement 103

    Phase 2 Transactions Simulation 104

    Phase 3 Ordering 105

    Phase 4 Transaction Validation 106

  6.7.4 Channels 106

  6.7.6 Membership Service Provider (MSP) 108

  6.7.7 The Authentication Process 109

Chapter 7 111

Blockless Distributed Ledger Technologies (DLT) 111

  7.1 IOTA 111

    7.1.1 The Vision Of IOTA 112

    7.1.2 The Tangle 113

    7.1.3 The Core Principles 113

    7.1.4 The Tangle Structure 114

    7.1.5 Unweighted Random Walk Algorithm 118

- 7.1.6 The Lazy Tips 119
- 7.1.7 Weighted Random Walk 120
- 7.1.8 The Parameter Alpha 121
- 7.2 R3 Corda 122
  - 7.2.1 Key Concepts of Corda 123
  - 7.2.2 The Corda Architecture 124
  - 7.2.3 The Corda Network 124
  - 7.2.4 How does Corda differ from other DLT Platforms? 125
  - 7.2.5 The Doorman 126

Chapter 8 127

Blockchain-Powered Financial Services 127

- 8.1 Cross-Border Money Transfer 127
- 8.2 Blockchain-Based P2P Lending 130
  - 8.2.1 The Hybrid P2P Lending Model 131
    - SALT 132
    - NEXO 133

- 8.2.2. Pure Cryptocurrency P2P Lending Model 135
  - ETHLend 135
  - Elix 136
- 8.3 Crypto Fund Management 137
  - 8.3.1 Bitwise 10 Private Index Fund 138
  - 8.3.2 Crypto20 140
  - 8.3.3 Coinbase 140
  - 8.3.4 Hodlbot 141

Chapter 9 Transaction and Provenance Tracking 142

- 9.1 Transaction Tracking 142
- 9.2 Provenance tracking and record keeping 143

Chapter 10 145

Blockchain-Powered Supply Chain Management 145

- Case 1 Blockchain-Powered Smart Supply Chain Management - Auto Parts Business Case Study 145
  - 10.1 Automotive Supply Chain Issues 145

10.2 Possible Benefits of Blockchain Usage in Automotive SCM 147

10.2.1 Identification and Tracking of Automotive Spare Parts 147

Counterfeit Protection – Verifying Authenticity and Origin 147

Protection of Aftermarket Business 148

Spare Parts Liability Resolution 148

Vehicle Recall Optimization 149

10.2.2 Optimizing the Supply Chain Process 149

Inbound Logistics and Smart Manufacturing 149

Outbound Logistics Planning 150

10.2.3 Business Model Innovation 150

Car Personalization and Customer Engagement 150

Dynamic Pricing Models in Automotive Insurance and Leasing 150

Digital Car Wallet 151

Car-to-Infrastructure Transactions 151

10.2 Current Auto Parts SCM Model 152

10.3 The Proposed Blockchain SSCM Model 152

Case 2 Blockchain-Powered Smart Supply Chain Management - Textile Industry 155

10.4 The Blockchain Solution 159

Chapter 11 161

Building a Digital Government Powered by Blockchain 161

The Proposed Model of a Digital Government Powered by Blockchain 163

11.1 National Digital Id Blockchain Net 163

11.2 A Short History of POA 163

11.3 Advantages of POA Consensus Protocol 164

11.4 The National Digital ID Blockchain Net Notary Nodes 164

11.5 The Role of Notary Nodes 165

11.6 Responsibilities of Notary Nodes 165

11.7 The Role of Registration Nodes 166

11.8 Government Agency Nodes 166

11.9 Storing Biometric Data 167

11.10 Data Storage in National Digital ID Blockchain Net
.... 167

Chapter 12 168

HR Digital Transformation-powered by Blockchain 168

12.1 Talent sourcing and management 169

12.2 Targeting productivity gains 169

12.3 Cross-border payments and mobility 170

12.4 Fraud prevention, cybersecurity, and data protection
.... 170

12.5 HR Blockchain Use Cases 171

12.5.1 ChronoBank.io 171

12.5.2 PeaCounts 172

12.5.3 bitWage 172

Chapter 13 174

17

Decentralized Finance 174

    13.1 The Advantages of DeFi 174

        13.1.1 Maintain Full Control of Your Own Digital Assets 174

        13.1.2 Increased Accessibility 175

        13.1.3 Opportunity to Own a Portion of An Expensive Asset 175

        13.1.4 Transparency 176

    13.2 Types of DeFi Products 176

        13.2.1 Maker DAO 178

        13.2.3 AAVE-The Decentralized Lending and Borrowing Platform 180

        13.2.3 Compound-A DeFi Money Market 182

        13.2.4 dYdX, a Lending, Borrowing and Trading Platform . 183

Chapter 14 185

Building Blockchain for Business 185

    14.1 Identify a suitable use case 186

        14.1.1 Data Authentication & Verification 187

- 14.1.2 Digital Asset Management 188
- 14.1.3 Smart Contracts 189
- 14.2 Assemble your Team 190
- 14.3 Designing the Blockchain Architecture 191

Chapter 15 Storing Data on Blockchain 194

- 15.1 What is IPFS? 195
- 15.2 Blockchain and IPFS 196

Chapter 16 Plasma-The Solution for Security and Scalability 198

- 16.1 The Scalability Issue 198
- 16.2 Plasma 199
- 16.3 The Plasma Structure 199
- 16.4 How does Plasma Works? 200
- 16.5 State Channels 201
- 16.6 Steps in Implementing Plasma 201
- 16.7 Plasma Exits 202

TECHNICAL SECTION 204

Chapter 17 Solidity and Smart Contracts 205

    17.1 Choosing the IDE to Develop Smart Contracts 205

    17.2 Writing Your First Smart Contract in Solidity 206

        17.2.1 Assigning variables 207

        17.2.2 Access Modifier 207

    17.3 The Remix IDE 208

17.4 Creating a cryptocurrency using Solidity 213

Chapter 18 218

Decentralized Applications (DApps) 218

    18.1 Event Management and Ticketing DApp 218

    18.2 Use Cases 220

        18.2.1 BitTicket 220

        18.2.2 GUTS 221

        18.2.3 LAVA 222

        18.2.4 PouchNATION 222

        18.2.5 EventChain 223

18.2.6 Event Management and Ticketing Platform - A Conceptual Model 224

18.3 Developing a DApp - KittyChain Shop 226

18.3.1 Steps to Build the Dapp 227

Step 1 Setting Up the Development Environment 227

Step 2 Creating the Project Using a Truffle Box 227

Step 3 writing the smart contract 229

Step 4 Compiling and Migrating the Smart Contract 230

Step 5 Testing the smart contract 234

Step 6 Creating a User Interface to Interact with The Smart Contract 236

Step 7 Instantiating the Contract 237

Step 8 Getting the Adopted Pets and Updating The UI ... 238

Step 9 Handling the Adopt() Function 238

Step 10 Interacting with The Dapp In A Browser 239

Step 11 Installing and Configuring Lite-Server 242

Chapter 19 247

Developing an Ethereum Cryptocurrency on Windows 247

    I. Installation of the Packages 248

        Step1: Install Chocolatey 248

        Step 2 Install Visual Studio Code, Git and Node.Js 249

        Step 3 Install Truffle Framework 250

    II. Configuring VS Code for Ethereum Blockchain Development 251

        Step 1 Choose the Folder for Your Project 251

        Step 2 Install Solidity in The Vs Code IDE 252

        Step 3 Install Material Icon Theme 252

    III. Creating a Blockchain Application 252

    IV Deploying the Contract 256

    V Interacting with the contract with Web3 259

    Checking Balance with the getBalance() method 261

    Send Coin with the sendCoin Function 263

Debugging the Transaction 265

VI Deploying Your MetaCoin Contract with Truffle 268

    Deploy to Ganache 268

    Deploy to Ropsten 271

    Deploy to Rinkeby 272

Chapter 20 273

Creating Your Own Token for ICO 273

Chapter 21 Setting up a Private Ethereum Blockchain Network on Windows 283

    21.1 Prerequisites 283

    21.2 Creating the Genesis Block 284

    21.3 Starting the Private Network 286

    21.4 Launching the Ethereum Wallet 287

    21.5 Creating a New Account Address 287

    21.6 Start Mining 288

    21.7 Stop Mining 289

Chapter 22 291

Deploying Smart Contracts on Ropsten Testnet through Ethereum Remix 291

    Step 1 292

    Step 2 292

    Step 3 296

Chapter 23 301

Creating Multisig Wallet 301

    23.1 Steps in Creating a Multisig Wallet 302

        Step 1 Installation of Electrum 302

        Step 2 Decide the number of co-signers 302

        Step 3 Creating the multisig Wallet 303

Chapter 24 316

Setting up Automotive Smart Supply Chain Management(SSCM) with Hyperledger Fabric 316

    24.1 Technical Requirements 316

    24.2 Installing cURL 317

24.3 Installing Docker 317

24.4 Uninstall old versions 318

24.5 Install using the repository 318

24.6 Set Up the Repository 318

24.7 Install Docker Ce 320

24.8 Install Docker Compose 321

24.9 Installing Go Language 323

24.10 Installing Hyperledger Fabric Docker Images and Binaries 324

24.11 Installing the Automotive Supply Chain Sample 325

24.12 Query All Part Recorded 327

24.13 Query a Specific Part Recorded 327

24.15 Record a Part 328

Appendix 330

White Paper#1 Blockchain Based School Ecosystem 330

    Abstract 330

25

White Paper#2 Chi Crypto Index fund 340

    Abstract 340

    References 378

Chapter 1

Introduction to Blockchain

Blockchain has been the most hyped technology in the last decade. A recent World Economic Forum report predicts that by 2025, 10% of GDP will be generated by blockchain. Though blockchain technology is being overhyped somewhat, it has the potential to disrupt many existing industries. Start-ups, MNCs, governments, non-profit organizations and even individuals have already developed and implemented blockchain-based applications. For example, Walmart has collaborated with IBM to implement blockchain for food traceability as part of its food safety initiative. Therefore everyone, particularly business owners and enterprises, should take notice of this trend.

Blockchain has slowly crept into our daily life as we are bombarded with news from social media, web portals and advertisements. As a result, nearly everyone is talking about cryptocurrency today. In fact, many have invested in cryptocurrencies such as Bitcoin, Ethereum and other altcoins. While many people have made lots of money, many others have experienced substantial losses too. However, most people still do not understand blockchain, the technology that powers cryptocurrency. Therefore, I have written this book with the aim to help everyone understand blockchain technology and cryptocurrency better.

1.1 A Short History of Blockchain

To begin with, the first blockchain was invented by Satoshi Nakamoto in 2008 to serve as the public transaction ledger of the cryptocurrency Bitcoin. That year, he or she posted a paper called Bitcoin – A Peer to Peer Electronic Cash System to a mailing list discussion on cryptography. Therefore, we can say that Satoshi Nakamoto invented Blockchain and Bitcoin as its application. However, Satoshi Nakamoto's real identity remains a mystery to this day. In fact, Satoshi Nakamoto may not be a person, but a group of people.

On the other hand, Satoshi Nakamoto might not be the first person to come up with the idea of blockchain technology. The idea behind blockchain technology can be traced back to 1991, when Stuart Haber and W. Scott Stornetta (Scott-Briggs, 2018) conceived the idea of a cryptographically secured chain of blocks. In 1992, they incorporated Merkle trees into the design, allowing several documents to be collected into a block.

In addition, there were also previous attempts at creating online currencies with ledgers secured by encryption, such as B-Money and Bit Gold. B-money was an early proposal created by Wei Dai for an "anonymous, distributed electronic cash system". His essay was published on the Cypherpunks mailing list in November 1998. Even Satoshi Nakamoto referenced B-Money when he invented Bitcoin. Another precursor of Bitcoin is Bit Gold, invented by Nick Szabo in 1998. Bit Gold is a decentralized digital currency but was never implemented.

However, blockchain technology did not gain traction until the emergence of Bitcoin. Since its debut in 2009, the price of Bitcoin has skyrocketed, though it turned south in the year 2018. Many people are actively involved in mining activities in the hopes of getting rich quick. From 2011 onwards, many alternative cryptocurrencies or altcoins have emerged, such as Ethereum, EOS, Ripple, Ethereum Classic (ETC), XRP, Litecoin and more. Currently, there are over 1,000 cryptocurrencies in circulation with new ones frequently appearing.

None of the cryptocurrencies came close to challenging Bitcoin until the invention of Ethereum by Vitalik Buterin in 2013. The Ethereum platform introduced the concept of smart contracts and the cryptocurrency Ether. It is also a platform for ICO, crypto crowdfunding. I shall elaborate on Ethereum and ICO in a later chapter.

1.2 Blockchain in a Nutshell

A blockchain is a distributed and decentralized digital ledger that can be used to record transactions and data across numerous computers in a decentralized peer-to-peer network. We can also define a blockchain as a distributed encrypted database, like a spreadsheet that is duplicated thousands of times across a network of computers. This network is designed to regularly update this spreadsheet. It is a subset of **distributed ledger technologies (DLT)**.

The main feature of blockchain is decentralization. To understand what decentralization is, first we need to understand the traditional centralized operation mode. For example, if you go to the supermarket to buy something, you pay with a credit card when you check out. This process requires the approval of a third party, the bank. The transaction is completed after the bank approves it. However, if you use the blockchain platform to perform a transaction, you do not need a third party. The buyer and the seller can trade directly and seamlessly in a transparent and secure blockchain ecosystem.

Another feature of the blockchain is that all participants in the network do not need to establish any trust relationships to perform transactions. It relies on cryptographic authentication technology, a decentralized network, and a consensus mechanism to ensure the security and integrity of funds and information. Therefore, information on the blockchain is highly transparent and not easily falsified. Thus, the blockchain system is particularly suitable for the financial industry. Indeed, blockchain is an incorruptible digital ledger of economic transactions that can record not only financial transactions but pretty much everything of value ((Don Tapscott, 2017).

In short, blockchain has the following advantages:

- Transparent
- Secure
- Decentralized
- Democratic

- Efficient
- Auditable
- Immutable
- Consensus

1.3 The Blockchain Network

The blockchain network is a peer-to-peer decentralized network. The peers, also known as nodes, are connected to this network in a synchronous way. The nodes can be a desktop, a laptop, a mobile phone, a mining rig, servers, or any other electronic devices. These nodes form the foundation of the blockchain network. They provide computing resources like disk storage space to keep the network alive and to maintain its integrity and security, and they do it voluntarily.

The decentralized peer-to-peer network is different from the traditional centralized client-server network, as shown in Figure 1.1 and Figure 1.2.

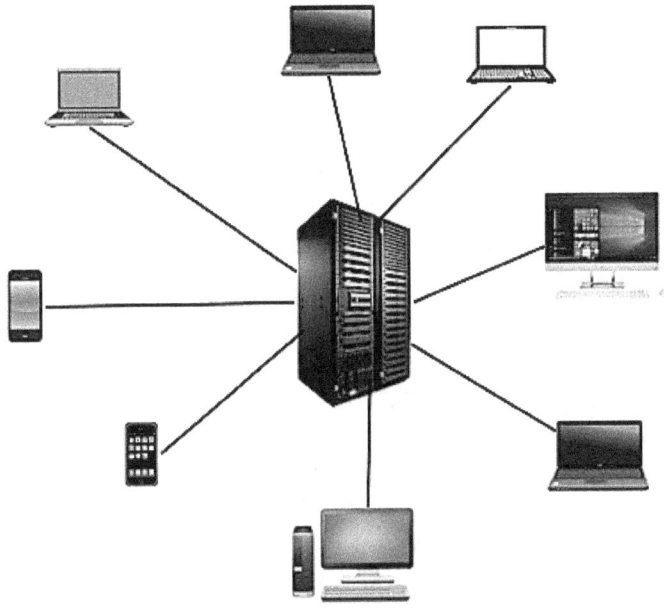

Figure 1.1 Centralized Client-Server Network

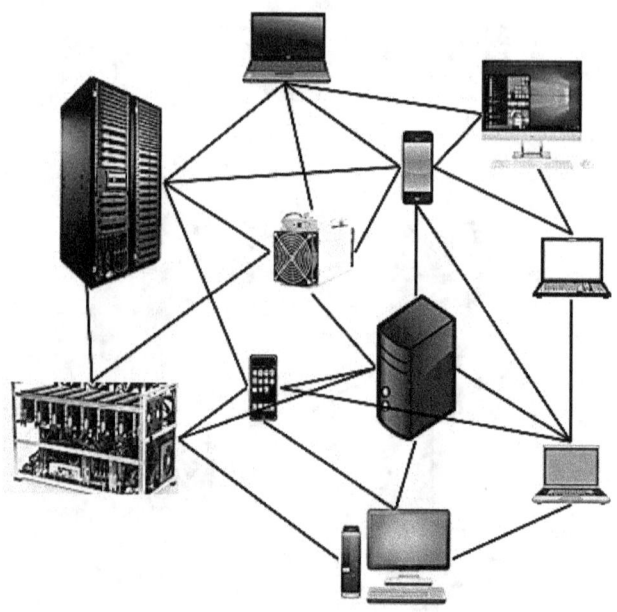

Figure 1.2 Decentralized Peer-to-Peer Network

A centralized network has an authoritative central point of control. All the clients are connected to this single point and all their data are stored in the central server. The client has not much control over how the central authority will use his or her data.

A good example is your bank account. The bank keeps your money, manages your account, and records all your transactions. They can also lend your money to other clients. Although this system has been quite reliable, it is prone to the vulnerability of a single point of failure. For example, if a bank's central server is hacked, all the accounts will be compromised.

On the contrary, in the peer-to-peer decentralized network, all the peers work together to upkeep the network via a consensus mechanism. The peers have 100% control of their data and how the data could be used. In addition, they do not need a third party or a middle entity to perform transactions.

More importantly, it eliminates the vulnerability of a single point of failure. If a node is hacked, only the data belonging to that node would be compromised while all other nodes would keep a copy of the ledger. Moreover, the cryptographic hashing algorithm makes it extremely difficult to hack the blockchain.

To ensure the nodes are motivated to maintain the network, blockchain incentivizes the nodes through a mechanism known as mining. By engaging in mining activities, the successful miners will be rewarded with cryptocurrencies such as Bitcoin, Ethereum or other coins.

1.4 The Composition of Blockchain

A blockchain is comprised of a chronological chain of blocks. The first block is known as the genesis block. A block refers to a set of transactions that are bundled together and appended to the blockchain. The second block is appended to the genesis block, the third block is appended to the second block and so forth, as shown in Figure 1.3.

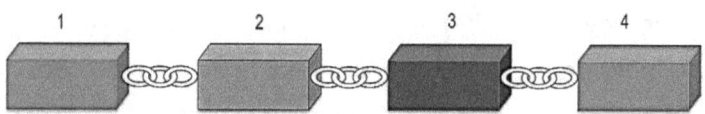

Figure 1.3 The Blockchain Structure

Every node in the network stores a copy of the distributed ledgers, or the blockchain, as shown in Figure 1.4.

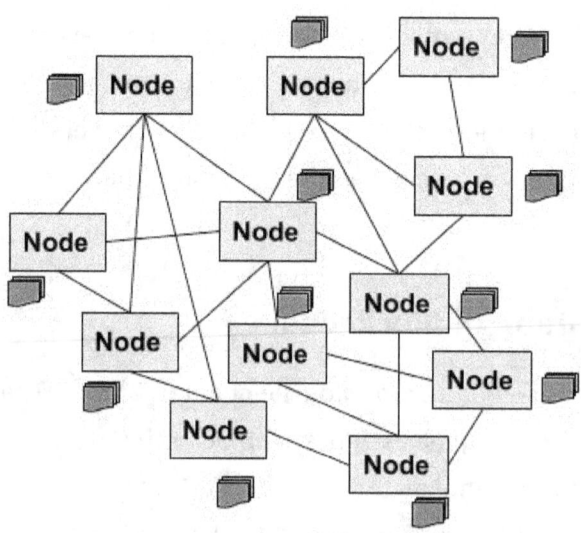

Figure 1.4 The Blockchain Network

1.5 The Block Structure

A block consists mainly of the block header containing metadata and a list of transactions appended to the block header. The blockchain metadata consists of information such as Hash, Block Height, Nonce, Difficulty, Timestamp and more, as shown in Figure 1.5.

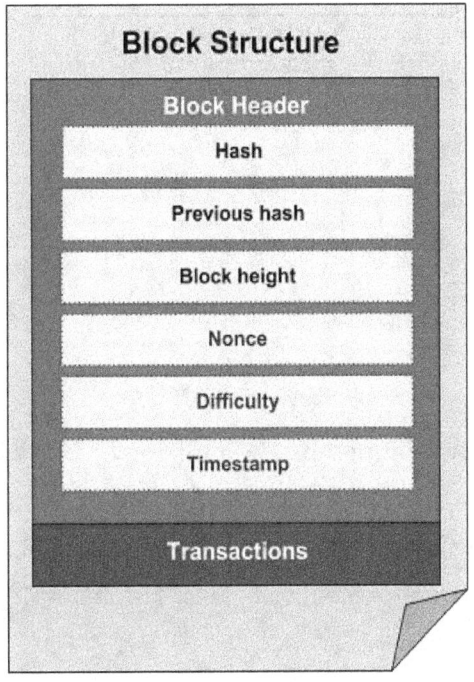

Figure 1.5 The Block Structure

Moreover, there is other information in the block, such as rewards, transaction fees and so on. If you want to find out the latest Bitcoin block information, you can browse the following link:

https://www.blockchain.com/explorer

Figure 1.6 shows the real data of Bitcoin block #631977

Home / Block - 0000000000000000000e76cc39b4da8ff77d9987d253cca33995003e650723f1					
Summary					
Height	631,977	Version	0x37ffe000	Block Hash	000
Confirmations	1	Difficulty	19.46 T / 15.14 T	Prev Block	000
Size	1,563,900 Bytes	Bits	0x171297f6	Next Block	
Stripped Size	809,809 Bytes	Nonce	0x157d9ff2	Merkle Root	7de
Weight	3,993,327	Relayed By	58COIN&1THash		
Tx Count	1,905	Time	2020-05-28 07:27:09	Other Explorers	

Figure 1.6

1.6 Block Height

The block height of a block is defined as the number of blocks preceding it in the blockchain (Investopedia). It is calculated as the length of the blockchain minus one. Genesis block has a block height of zero as it does not have preceding blocks. For example, the height of block 631977 is 631977.

1.7 Nonce

A nonce is a random number the miners use to solve a mathematical puzzle in the mining process, which is also known as proof of work. The nonce in the Bitcoin block is a 32-bit (4-byte) field whose value is adjusted by the miner to make the hash of the block smaller than or equal to the current target of the network. The concept of proof of work will be explained in a later chapter.

1.8 Difficulty

Difficulty is a value that measures the degree of difficulty to find a hash value for a given target, which represents the difficulty of mining. The value of difficulty will be changed once every 2016 blocks. The value will usually increase.

1.9 Timestamp

A timestamp is a sequence of characters or encoded information identifying when a certain event occurred, usually giving date and time of day. The term derives from rubber stamps used in offices to stamp the current date, and sometimes time, in ink on paper documents, to record when the document was received, as shown in Figure 1.7.

Figure 1.7 Timestamp (Image adapted from Wikipedia)

In this digital age, the term has been expanded to refer to the date and time information attached to digital data. For example, computer files contain timestamps that tell when the file was created and when was it last updated. Digital cameras add timestamps to the pictures by recording the date and time the pictures were taken.

The Unix timestamp is the number of seconds passed since midnight on January 1, 1970 (UTC / GMT), ignoring leap seconds. When I wrote this book, the Unix timestamp was 1540130658. You can check the current timestamp at the link below:

https://www.unixtimestamp.com/

Timestamping is an important feature of blockchain technology. Each block is timestamped, with each new block referring to the previous block using the cryptographic hash. Combined with cryptographic hashes, this time stamped chain of blocks provides an immutable record of all transactions in the blockchain, as shown in Figure 1.8:

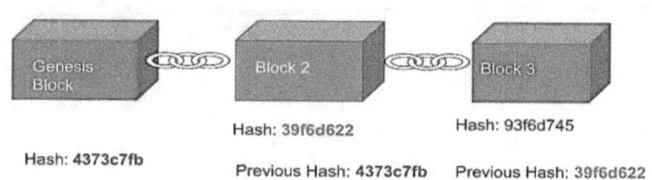

Figure 1.8

1.10 Hash

A hash or hash value is the result of a hash function. A hash function takes an input of any length, performs an algorithmic transformation, and produces an alphanumeric value of a predetermined length. The input could be a spreadsheet file, a music file, a video file, an image file, a financial statement, an invoice, a contract and more.

A hash value consists of 256 randomly generated bits, which are represented with 64 hexadecimal characters. Here is an example: "4373c7fb1437035365d9228c77eca2cfd240523e274163e78c1e ba11effd8b38"

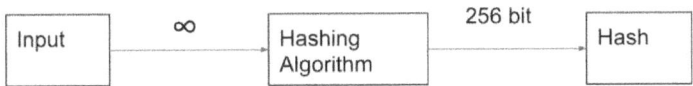

Figure 1.9 Hash

You can generate a hash online using the following link:

https://passwordsgenerator.net/sha256-hash-generator/

A hash has the following properties:

- A given input has a precisely predictable output of a specified length, usually but not necessarily much shorter than the input.

- Even if the input is only slightly changed, the output differs dramatically.
- If the hash function is of the cryptographic variety, it is exceedingly difficult, if not practically impossible, to infer the original input given only the output. The degree of difficulty/impossibility depends on the strength of the encryption used.

Every transaction occurring on the blockchain network is encoded with a hashing algorithm to produce a hash that is impossible to decrypt. Hashes are used to represent the current state of the blockchain. It means all the transactions that have taken place so far have been hashed, and the resulting output hash represents the current state of the blockchain. The hash is used for all parties to agree that the state is the same.

The purpose of the hash is for validation. Data on the blockchain is "hashed" in each block. Each block is linked with the previous block via the hash value. If someone tampers with a block, everyone will know the block is corrupted. Therefore, it preserves the integrity and immutability of the blockchain.

1.11 Merkle Tree

Merkle tree is one of the metadata in a block of the blockchain. In computer science, the Merkle tree is a branching data structure that is used to store hashes of individual data in a large dataset. The purpose is to make the verification of the dataset efficient and fast. It is an anti-tamper mechanism to ensure that the large dataset has not been tampered with.

In blockchain, the Merkle tree(also known as the hash tree) encodes the blockchain data in an efficient and secure manner. Every transaction occurring on the blockchain network is subjected to a hashing algorithm to produce a hash, as shown in Figure 1.9. Therefore, every transaction has a hash associated with it.

As there are thousands of transactions stored on a block, it will be very time consuming if every node must deal with hundreds of thousands of transactions across the blockchain, synchronization and mining will take a long time. To solve this issue, all the transactions hashes in the block are also hashed. As illustrated in the following figure, two hashes are hashed into a single hash, as shown in Figure 1.10

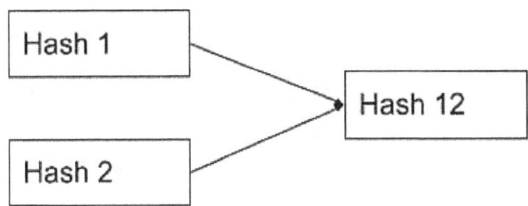

Figure 1.10

These hashes are not stored in a sequential order on the block, rather in the form of a tree-like structure such that each hash is linked to its parent following a parent-child tree-like relation. The hashing will go on until it produces a singular hash, the **Merkle root**. This Merkle root is the hash of the block and it is stored on the header of the block. The process is illustrated in Figure 1.11.

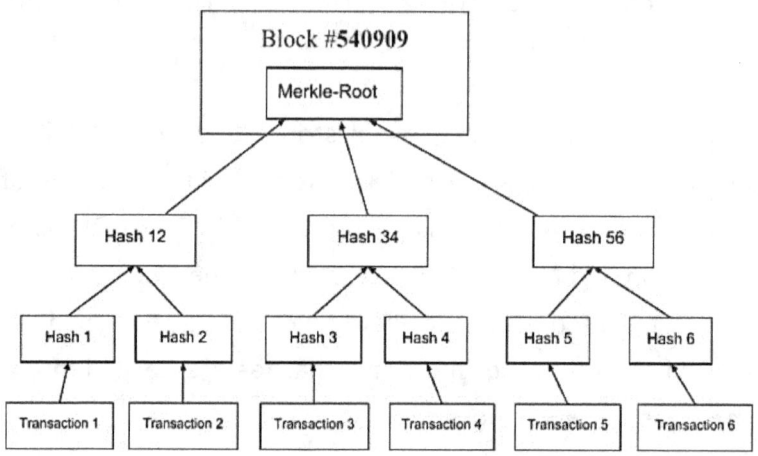

Figure 1.11

The Merkle Tree structure will enable the quick verification of blockchain data and quick movement of large amounts of data from one computer node to the other on the peer-to-peer blockchain network.

Chapter 2

Bitcoin- The First Application of Blockchain

2.1 A Brief History of Bitcoin

In contrary to popular belief, the idea of creating a digital money without a trusted third party was not conceived by Satoshi Nakamoto, but was proposed by advocates such as Wei Dai and Nick Szabo more than a decade before the successful launch of Bitcoin. The biggest issue surrounding the implementation of a decentralized digital currency is double spending. Double-spending is a potential problem in which the same digital currency can be spent more than once.

As we know, we can send any number of an electronic copy of a digital asset to anyone. This includes sending emails, documents, music files, video files and more. However, we cannot do the same with digital money. If you pay someone using cash, the value of money is transferred to another party and the money no longer belongs to you. However, if you send someone digital money, you still can retain the same amount of money and can send it to someone else. In fact, there is no limit to how many copies of the digital money you can send.

Wei Dai, a computer engineer and cypherpunk, tried to solve the double-spending issue by publishing a paper on cryptocurrency with the title "b-money, an anonymous, distributed electronic cash system" in 1998. In the paper, Dai outlines the basic properties of all modern-day cryptocurrency systems as *"a scheme for a group of untraceable digital pseudonyms to pay each other with money and to enforce contracts amongst themselves without outside help"*. In the same year, Szabo designed a mechanism for a decentralized digital currency he called "Bit Gold". Though Bit Gold was never implemented, it has been called a direct precursor to the Bitcoin architecture.

Satoshi sent an email to Wei Dai in the year 2008 to announce that he had solved the double-spending issue and was ready to implement the first decentralized digital cash without the need of a trusted third party. His email (Branwen) is as follows:

"From: "Satoshi Nakamoto" <satoshi@anonymousspeech.com>

Sent: Friday, August 22, 2008 4:38 PM

To: "Wei Dai" <weidai@ibiblio.org>

Cc: "Satoshi Nakamoto" <satoshi@anonymousspeech.com>

Subject: Citation of your b-money page

I was very interested to read your b-money page. I'm getting ready to release a paper that expands on your ideas into a complete working system. Adam Back (hashcash.org) noticed the similarities and pointed me to your site.

I need to find out the year of publication of your b-money page for the citation in my paper. It will look like:

[1] W. Dai, "b-money," http://www.weidai.com/bmoney.txt, (2006?).

You can download a pre-release draft at

http://www.upload.ae/file/6157/ecash-pdf.html   Feel free to forward it to anyone else you think would be interested.

Title: Electronic Cash Without a Trusted Third Party

Abstract: A purely peer-to-peer version of electronic cash would allow online payments to be sent directly from one party to another without the burdens of going through a financial institution. Digital signatures offer part of the solution, but the main benefits are lost if a trusted party is still required to prevent double-spending. We propose a solution to the double-spending problem using a peer-to-peer network. The network timestamps transactions by hashing them into an ongoing chain of hash-based proof-of-work, forming a record that cannot be changed without redoing the proof-of-work. The longest chain not only serves as proof of the sequence of events witnessed, but proof that it came from the largest pool of CPU power.

As long as honest nodes control the most CPU power on the network, they can generate the longest chain and outpace any attackers. The network itself requires minimal structure. Messages are broadcasted on a best effort basis, and nodes can leave and rejoin the network at will, accepting the longest proof-of-work chain as proof of what happened while they were gone.

Satoshi"

Later in the same year on 31 October 2008, he published the Bitcoin whitepaper titled "Bitcoin: A Peer-to-Peer Electronic Cash System". This whitepaper is now available for download from the link https://bitcoin.org/bitcoin.pdf.

Bitcoin's peer-to-peer electronic cash system allows a party to send payments to another party directly using digital signatures, without the need to go through a trusted third party such as a bank or a financial institution. However, digital signatures alone still cannot avoid the issue of double spending. Therefore, Satoshi proposed a solution to the double-spending problem using a peer-to-peer distributed timestamp server to generate computational proof of the chronological order of transactions (a.k.a. proof of work), in a process generally known as mining. The system is secure if honest nodes collectively control more CPU power than any cooperating group of attacker nodes. We shall describe digital signatures and mining in the following paragraphs.

2.2 What is a Digital Signature?

The Bitcoin whitepaper defines an electronic coin as a chain of digital signatures. Each owner transfers the coin to the next by digitally signing a hash of the previous transaction and the public key of the next owner and adding these to the end of the coin. A payee can verify the signatures to verify the chain of ownership.

According to Wikipedia,

"A digital signature is a mathematical scheme for presenting the authenticity of digital messages or documents. A valid digital signature gives a recipient reason to believe that the message was created by a known sender (authentication), that the sender cannot deny having sent the message (non-repudiation), and that the message was not altered in transit (integrity)."

A digital signature is generated using asymmetric cryptography, which is more secure than handwritten signatures that can be easily forged. It is used to prove that a message originates from a specific individual and not from someone else.

Asymmetric cryptography, also known as public key cryptography (PKI), uses public and private keys to encrypt and decrypt data. In the asymmetric encryption system, a user generates the key pair, which comprises a public key and a private key using a known algorithm. The public key and private key are associated with each other via a mathematical relationship.

The public key is meant to be distributed publicly to serve as an address to receive messages (including cryptocurrencies) from other users, like your Bitcoin or Ethereum address. The private key is meant to be kept secret and is used by the sender to send digitally signed messages to other users. The signature is included in the message so that the recipient can verify using the sender's public key. This way, the recipient can be sure that only the sender could have sent this message key pair, which is a public key and a private key using a known algorithm. For example, every transaction on the blockchain is digitally signed by the sender using their private key. This signature ensures that only the owner of the account can move money out of the account.

The steps are explained below:

Step 1 Signing the message with the private key

To create a digital signature, the user can use a signing software to create a one-way hash of the electronic data. The private key is then used to encrypt the hash. The encrypted hash, along with other information, is the digital signature. The process of creating a digital signature is illustrated in Figure 2.1.

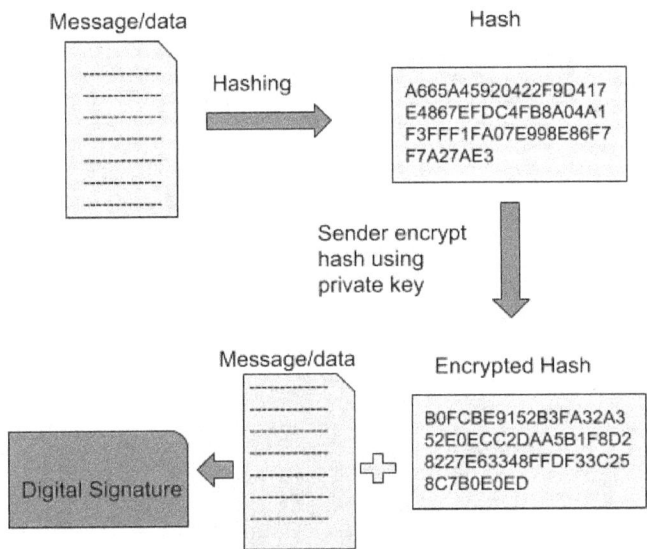

Figure 2.1 Creating Digital Signature

Step 2 Verifying the message with the public key

To verify the message, the receiver uses the sender's public key to decrypt the hash. If this decrypted hash matches a second computed hash of the same data, it proves that the data has not changed since it was signed. If the two hashes do not match, the data has either been tampered with in some way or the signature was created with a private key that does not correspond to the public key presented by the sender. The verification process is illustrated in the following figure:

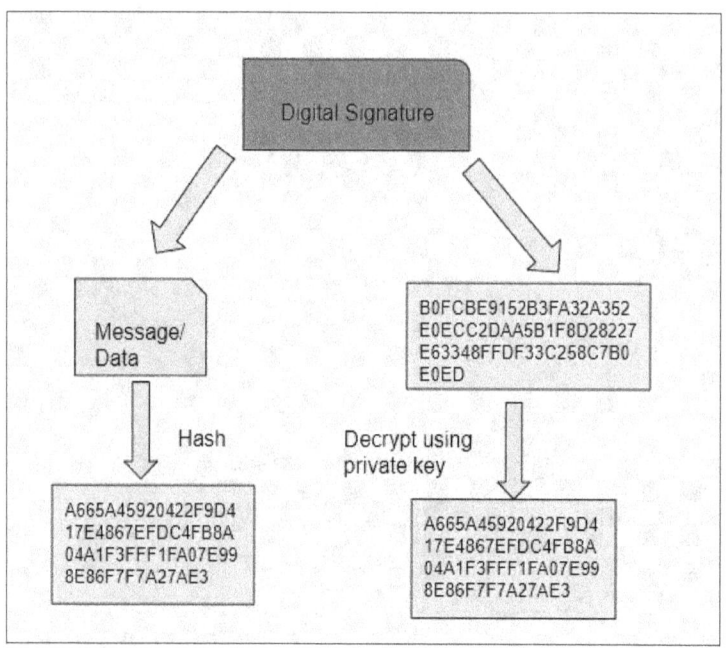

Figure 2.2 Verification Process

To sum it all, blockchain could not exist without hashing and digital signatures. Hashing provides a way for everyone on the blockchain to agree on the current world state, while digital signatures provide a way to ensure that all transactions are only made by the rightful owners. We rely on these two properties to ensure that the blockchain has not been corrupted or compromised.

2.3 What is Mining?

According to Investopedia,

"Bitcoin mining is the process by which transactions are verified and added to the public ledger, known as the blockchain, and the means through which new bitcoins are released. Anyone with access to the internet and suitable hardware can participate in mining. The mining process involves compiling recent transactions into blocks and trying to solve a computationally difficult puzzle. The participant who first solves the puzzle gets to place the next block on the block chain and claim the rewards. The rewards, which incentivize mining, are both the transaction fees associated with the transactions compiled in the block as well as newly released bitcoin. "

As quoted in the Bitcoin whitepaper, the continuous addition of a constant amount of new coins is like gold miners expending resources to add gold to circulation, therefore the term mining.

While Bitcoin is the first cryptocurrency generated using the mining process, it is certainly not the only platform that has adopted this algorithm. Most of the alternative coins (altcoins) are using the mining algorithm to generate their crypto money.

2.4 The Purpose of Mining

Generally, people think of mining in blockchain to obtain bitcoins or other cryptocurrencies. While this is partially true, it is not the main purpose of mining. In fact, the main objective of mining is to ensure the perpetuity and security of the decentralized network. The network comprises nodes that store the distributed ledgers in the form of the blockchain. Bitcoins are awarded to the miners for their effort in maintaining the integrity of the blockchain by validating the transactions in the blockchain. Because of the reward system, miners (nodes) will stay on in the network and help to prevent network downtime. Just imagine: if there was no reward, nobody would want to connect to the network, and it would just cease to exist.

2.5 How Does Mining Work?

The mining process starts when miners are trying to validate new transactions and record them on the blockchain. The miners are competing to solve a difficult mathematical puzzle based on a cryptographic hash algorithm. The solution found is called the **Proof of Work**, a.k.a. **PoW**. When a block is 'solved', all the transactions contained in the candidate block are considered validated, and the new block is confirmed. This new block will be appended to the blockchain. The time taken to confirm a new block is approximately 10 minutes for Bitcoin, but for other coins it is much faster. So, if you send or receive bitcoins, it will take approximately 10 minutes for the transaction to be confirmed.

Miners receive a reward when they solve the complex mathematical problem. There are two types of rewards: new bitcoins and transaction fees. The number of bitcoins created decreases every 4 years, or every 210,000 blocks to be precise. Today, a newly created block creates 6.25 bitcoins. This number will keep going down until no more bitcoin will be issued. This will happen around 2140, when 21 million bitcoins will have been created. After this date, no more bitcoin will be issued. However, miners can still receive rewards in the form of transaction fees. The winning miner can collect all the transaction fees in the block. As the amount of bitcoin created with each block diminishes, the transaction fees received by the miner will increase. After the year 2140, the winning miner will only receive transaction fees as their reward.

2.6 Technical Explanation of Mining

Let us examine the technical aspects of crypto mining. In the blockchain, every block has a previous block except the very first block or the genesis block. Miners are competing to validate a new block by solving a complex mathematical puzzle. Let us look at the latest Bitcoin mined block, block # 631977 at the time of writing. This block is shown in Table 2.1.

Table 2.1 Block 631977

Hash	0000000000000000000e76cc39b4da8ff77d9987d253cca33995003e650723f1
Confirmations	1
Timestamp	2020-05-28 07:27
Height	631977
Miner	Unknown
Number of Transactions	1,905
Difficulty	15,138,043,247,082.88
Merkle root	7de3e90dad93273ac22d1db9c1721264790cd1e6ca2eec4b6d73799f7f37b0a0
Version	0x37ffe000
Bits	387,094,518
Weight	3,993,327 WU
Size	1,563,900 bytes
Nonce	360,554,482
Transaction Volume	6633.39891611 BTC
Block Reward	6.25000000 BTC
Fee Reward	1.36240641 BTC

Notice that the block height is 631977, which means there are 631977 blocks in the Bitcoin blockchain that have been confirmed since the genesis block.

Let us call the successful miner for this block Mr. John. Before John successfully mines block #631977, he was competing with other miners in mining the previous block #631976. However, he lost in the contest and block #631976 was mined by a fellow miner. As soon as block #631976 was mined, he needs to quickly update his blockchain and start mining for a new unvalidated block, known as the candidate block.

In fact, while John's computer (also known as a node) was searching for the Proof of Work for the previous block, it was also searching for new transactions. Those new transactions are added to the memory pool or transaction pool. The memory pool is a node's temporary storage area for transaction data. This is where transactions wait until they can be included in a new block and validated.

In constructing the candidate block, John's node starts gathering the transactions in the transaction pool. It removes the transactions already present in the previous block if there are any. The block is called a candidate block because it does not have a valid Proof of Work yet.

As you can see in Table 2.1, block #631977 has 1905 transactions inside it. This was the number of transactions present in John's transaction pool when he created his candidate block. The mining process is illustrated in Figure 2.3.

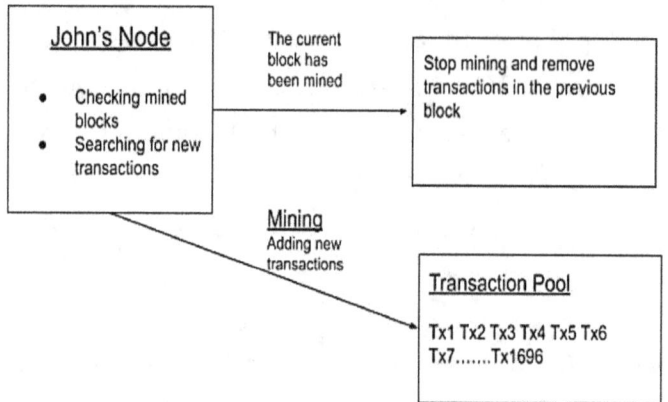

Figure 2.3 The Mining Process

In the mining process, John's node is creating a Coinbase transaction. This transaction will create bitcoins and deposit them into John's wallet as a reward for finding a valid Proof of Work. This transaction is different from the other ones because the bitcoins in the reward are created out of nothing. They do not come from someone's wallet. Besides that, John's node also calculates the transaction fees in the block.

John's reward for mining block #631977 is as shown in Figure 2.4 is

Total reward = Reward for mining block + Transaction fees

= 6.25 BTC + 1.36240641 BTC

= 7.61240641 BTC

*BTC block reward has been reduced to 6.25 BTC since Bitcoin halving occurred on 11th March 2020, down from 12.5 BTC.

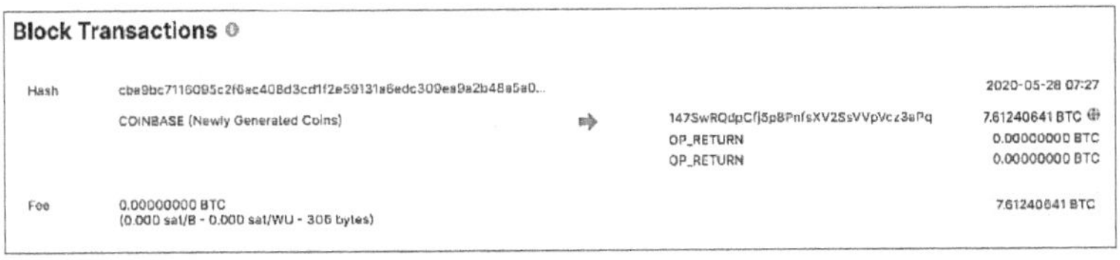

Block Transactions			
Hash	cbe9bc71160B5c2f6ac408d3cd1f2e59131a6edc300ea9a2b48a5a0...		2020-05-28 07:27
	COINBASE (Newly Generated Coins)	147SwRQdpCfj5pBPnfsXV2SsVVpVcz3ePq OP_RETURN OP_RETURN	7.61240641 BTC 0.00000000 BTC 0.00000000 BTC
Fee	0.00000000 BTC (0.000 sat/B - 0.000 sat/WU - 306 bytes)		7.61240641 BTC

Figure 2.4

From Figure 2.4, you can see that it is a Coinbase transactions which means the newly minted Bitcoin do not come from anyone's wallet. You can only see the winning miner's wallet address here.

2.7 How to achieve Proof of Work?

Mining involves the process of producing a hash whose value is less than the target value. When this hash has been found, it is called a valid hash and hence proof of work is achieved.

The mining algorithm uses a counter known as the nonce to generate the hash using the SHA256 cryptographic function. A hash algorithm always produces the same arbitrary length data given the same inputs. It is impossible to compute the same hash with two different inputs. It is also impossible to predict the output of any given data in advance.

The value of nonce is initialized to 0. Mining is finding the nonce, the only input that changes every time we run the hash function.

The goal is to find a value for the nonce that will result in a hash lower than the target. So, the mining node might need to try billions or trillions of nonce values before it gets a valid hash. As you can see, mining is like playing the slot machine, there is no way to predict when can you strike a jackpot.

It is quite easy to prove that the nonce found indeed produces a valid hash. All the information is available, everyone in the network can run the hash function and confirm if the hash is valid or not. Because it is also impossible to predict what the nonce will be, it also acts as a proof that the miner has indeed achieved Proof-of-Work.

Calculation of a valid hash is as follows (based on block #540909):

The formula to calculate the current target of the block is

Current target = Maximum target / Difficulty

Maximum target is

0x00000000FFFF0000000000000000000000000000000000000000000000000000

This is a hexadecimal number. After conversion to a decimal number, the maximum target is

26959946667150639794667015087019630673637144422540572481103610249215

Difficulty is (as given in the block)

7019199231177.17

Therefore, the current target is

26959946667150639794667015087019630673637144422540572481103610249215)/7019199231177.17

= 3.84089×10^{54}

The hash of the block is

0000000000000000000ef17668e407e78c5a247f731b1138ad16f5bf79f1c0d

Converted to a decimal number, the value is

8945471620549523954887101684606026470871856158494 6189

The hash value is approximately 8.95×10^{51}. Clearly, the hash value is less than the current target, therefore it is a valid hash.

Chapter 3

Ethereum - The Programmable Blockchain and DApps Platform

Many alternative cryptocurrencies or simply altcoins have emerged since the successful launch of Bitcoin in 2009. There are more than a thousand at the time of writing this book. However, none of the cryptocurrencies came close to challenging Bitcoin until the invention of Ethereum by Vitalik Buterin.

3.1 A Brief History of Ethereum

Ethereum was first conceptualized by Vitalik Buterin in 2013. He is a young Russian Canadian programming genius (born 1994). In 2014, he cofounded the Ethereum platform with Mihai Alisie, Anthony Di Iorio and Charles Hoskinson.

The Ethereum Foundation held an Ether crowdsale in July 2014 during which they sold 60 million tokens. A total of 12 million Ether (ETH) tokens were created so the Ethereum Foundation could expand its development and marketing efforts. The Ethereum Mainnet went live on 30 July 2015, with 72 million coins "premined".

Ethereum broke into the mainstream in early 2017 when the price of ETH increased by 1000 percent over the course of a couple of months. This led to a similar rise in the price of alternative blockchain tokens, also known as altcoins. It is still ranked second behind Bitcoin on Coinmarketcap at the time of writing. Currently there are over 1600 altcoins, and this number is still growing.

3.1.1 What is Ethereum?

Ethereum is an open-source blockchain-based decentralized platform featuring smart contracts. Besides that, Ethereum is a programmable blockchain that enables developers to build and deploy decentralized applications. Of course, it also offers Ether, an alternative cryptocurrency to Bitcoin. It is also a platform for running an Initial Coin Offering (ICO), which is a crypto crowdfunding initiative. I shall explain ICO in another chapter.

Ethereum runs on a distributed public blockchain network. Every node connected to the Ethereum network helps to maintain and update the blockchain database. The nodes of the network run the Ethereum Virtual Machine (EVM) and execute the instructions according to the smart contracts. Ethereum nodes run the EVM to maintain consensus across the blockchain.

Ethereum Virtual Machine ("EVM") is the core engine that runs the Ethereum Platform. It is the runtime environment that executes all the smart contracts on the Ethereum network. The EVM can be considered a Turing complete virtual machine, which means it can perform any logical step of a computational function. Rather than providing users with a set of predefined applications like the Bitcoin protocol, Ethereum serves as a platform for users to create many different types of decentralized blockchain applications (DApps), including but not limited to cryptocurrencies.

3.1.2 Gas, Gas Price and Gas Limit

A term everyone must know about Ethereum is gas. In addition, you need to understand its associated terms: gas price and gas limit.

3.1.3 What is Gas?

Gas is a unit that measures the amount of computational effort that it will take to execute certain operations on the Ethereum blockchain. The operations include sending tokens, deploying a smart contract, interacting with a contract, sending ETH, launching an ICO, or anything else on the blockchain. Gas is needed to power the Ethereum Ecosystem, just like fuel is needed to power a car.

3.1.4 What is Gas Price?

As I have mentioned earlier, we need to use gas for every operation made on Ethereum, regardless of whether your transaction succeeds or fails. Gas does not come free. We need to pay for it, just like paying for gasoline to drive our cars. The transaction fee depends on the gas price and the gas limit.

Gas price is the amount of Ether you need to pay per unit of gas. It is measured in Gwei (1 Gwei = 0.0000000001 ETH). Its value is determined by the miners, who can refuse to process the transaction with less than a certain gas price. The transaction fee is paid to the successful miner as a form of incentive that motivates the miners to maintain the nodes. Therefore, they have the controlling power over the gas price. We must have enough Ether in our wallet to pay for the gas fees. The transaction fee is calculated using the following formula:

Transaction fee = Gas used x Gas price

For example, for a certain transaction:

Gas used = 21,000

Gas price = 6 Gwei or 0.000000006 ETH

Transaction fee = 21,000 ×0.000000006 ETH = 0.000126 ETH

You can see the actual output in a smart contract deployment on Etherscan, as shown in Table 3.1.

Table 3.1 Block #10151194

Block	10151194
Timestamp	18 mins ago (May-28-2020 01:01:20 AM +UTC)
From	0x5a0b54d5dc17e0aadc383d2db43b0a0d3e029c4c (Spark Pool)
To	0x8fd00f170fdf3772c5ebdcd90bf257316c69ba45_
Value	109.62091869961092145 Ether ($22,796.77)

Transaction Fee	0.000126 Ether ($0.03)
Gas Used by Transaction:	21,000
Gas Limit	100,000
Gas Price	0.000000006 Ether (6 Gwei)

In addition, you can incentivize the miners to do your work first by paying more gas fees. In this way, you can jump to the front of the queue so that your transaction can be processed first. Even if the transaction fails, you still need to pay for the transaction fee because the miners must validate and execute your transaction.

3.1.5 Gas Limit

The gas limit is an estimation of the total amount of work to perform a transaction. It is not easy to compute the gas limit. Fortunately, there are many apps that set the limit for us. Typically, 21,000 gas will satisfy most transactions. However, for more complex transactions such as sending ETH to an ICO smart contract, the gas limit will be much higher. The reason is because such a transaction requires much more computational power.

If you set the limit too low, your transaction may take too long to process and even fail. As a result, you will lose ETH for nothing. On the other hand, if your transaction was completed before reaching the gas limit, you get back the balance ETH. The gas limit protects you from spending unlimited ETH, just like how banks set your credit card limit so that you will not overspend.

3.2 Smart Contracts

A smart contract is a computer code that can facilitate the exchange of money, content, property, shares, digital assets, or anything of value among disparate and anonymous parties without a middle entity.

When a smart contract is installed in a blockchain system, it behaves like a self-operating computer program that automatically executes when specific terms and conditions are met. Because smart contracts run on the blockchain, they run exactly as programmed without any possibility of censorship, downtime, fraud, or third-party interference.

On the Ethereum Blockchain Platform, a user can send some Ether to another user in exchange for something of value where the transaction is executed automatically based on a smart contract. In the case of Cryptokitties, a smart contract is executed when a user acquires a unique virtual kitty from the Cryptokitties collectible marketplace via a bidding process, where the highest bidder gets to own the digital asset.

On the other hand, a transaction can occur automatically between two smart devices using an integrated system of IoT technology and blockchain. For example, smartphone A can top up data for another smartphone B after A receives money from B. The transaction occurs based purely on a smart contract without the awareness of the owners.

Contrary to popular belief, the smart contract was not invented by Vitalik Buterin, the founder of Ethereum. In fact, the idea of the smart contract was first conceived by computer scientist and cryptographer Nick Szabo in 1993 as a kind of digital vending machine. In his famous example, he described how users could input data or value, and receive a finite item from a machine, in this case, a real-world snack or a soft drink. Nick Szabo is so smart that some people believe that he could be Satoshi Nakamoto, who invented Bitcoin.

In addition, though Ethereum was the first blockchain system to adopt smart contract technology, it is not the only one using smart contracts. Many non-Ethereum blockchain platforms such as Tron, Hyperledger Fabric, Hyperledger Sawtooth and Corda implement their own versions of smart contracts. The smart contract in Hyperledger Fabric is called Chaincode that runs in a container known as docker.

Today, most blockchain platforms run on the Ethereum Virtual Machine (EVM) and implement Ethereum smart contracts, while a few enterprise blockchain platforms implement their own version of smart contracts. However, there could be interoperability between the Ethereum platform and the enterprise platforms. For instance, in the Sawtooth-Ethereum integration project, EVM (Ethereum Virtual Machine) smart contracts can be deployed to

Sawtooth using the Seth transaction family. I will discuss Hyperledger technologies in another chapter.

3.2.1 Solidity

Solidity is a high-level programming language that is used to create and implement smart contracts on the Ethereum platform. The smart contracts created using Solidity can be used for financial transactions, crowdfunding, voting, supply chain management, IoT implementation, ride sharing automation, smart city administration and more. Besides that, it can be used to develop decentralized applications.

Solidity has Python, C++ and JavaScript influences. Therefore, it is convenient and easy to grasp for those that are already familiar with Python, C++ Or Javascript.

3.2.2 Writing and Deploying the Smart Contract

The best tool to write, compile, test and deploy smart contracts is Remix. Remix is a browser-based IDE that provides an inbuilt compiler as well as a run-time environment without server-side components. You can access Remix from the following link: https://remix.ethereum.org

We can also use other code editors for Solidity. I suggest you use Visual Studio Code or Solidity Plugin for Visual Studio. You need to download the Solidity Plugin from https://marketplace.visualstudio.com/items?itemName=ConsenSys.Solidity

Besides that, you need to install Visual Studio 2019. I shall skip the technical details as this is a book written for non-technical guys.

3.2.3 The Smart Contract Code

A smart contract is a collection of code (its functions) and data (its state) that resides at a specific address on the Ethereum blockchain. Let us begin with the most basic example. It is fine if you do not understand everything here. However, if you are keen to test it out, you can enter the following code in the Remix IDE and save the file as MyStorage.sol.

```
pragma solidity ^0.5.0;

contract MyStorage {

    uint storedData;

    function set(uint x) public {

        storedData = x;

    }

    function get() public view returns (uint) {

        return storedData;

    }
```

}

3.2.4 Understanding the Code

The first line simply states that the source code is written for Solidity version 0.5.0 or anything newer that does not break functionality. This is to ensure that the contract does not suddenly behave differently with a new compiler version. The keyword pragma is called that way because, in general, pragmas are instructions for the compiler about how to treat the source code.

A contract in the sense of Solidity is a collection of code (its functions) and data (its state) that resides at a specific address on the Ethereum blockchain. The line uint storedData; declares a state variable called storedData of type uint (unsigned integer of 256 bits). You can think of it as a single slot in a database that can be queried and altered by calling functions of the code that manages the database. In the case of Ethereum, this is always the owning contract. And in this case, the functions set and get can be used to modify or retrieve the value of the variable.

To access a state variable, you do not need to use the prefix that is commonly used in other programming languages. This is just a simple contract that does not do much yet apart from allowing anyone to store a single number. This number is accessible by anyone in the world without a feasible way to prevent you from publishing this number. Of course, anyone could just call set again with a different value and overwrite your number. However, the number will still be stored in the history of the blockchain.

3.2.5 Decentralized Applications (DApps)

DApp is an abbreviation for decentralized application. A DApp has its backend code running on a decentralized peer-to-peer network such as the Ethereum blockchain network. On the contrary, an app's backend code is running on centralized servers.

A DApp can have frontend code and user interfaces written in any language that can make calls to its backend. Furthermore, its frontend can be hosted on decentralized storage such as Swarm or IPFS.

One of the most famous Ethereum-based DApps is CryptoKitties (https://www.cryptokitties.co/). CryptoKitties is a game centered around breedable, collectible, and adorable creatures that are known as CryptoKitties. Each cat is unique and is 100% owned by an owner; it cannot be replicated, taken away, or destroyed. The game is so popular that it congested the Ethereum Mainnet in December 2017, causing it to reach an all-time high in number of transactions and slowing it down the network significantly. Many DApps have been developed on the Ethereum platform since its inception. You can check out the DApp Store from this link: https://www.dapp.com/. To learn more about smart contracts and DApp, please read our technical section.

Chapter 4

Storing your Cryptocurrencies

Since the introduction of bitcoin by Satoshi Nakamoto in 2009, and the exponential price hike of bitcoin in recent years, using bitcoin as an investment instrument is becoming more and more popular. The emergence of Ethereum and altcoins has further pushed the craze of investing in cryptocurrencies to new heights.

As more and more people buy and trade cryptocurrencies, storing the digital currencies securely has become a topmost concern. The frequent incidents of exchange hacking causing the loss of billions of dollars in crypto assets have triggered a wave of fear among cryptocurrency holders. Therefore, choosing a secure wallet is the first step you must undertake before investing in cryptocurrencies.

However, transacting cryptocurrencies is not as easy as transacting the fiat currencies. The technical difficulties in transferring cryptocurrencies could be a nightmare for many people. Since cryptocurrencies are managed by decentralized platform without interference from any third-party entity, anything goes wrong in the transaction can result losing your cryptoassets forever. In the contrary, if anything goes wrong in a traditional transaction, you could seek help from the bank or a third-party entity to recover your funds.

On top of that, storing your cryptocurrencies is more difficult than keep your fiat currencies. You need special wallets to store your cryptocurrencies with a password constitutes of 12 or 24 words seed phrase which is difficult to remember. Worse still if you lose the seed phrase, there is no way for you to recover your money. On the other hand, if you forgot your bank account password, you could click forget password and reset your password through an email.

To alleviate your fear, I would like to discuss how to choose a wallet to store your cryptocurrencies securely.

4.1 Crypto Wallet

To store and transact your cryptocurrencies, you must use a crypto wallet. Crypto wallet is a secure digital wallet used to store, send, and receive bitcoin as well as other digital currencies. It is a software that allows you to monitor and conduct cryptocurrency transactions. Technically the crypto wallet is connected to the blockchain via a node and uses a method called simplified payment verification (SPV) to verify transactions. Most cryptocurrencies have official wallets, or some officially recommended third-party wallets.

The crypto wallet does not actually store the cryptocurrency in the wallet. It is a support system for storing the addresses of public and private keys of cryptocurrencies, cryptocurrency settlement, and cryptocurrency transactions. Sometimes the system even includes the accounting and maintenance of the entire blockchain.

The actual amount is based on the final recorded result of the blockchain.

4.2 Types of Crypto Wallets

Due to the rapid development of cryptocurrencies, different types of crypto wallets have been developed to cope with various usage scenarios.

According to the degree of decentralization, crypto wallets can be divided into full-node wallet, light wallet, and centralized wallet.

In terms of the private key storage method, the crypto wallet can be divided into cold wallet and hot wallet

4.2.1 Full Node Wallet

This kind of wallet must be installed with a software. After installation, it will synchronize with the entire blockchain and store the entire blockchain, so when the new wallet starts to synchronize, it must be downloaded from the first data, which will take hours to days and takes up a lot of storage space and online traffic. Such a wallet is also called a full node. Ethereum Wallet is one of the full-node wallets.

4.2.2 Hot Wallet

A hot wallet refers to a crypto wallet that is online and connected to the blockchain via a node . The hot wallet is generally designed as a web page. After the website generates the private key, it is kept by an individual. When you want to access the wallet in the future, you must enter the private key. The website is not responsible for saving it for the user.

One class of hot wallet is known as SPV wallet (simplified payment verification) wallet, also known as light wallet. This kind of wallet only stores private keys and settlement, and does not store the entire blockchain, so it occupies few resources and is more suitable for mobile devices. One of the most used web versions of SPV wallet is MetaMask, which stores Ethereum and ERC20 tokens . For Bitcoin, a good example of the SPV wallet is Electrum, one of the best Bitcoin wallets. You can easily install the mobile version of Electrum from Google Play Store. It allows you to create a standard wallet or a multisig wallet.

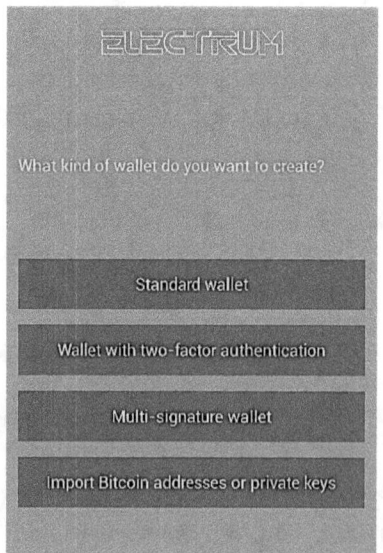

Figure 4.1

4.2.3 Centralized Wallet

4.2.4 Cold Wallet

Cold Wallet is also known as offline wallet. Cold wallets usually rely on "cold" devices (non-networked computers, mobile phones, hardware wallets, paper wallets etc.) to ensure the security of the cryptocurrency private key. It uses QR code communication to keep the private key from connecting to the network, avoiding the risk of private key theft. However, cold wallets may still face physical security risks (such as computer loss, damage, etc.).

Hardware wallets are physical devices that store public addresses and private keys for cryptocurrencies offline in an encrypted device. It is a USB-like device with an OLED screen and side buttons to navigate through the interface of the wallet and comes with native desktop apps for different cryptocurrencies. It can be connected to a PC or mobile device via USB when you need to transfer funds in and out of the wallet.

A hardware USB wallet typically costs between $70-$150 but it is still cheap compared to the value of your cryptocurrencies stored in the hardware wallet. Two of the most popular hardware wallets that allow you to store more than 22 cryptocurrencies and 500 ERC-20 tokens are Ledger Nano S and Trezor.

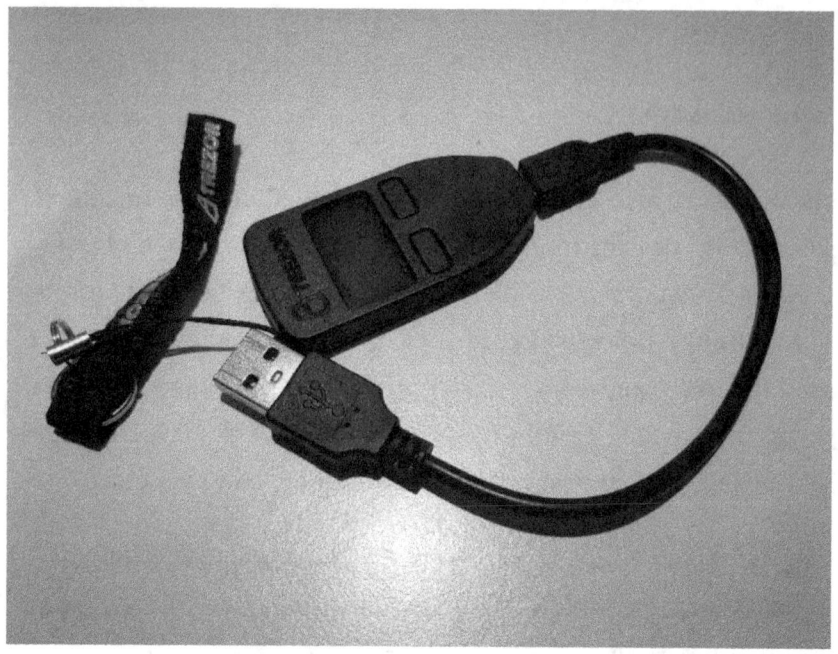

Figure 4.2 Trezor Wallet

For less expensive option, you can use a paper wallet. To generate the public key and the private key into QR code, you can use an online paper wallet generator. The best one is https://www.bitaddress.org which only generate Bitcoin paper wallet. Generating the wallet is easy, simply visit the website, select the number of addresses you wish to create and the click the generate button. The addresses will be generated instantly, as shown in Figure 4.3.

Figure 4.3

To generate Ethereum paper wallet, visit the following website:

https://generatepaperwallet.com/ethereum/index.html

Move your mouse random on the webpage and the QR addresses will be generated, as shown in Figure 4.4.

Figure 4.4

4.3 How Should You Store your Cryptocurrencies?

Basically, you can choose to store your cryptocurrencies in an exchange wallet, in a hot wallet or in a cold wallet. All the wallets have their advantages and disadvantages. How to decide which wallet to use is always a tradeoff between convenience and security.

Keeping your cryptocurrencies on an exchange is convenience but also subject to security issues. It is easy to trade and cash out your cryptocurrencies by storing your cryptocurrencies in an exchange wallet. However, exchanges are mostly hosted on centralized servers therefore prone to cyberattack and hacking. If an exchange lost a substantial amount of money, they may not be able to pay you back your money. In addition, since the exchange is controlling your private key, it may subject to misappropriation of your funds.

Another choice is to keep your cryptocurrencies in a hot wallet installed on your mobile devices , your laptop, or your PC. The advantage of storing your cryptocurrencies in a hot wallet is that you can control your own private key. However, as the hot wallet is always connected to the Internet once you on your devices, it is also subject to hacking and cyberattack. To improve security, you may enable two factor encryptions.

The third option is the cold wallet. The cold wallet is most secure since it is always offline therefore will avoid cyberattack and online theft. However, it is still prone to physical risks like natural disaster, robbery, coercion, carelessness and more. Moreover, it is not as easy to move the funds out as other kinds of wallets.

So, what kinds of wallets should you use? The answer is using a combination of all three kinds of wallets. I would suggest keeping some of your funds , like 20% of your funds in exchange wallets for short-term trading. Another portion of your funds perhaps like 30% in the hot wallet for quick access to the funds. Last, set aside 50% of your funds and keep them in a hardware wallet for long-term safe keeping of your funds.

Chapter 5 - Crypto Fundraising

Fundraising is always the primary concern of start-ups as they need funds to kickstart their projects. However, traditional fundraising from the public via an IPO is a huge barrier for start-ups as they do not have the resources and expertise to initiate it. Therefore, they often opt for a much easier fundraising method known as crowdfunding, which is a project or venture funded typically by raising small amounts of money from a large community.

With the growth of the Internet, many crowdfunding platforms have emerged to cater for the need of the start-ups who are hungry for funds. To protect investors' interests, if a project fails to reach its funding goal, it is usually dropped from the fundraising platform and the pledged funds are returned to the investors. One of the most successful ones is Kickstarter, which launched in 2009 and has received almost $4 billion in pledges from 15.5 million backers to date (Aitken, 2019).

With the invention of Bitcoin by Satoshi Nakamoto in 2009 and the subsequent emergence of numerous altcoins, cryptocurrencies have been utilized to conduct crowdfunding in recent years with great success, which has reached its peak in 2017 where an estimated $4.9 billion was raised through ICOs (Page, 2018). Though ICOs are an innovative way to raise funds for start-ups, unfortunately many projects have turned out to be scams. Therefore, you need to understand and study an ICO project carefully before you invest in its coin. Let us delve deeper into ICO to get a better picture of what it is about.

5.1 Initial Coin Offering (ICO)

According to Investopedia, an Initial Coin Offering (ICO) is akin to an Initial Public Offering (IPO). However, instead of issuing shares to the public, ICO projects issue cryptocurrencies, often in the form of coins or tokens. The objective of an ICO is to raise funds to create a new coin, app, or service.

During the ICO campaign, interested investors can buy into the offering and receive a new cryptocurrency token issued by the company. Therefore, ICO is also known as a token sale. Most ICOs design their coins as a utility token that is used to power their native platforms and decentralized applications (DApps) rather than for investment. As a result, most ICO projects can evade legal frameworks and do not have to comply with the strict governance of regulatory bodies. Investors usually need to pay for the token with fiat money or established cryptocurrencies like Bitcoin, ETH, USDT and more. This token will usually be listed on crypto exchanges at a specific listing price where investors can trade and hopefully gain profit when its value appreciates.

Many people would have thought Vitalik Buterin was the inventor of the concept of ICO, but the fact is that he was not the first one to come out with this idea, let alone launch it. There were five predecessors before the massively successful Ethereum ICO campaign. According to Merre (2019), J.R. Willett first conceived the idea in 2013 where he proposed a Mastercoin protocol that adds a layer on top of the Bitcoin protocol and provides additional features. He used the Kickstarter crowdfunding method to solicit bitcoins from investors in exchange for his Mastertokens to enjoy the features provided by the Mastercoin protocol.

The ICO campaign was largely successful. The project managed to raise 4740 bitcoins, which was worth around US $500K at the time. Not a crazy amount, but it is worth a whopping US $33 million at the market value at the time of writing this book. Although Mastertoken itself is not particularly useful today, the Mastertoken protocol was rebranded as the Omni Layer and went on to be an incredibly successful invention. It now serves as the underlying protocol for the Tether Token, better known as USDT, which is the most traded cryptocurrency beside BTC and ETH.

Following the successful ICO campaign of Mastertoken, four more ICO projects were launched: NextCoin (#NXT), CounterParty (#XCP), MaidSafeCoin (#MAID) and Swarm. However, the real game changer was the invention of Ethereum by Vitalik Buterin and the successful campaign of the Ethereum ICO. Vitalik claimed that Ethereum Virtual Machine is the world's first zero-infrastructure platform. Ethereum's token sale managed to garner 3700 BTC in 12 hours, approximately US $2.3 million at that time. It went on to raise US $18.3 million at the end of the campaign. Ethereum now ranks second on Coinmarketcap, with a market capitalization of US $14,316,813,733 at the time of writing.

When a start-up initiates an ICO campaign, the founder team needs to write a comprehensive whitepaper. During the height of ICO campaigns in 2017, you would have noticed that many whitepapers were badly written, especially whitepapers done by scam projects. The founders should avoid this pitfall.

The whitepaper should outline what the project is about, the need the project will fulfil upon completion, how much fund is needed, how many of the crypto tokens are to be minted, how the tokens will be distributed, what type of money (fiat or cryptocurrency) will be accepted, how long the ICO campaign will run for and so forth.

For more details on how to conduct an ICO campaign, please refer to the section on how to conduct an IEO campaign as the steps are largely the same.

5.2 Initial Exchange Offering (IEO)

After the craze of ICOs subsided, two new crypto crowdfunding methods emerged, namely Security Token Offering (STO) and Initial Exchange Offering (IEO). Among the two, IEO is more popular as STO poses a higher barrier of entry, is more expensive, and is subjected to more stringent regulations by the security commission.

In a recent article, Reuters reported that IEOs have raised $1.5 billion so far in 2019, compared with just $836 million raised from ICOs. A dozen of amazingly successful cases of IEOs have driven more project owners to embark on their own IEO journeys. Famous

IEO cases include the sale of the BitTorrent (BTT) token on the Binance Launchpad, raising $7 million in just the first 14 minutes of the sale opening. Veriblock did even better, raising $7 million in April through an IEO on the Bittrex exchange in just 10 seconds. An utterly amazing feat! It is safe to say that IEO has taken over ICO as the preferred choice of fundraising in the cryptocurrency industry.

Investors who are still thinking of the good old days of ICO should start changing their mindset and focus on investing in IEO projects instead. On the other hand, start-ups or enterprises who wish to raise funds in the crypto industry must realize that ICO is already dead and IEO is the way to go. Lastly, more exchanges should create IEO launchpads to assist projects that wish to raise funds through IEO, as this is an untapped niche with immense potential.

5.2.1 What is IEO?

According to Binance, an Initial Exchange Offering (IEO) is a fundraising campaign that is administered by a crypto exchange platform. An IEO allows investors to purchase a new cryptocurrency (or token) while raising funds for its crypto project.

Though ICOs and IEOs both raise funds through token sales, the way they sell tokens is different. For ICOs, the project team themselves conduct the fundraising campaign. Meanwhile, IEO fundraising is conducted on a crypto exchange platform, where the users of the exchange can buy tokens with funds directly from their own exchange wallet.

5.2.2 Advantages and Disadvantages of IEO

Advantages

Increased Investor Confidence

Investors are more confident in investing in IEO tokens as the project must undergo stringent KYC/AML checks by the exchange platform that handles the IEO projects. The exchange platform will also evaluate the business model of the project and audit its technical infrastructure, including its blockchain system and smart contracts. Therefore, many scam projects will be filtered and eliminated. The exchange platform acts as a trusted third party that can reduce considerable risk in crypto investment.

Win-Win for The Project Owner and The Exchange

For the project owner, it is a cheaper and easier way to raise the necessary funds for the project, while not embarking on long marketing campaigns and roadshows. The token is also listed on the exchange immediately after the IEO campaign.

For the exchange, conducting an IEO means more revenue for them. An exchange that hosts an IEO will typically charge a fee for the campaign and get a cut from the token sales. They also get fees when the token starts trading on their exchange.

Disadvantages of IEO

Ambiguous Regulations and Restrictions

Many countries still ban or restrict fundraising activity in the cryptocurrency industry while some countries impose stringent regulations on crypto activities. Therefore, it is still uncertain whether IEO will be fully accepted and recognized as the legal way of fundraising in the crypto industry.

All Investors Subjected to Stringent AML/KYC

While a stringent KYC/AML check for the project can increase investor confidence, some individuals may be reluctant to expose their identities, so going through a stringent AML/KYC procedure may deter these people from investing in the IEO project.

Limited Number of Tokens

There have been many complaints from investors that not everyone manages to purchase tokens during IEOs as the number of tokens available for sale is usually limited.

Botting Concerns

Using bots for trading and investing is ubiquitous nowadays. In the crypto space, there are concerns about bots that can be programmed to participate in IEOs and beat out human investors. In such a scenario, all parties lose out.

5.2.2 How to Conduct an IEO?

Although an IEO is a promising method for fundraising, especially for startups that do not have the resources and expertise to do an IPO, it is by no means an easy feat. The project owner needs to plan and make the necessary preparations before embarking on the IEO initiative. The following are suggested steps that a project must follow before going IEO.

Step 1 Design the Business Model

Before embarking on an IEO campaign, the founding members of the project must have a clear vision of what their business wants to achieve. They also must design a business model and draw up plans to attain the vision.

For instance, the vision of a project is to build the world's largest digital platform for global entrepreneurs, which has the potential to create a vibrant token economy for the closed-loop ecosystem. The business model is to create a blockchain-based utility token that will power the digital platform for entrepreneurs, enabling them to perform all forms of economic activities that will create huge economic value.

Step 2 Assemble a Formidable Team

In this internet era where information is readily available, potential investors and exchanges can easily check the background of the project team members. If the project team is comprised of mostly inexperienced people, it will seriously affect the confidence of the investors and the exchanges. Therefore, the project owner needs to assemble a formidable team that includes experts in business, law, technology, marketing, and other related disciplines. As most IEO projects are blockchain-based, it is a must to hire blockchain experts.

Step 3 Preparing the Whitepaper and Other Documents

The whitepaper is a document that contains a thorough description of the project, distribution of tokens, business model, tokenomics and more. It also includes information about the project team which usually comprises the board members, the marketing team, the technical team, the legal team, and the advisers.

Writing the whitepaper is an especially important step in the IEO campaign. It is an important document that showcases the project. Whether the investors will be impressed and looking forward to investing in the project depends on how well the paper is written.

Besides the whitepaper, the project team should also prepare a one-pager, website, pitch decks, social media pages and more. These are the components that contain the primary source of knowledge about the project for potential investors and exchanges to evaluate the IEO project.

Step 4 Develop the Token

The token is an integral part of the IEO project. Without a native token, what can you sell to the investors? Therefore, it is crucial to design the token from day 1 and start developing it as soon as possible.

Most tokens for IEO projects are ERC20 tokens. The ERC20 standard is chosen because it can be easily designed and deployed to the Ethereum Mainnet. However, if you want a customized token and your team has the expertise and programming skills, you can develop a different protocol from the Ethereum Mainnet, or even develop your own blockchain system.

To mint the ERC20 token, the blockchain developers must write a robust smart contract and have it tested and audited by a trusted third-party contract auditor to ensure the contract is secure and free of bugs. The audited token can then be deployed to the Ethereum Mainnet or a private network.

Step 5 Marketing

The project team must carry out an aggressive marketing campaign for its IEO initiative to broadcast the news to as many investors as possible. The marketing campaign can be conducted through websites, blogs, as well as social media platforms such as Facebook, Twitter, WhatsApp, WeChat and more. They should also organize events and conferences to promote their token, but they must check whether these activities can be conducted in certain countries. For example, you cannot do so in Malaysia and China.

Step 6 Engage a Crypto Exchange

The project team also must sign an agreement with a crypto exchange to start their IEO campaign. They must conduct due diligence in searching for a trusted exchange before deciding to engage one. A good guide is to look for exchanges that rank within the top 50 on Coinmarketcap. Besides that, they also need to analyze reviews of the exchanges on various crypto platforms. IEO fees may also be another concern, as top rank exchanges may charge an extremely high fee. Therefore, there is always a trade-off between the fee and the reputation of the exchange.

5.3 Security Token Offering (STO)

Security Token Offering (STO) has emerged as a new option in fundraising in the blockchain/crypto space, since ICOs have been banned or heavily regulated in many countries. ICO projects were banned because many of the projects were scams and the coins or tokens issued by them had neither utility nor monetary value. In China, they called such coins "Air Coins" and in the west they called them "S**t Coins".

In contrast to ICO tokens which are mostly utility tokens, security tokens are backed by underlying tangible assets that have monetary value, like stocks, bonds, funds, bank reserves, properties, minerals and more. In fact, Security Token Offering

(STO) can be considered a hybrid model between Initial Public Offering (IPO) and cryptocurrency ICOs.

Security tokens represent the ownership of the tokenized underlying assets that are stored on the blockchain. Security token holders are entitled to an array of rights including equity, dividends, profit sharing, voting rights and more. These rights are written into a smart contract and traded freely as a token. In blockchain, tokenization is a method that converts rights to an asset into a digital token. Thus, we can take an asset, tokenize it and create its digital representation that lives on the blockchain. Blockchain guarantees that the ownership information is immutable. The tokens created in this way are also known as crypto tokens or better still security tokens.

For example, you can tokenize an asset such as a book that you authored. The book is kept somewhere while the book token is uploaded to the blockchain network. The book crypto token is a representation of the book ownership. You can specify how many tokens must be transferred to your crypto wallet before you can transfer the book ownership to a buyer by means of a smart contract. CryptoKitties is a brilliant example of a crypto token that allows users to acquire an adorable collectible by transferring cryptocurrencies to the owner. The owner will then transfer the digital collectible to the buyer. The transaction occurs automatically via the smart contract.

STOs are usually more acceptable to regulatory bodies as they are asset-backed and comply with regulatory governance. They are a more legitimate method of fundraising. Compared to ICO, it is much more difficult to launch an STO, as it is governed by strict securities law. Therefore, STO projects will have to conduct due diligence work of making sure they comply with the relevant regulations that are usually imposed by the security commission of a country. They would typically only be able to raise funds from accredited investors who need to pass stringent whitelisting and KYC processes. In addition, the financial cost of launching an STO is much higher compared to ICO, though it is cheaper than the traditional IPO.

The process of launching an STO is nearly the same as IEO and ICO but drafting legal documents with the help of a qualified legal adviser is more important than the latter two. They may need to furnish a prospectus as you would with an IPO, depending on the amount of money they wish to raise and the jurisdiction of different countries. Despite the additional legal restrictions and financial cost, STO campaigns have been successful. For example, the blockchain venture capital firm Blockchain Capital was able to raise US $10 million via its STO initiative in 2017. NEXO, a company that operates crypto-backed loans worldwide, successfully raised US $52,500,000 in 2018.

The success of Polymath was even more astounding. Its STO campaign managed to raise a total of US $207,300,000 in 2018. Polymath is an interface between financial securities and the blockchain, helping issuers to overcome the complex technical and legal challenges related to issuing regulated securities on the blockchain. This cutting-edge blockchain platform offers a comprehensive tokenization process with decentralized protocol. Polymath allows a company to raise capital and mint security tokens quickly and conveniently.

Chapter 6

Hyperledger - A Framework for Enterprise Blockchain

In previous chapters, we have learned about the Bitcoin blockchain, the flagship of cryptocurrency. Subsequently, we learned about Ethereum, which features smart contracts on top of its cryptocurrency Ether. Smart contracts allow developers to create decentralized applications (DApps) on the Ethereum ecosystem.

Both Bitcoin and Ethereum are amazing blockchain platforms. However, both are facing incredibly challenging issues, one of which is scalability. The transaction processing capacity of the Bitcoin network is limited by the average block creation time of 10 minutes and the block size limit. The transaction rate for Bitcoin is between 3.3 and 7 transactions per second.

Ethereum does not fare better, with a transaction rate of 15 transactions per second. Comparatively, VISA's transaction rate is 45,000 transactions per second. Therefore, both platforms fall short in developing practical enterprise applications now.

To overcome the limitations of the blockchain technologies for enterprise usage, Hyperledger was created with the vision to provide viable blockchain solutions for industries and businesses.

Hyperledger is an open source effort created to advance cross-industry blockchain technologies hosted by the Linux Foundation.

6.1 The Mission of Hyperledger

The philosophy of Hyperledger is:

"Only an Open Source, collaborative software development approach can ensure the transparency, longevity, interoperability, and support required to bring blockchain technologies forward to mainstream commercial adoption." –hyperledger.org

Indeed, the Hyperledger project has been a collaboration of players from various industries and organizations in technology, finance, banking, supply chain management, manufacturing, IoT and more. Since its inception in December 2015, it has managed to enlist many prominent members that include IBM, Intel, NEC, Cisco, J.P Morgan, AMN AMRO, ANZ Bank, Wells Fargo, Accenture, SAP and more.

The mission of Hyperledger comprises some ambitious goals:

- Create enterprise grade, open source, distributed ledger frameworks and code bases to support business transactions.
- Provide neutral, open, and community-driven infrastructures supported by technical and business governance.
- Build technical communities to develop blockchain and shared ledger POCs, use cases, field trials and deployments.

- Promote our community of communities - taking a toolkit approach with many platforms and frameworks.

6.2 The Hyperledger Greenhouse

Hyperledger itself is not a platform. It is an umbrella body that incubates and promotes a range of business blockchain technologies. The technologies include distributed ledger frameworks, smart contract engines, client libraries, graphical interfaces, utility libraries, and sample applications. The umbrella strategy was able to accelerate innovation of DLT components by encouraging the re-use of common building blocks and components (hyperledger.org, 2019).

The Hyperledger projects known as The Hyperledger Greenhouse consists of six distributed ledgers, five tools, four libraries and a domain-specific platform:

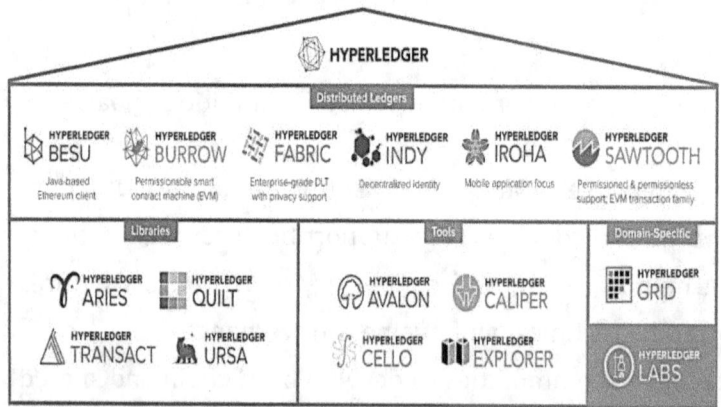

Figure 6.1 Hyperledger Greenhouse (Source: hyperledger.org

Each of the Hyperledger frameworks operates differently but they also allow certain interoperability among themselves. Hyperledger frameworks are generally permissioned (private) blockchains. It means that the parties need authentication and authorization to participate on the blockchain networks.

6.3 Open Source and Open Governance

The success of Hyperledger is based on the concepts of open source and open governance. The concept of open source means that an open source software is a software that is made freely available and may be redistributed and modified. In other words, anyone could view the code, use the code, copy the code, modify the code, and depending on the open source license, contribute back changes. (hyperledger.org, 2019)

On the other hand, open governance means that technical decisions for an open source project are made by a group of community-elected developers voted in from a pool of active participants. These decisions include things such as which features to add, how, and when to add them. (hyperledger.org, 2019). Hyperledger has formed a Technical Steering Committee (TSC) to implement open governance pertaining to the Hyperledger projects. You can read about Hyperledger's open governance by following this link:

https://www.hyperledger.org/blog/2017/09/06/abcs-of-open-governance

6.4 Hyperledger Fabric

Hyperledger Fabric is the first blockchain project developed and hosted by the Linux Foundation. It was initially contributed to by Digital Asset and IBM, because of the first hackathon. According to the Linux Foundation, it was intended as a foundation for developing DLT applications or solutions with a modular architecture.

Hyperledger Fabric is an open-source enterprise-grade permissioned distributed ledger technology (DLT) platform, designed for use in developing enterprise applications. In contrast, Bitcoin protocol and Ethereum are public permissionless blockchain, though Ethereum can be configured to be a private permissioned blockchain using a consensus protocol such as proof of authority (PoA).

Hyperledger Fabric features some key differentiating capabilities over other popular distributed ledger or blockchain platforms. One special feature of Hyperledger Fabric is that it allows components, such as consensus and membership services, to be plug-and-play. Besides that, Hyperledger Fabric uses container technology to host smart contracts called chaincode that comprises the application logic of the system.

Channels are another unique feature of Hyperledger Fabric. They allow transactions to be private between two actors, while still being verified and committed to the blockchain.

6.5 The Hyperledger Fabric Architecture

Hyperledger Fabric has a highly modular and configurable architecture. Therefore, enterprises can make use of its versatility to develop innovative business applications. Besides that, it can be used to optimize applications. Indeed, Hyperledger Fabric is well suited to develop a broad range of industry use cases including banking, finance, insurance, healthcare, human resources, supply chain and even digital music delivery.

Like Ethereum, Hyperledger Fabric also features smart contracts. However, it does not use Solidity as the programming language to code smart contracts. Hyperledger Fabric smart contracts are written in general-purpose programming languages such as Java, Go and Node.js. This means that most enterprises already have the skill set needed to develop smart contracts and no additional training to learn a new language is required.

Unlike Ethereum and many other public blockchains or DLT platforms, Hyperledger Fabric is a permissioned platform. It means the participants are known to each other, rather than anonymous and fully untrusted. In the Hyperledger Fabric ecosystem, while the participants may not fully trust one another, it can be operated under a governance model that is built with trust between participants, such as a legal agreement or framework for handling disputes.

6.6 Consensus Protocol

One key difference between Hyperledger Fabric and other DLT platforms is its support for pluggable consensus protocols. It enables the platform to be more effectively customized to fit particular use cases and trust models.

For example, when Hyperledger Fabric is implemented within a single enterprise or operated by a trusted authority, fully Byzantine fault tolerant consensus might be considered unnecessary as it might cause excessive drag on performance and throughput. Instead, a crash fault tolerant (CFT) consensus protocol is more than adequate. However, in a multi-party, decentralized platform, a more traditional Byzantine fault tolerant (BFT) consensus protocol might be required.

Another significant difference between Hyperledger Fabric and other DLT platforms is that it can implement consensus protocols that do not require a native cryptocurrency. That means it does not need a cryptocurrency to incentivize costly mining or to fuel smart contract execution. The avoidance of a cryptocurrency reduces some significant risk due to hacking via attack vector. Besides that, the absence of cryptographic mining operations means that the platform can be deployed with the same operational cost as other distributed platforms.

The combination of the differentiating features makes Hyperledger Fabric one of the better performing DLT platforms available today both in terms of transaction processing and transaction confirmation latency. Besides that, it enables privacy and confidentiality of transactions and the smart contracts (chaincode) that implement them.

6.7 Hyperledger Fabric Network

Hyperledger Fabric is a permissioned blockchain network that provides ledger services to application clients and administrators. It allows multiple organizations to collaborate as a consortium to form the network. The permissions to join the network are determined by a set of policies that are agreed to by the consortium when the network is configured. The network policies may change over time, subject to the agreement of the organizations in the consortium.

The Hyperledger Fabric network comprises the following components:

- Ledger
- Peers
- Ordering service
- Chaincode (aka smart contract)
- Channels
- Membership service provider

The Hyperledger ecosystem also consists of the client applications that allow users to interact with the network. Moreover, the Hyperledger Fabric application SDK provides a powerful API for developers to program applications to interact with the blockchain network on behalf of the users.

6.7.1 Peers

The Fabric network is comprised primarily of a set of peers or nodes. Peers maintain the state of the network and a copy of the ledger. In addition, they also host smart contracts (chaincode).

There are two different types of peers in Fabric, the endorsing peer, and the committing peer. The endorsing peers (aka endorsers) simulate and endorse transactions. On the other hand, the committing peers (aka committers) verify endorsements and validate transactions before committing transactions to the blockchain. On a separate note, the endorsing peers can also commit transactions to the blockchain. Indeed, the endorsers are a special kind of committer. However, committers cannot be the endorsers. All peers can commit blocks to the distributed ledger.

6.7.2 Ordering Service

The ordering service is made up of a cluster of special nodes known as orderers. The ordering service accepts the endorsed transactions and specifies the order in which those transactions will be committed to the ledger. However, it does not process transactions, smart contracts, or maintain the shared ledger.

6.7.3 The Transaction Workflow

Let us examine the transaction workflow that involves the client applications, the peers and the orderers. By examining the entire transaction workflow, we will learn how consensus is reached in the process.

The transaction flow to reach consensus consists of three phases:

1. Transaction endorsement
2. Ordering
3. Validation and commitment

Phase 1 Transaction Endorsement

Transactions begin with client applications sending transaction proposals to the endorsing peers, as shown in the following diagram:

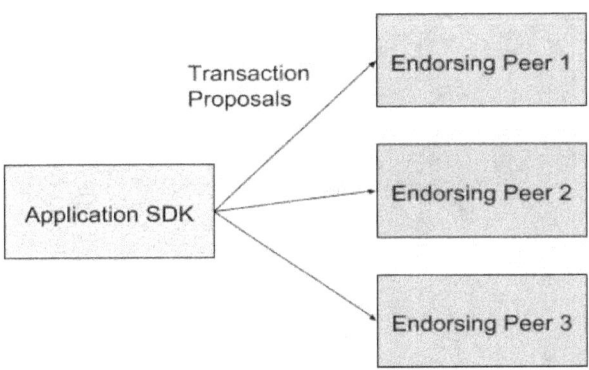

Figure 6.2 Transaction Flow

Phase 2 Transactions Simulation

At this phase, the endorsers will simulate the proposed transactions, without updating the ledger. The endorsers must hold smart contracts to simulate the transaction proposals. In the simulation process, the endorsing peers will capture the set of Read and Written data, known as **RW Sets**.

These RW sets contain data that was read from the current world state while simulating the transaction, as well as data that would have been written to the world state had the transaction been executed. The endorsing peers then sign these RW sets and send them back to the client application for use in the next phase of the transaction flow, as shown below:

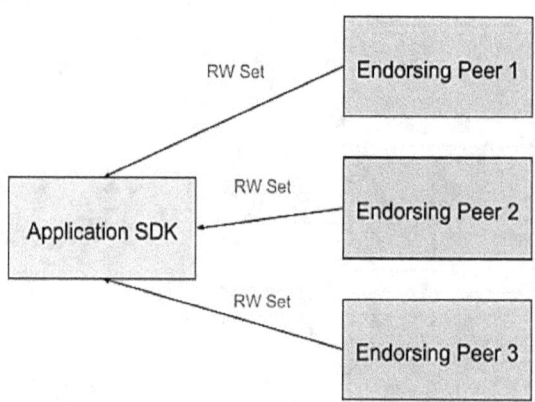

Figure 6.3 RW Set

Phase 3 Ordering

At this phase, the client application submits the endorsed transactions and the RW sets to the ordering service. The ordering service will take the endorsed transactions and RW sets, orders them into a block and delivers the block to all committing peers.

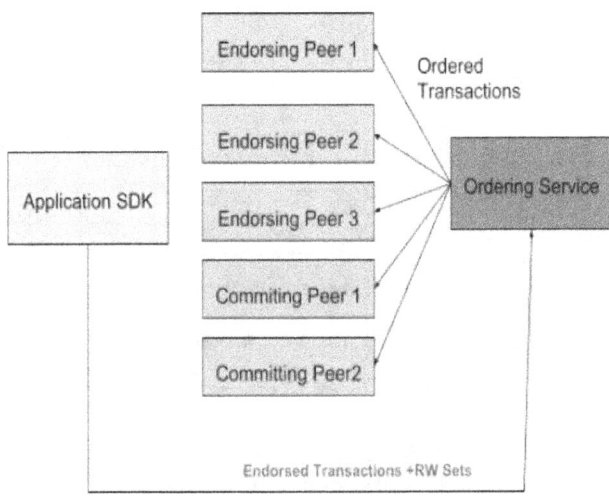

Figure 6.4 Ordering

The order of transactions needs to be established to ensure that the updates to the world state are valid when they are committed to the network. Unlike the Bitcoin blockchain or Ethereum, where ordering occurs through mining, Hyperledger Fabric allows organizations to choose the ordering mechanism that best suits that network.

Hyperledger Fabric provides three ordering mechanisms i.e. SOLO, Kafka, and Simplified Byzantine Fault Tolerance (SBFT). However,

SOLO is used only for experimentation purposes and SBFT has not yet been implemented. Therefore, Kafka is the default ordering mechanism for production use. The Kafka mechanism provides a crash fault tolerant solution to ordering.

Phase 4 Transaction Validation

At this final phase, the committing peers validate the transactions by checking that the RW sets still match the current world state. In addition, they need to ensure that Read data that existed during the simulation process is identical to the current world state.

After the committing peers validate the transactions, the transactions are then written to the ledger, and the world state is updated with the Write data from the RW Set. Committing peers are responsible for adding blocks of transactions to the blockchain and updating the world state. Lastly, the committing peers asynchronously notify the client application the results of the transactions.

6.7.4 Channels

In permissionless blockchains like Bitcoin and Ethereum, all peers share and have access to the same ledger. However, this kind of blockchain may not be suitable for business applications. For example, a supplier may want to set different prices for different wholesalers, and he would not want everyone in the supply chain to view this information. In this scenario, he or she will prefer to deal with the different wholesalers separately. To solve this issue,

Hyperledger Fabric came out with the novel concept of channels that allow private transactions within the same network.

Channels partition the Fabric network in such a way that only the stakeholders can view the transactions. In this way, organizations can utilize the same network while maintaining separation between multiple blockchains. The mechanism works by delegating transactions to different ledgers. Members of the channel can communicate and transact privately. Other members of the network cannot see the transactions on that channel. The concept is illustrated in the following diagram:

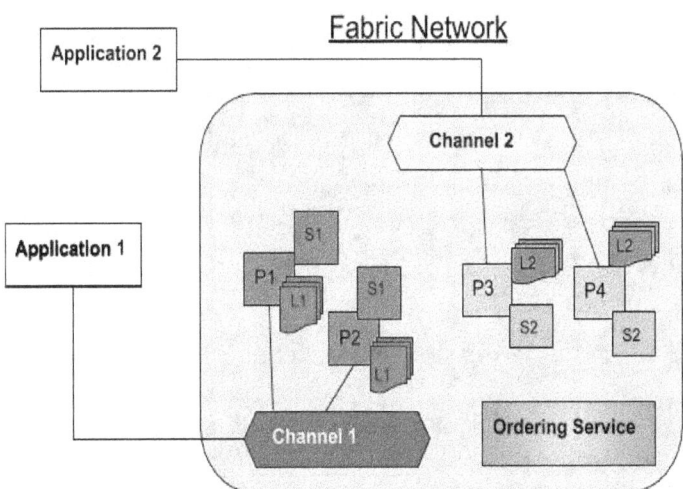

Figure 6.5 Fabric Network

The diagram above shows two channels, channel 1 and channel 2. Each channel has its own application, peers, ledger, and smart contract (chaincode). In this example, channel 1 has two peers, P1 and P2, and channel 2 also has two peers, P3 and P4. Ordering service is the same across any network and channel.

Application 1 will send transaction proposals to channel 1. P1 and P2 will then simulate and commit transactions to ledger L1 based on chaincode S1. On the other hand, Application 2 will send transaction proposals to channel 2. P3 and P4 will simulate and commit transactions to ledger L2 based on chaincode S2.

Though our example shows peers belonging to two distinct channels, in actual case peers can belong to multiple networks or channels. Peers that participate in multiple channels simulate and commit transactions to different ledgers. In addition, the same chaincode can be applied to multiple channels.

6.7.6 Membership Service Provider (MSP)

Hyperledger Fabric is a permissioned blockchain. Therefore, every user needs permission to join the Fabric network. To obtain permission to join the Fabric blockchain network, the identity of every user must be validated and authenticated. The identity is important because it determines the exact permissions over resources and access to information that the user has in the Fabric network.

To verify an identity, we must employ a trusted authority. In Hyperledger Fabric, the trusted authority is the membership service provider (MSP). The membership service provider is a component that defines the rules in which identities are validated, authenticated, and allowed access to a network. The MSP manages user IDs and authenticates clients who want to join the network. This includes providing credentials for these clients to propose transactions, defining specific roles a member might play and defining access privileges in the context of a network and channel.

The MSP uses a Certificate Authority to authenticate or revokes user certificates upon confirmed identity. In Fabric, the default Certificate Authority interface used for the MSP is the Fabric-CA API. However, organizations can choose to implement an External Certificate Authority of their choice. Hyperledger Fabric supports many types of External Certificate Authority interfaces. As a result, a single Hyperledger Fabric network can be controlled by multiple MSPs.

6.7.7 The Authentication Process

In the authentication process, the Fabric-CA identifies the application, peer, endorser and orderer identities, and verifies them. Next, a signature is generated using a Signing Algorithm and a Signature Verification Algorithm. The Signing Algorithm utilizes the credentials of the entities associated with their respective identities and outputs an endorsement. The generated signature is a byte array that is bound to a specific identity.

In the following step, the Signature Verification Algorithm will accept the request (to join the network) if the signature byte array matches a valid signature for the inputted endorsement or reject the request if not. If the user is accepted, he or she can see the transactions in the network and perform transactions with other actors in the network. On the other hand, if the user is rejected, he or she will not be able to submit transactions to the network or view any previous transactions.

Chapter 7

Blockless Distributed Ledger Technologies (DLT)

So far, we have discussed blockchain platforms that are made up of blocks. However, blockchain is only a subset of distributed ledger technologies (DLT). In this chapter, we shall explore two blockless DLT platforms that have evolved alongside Bitcoin, Ethereum and other blockchain and DLT systems.

7.1 IOTA

From connected mobile devices to wearable devices to smart homes, the Internet of Things is beginning to permeate every aspect of our lives. The adoption of IoT technologies is fostering a new economy nurtured by these technologies. As this kind of economy is powered by machine to machine (M2M) communication, it is also known as the **machine economy**. Foreseeing the huge growth potential in machine economy, the IOTA platform was developed to tap into the IoT industry.

According to the IOTA foundation, the number of connected devices is estimated to reach 75 billion by 2025. Internet of Things (IoT) includes tiny sensors on roads, bridges, railway tracks, mobile phones, smart washing machines, smart drones, wearable electronics like smartwatches and more. The amount of data being produced and consumed by all these devices is becoming astronomical.

Over the next five years, it is predicted that the global IP traffic on the IoT network will increase five-fold by 2021, and monthly IP traffic is expected to reach 31 Gigabytes per capita. However, for the same period, broadband speeds are expected only to double, and the global data pipelines will experience congestion. By then, it will not be possible for all these devices to stay connected 24/7 to the centralized cloud silos for all the data they will generate.

Recently, the emergence of 'Fog' and 'Mist' computing might provide a solution to the issue. However, how to distribute resources efficiently across the IoT ecosystem remains a huge challenge in this new machine economy. Therefore, IOTA was conceptualized with the mission to tackle the congestion issue. By implementing zero fee transactions, these devices could share the technological resources in real-time locally in a distributed network. In this way, it can avoid the centralized points of failure, eliminating the resource infrastructure bottleneck.

7.1.1 The Vision Of IOTA

The vision of IOTA is to enable all connected devices through verification of truth and transactional settlements, which incentivize devices to make available its properties and data in real time. In addition, the IOTA cryptocurrency was developed to enable machine to machine (M2M) transactions, thus creating the machine economy powered by IoT.

The main objective of IOTA is to serve the machine economy by enabling zero fee M2M payments. IOTA has established itself as the leader in the IoT fintech landscape by providing efficient, secure, lightweight, real-time microtransactions without fees. It is open source and engineered specifically for the Internet of Things. Its real-time microtransactions using the IOTA cryptocurrency has created an ecosystem that is ready and flexible for scale.

7.1.2 The Tangle

IOTA technology is like the blockchain technology, but it is not blockchain-based. In fact, it utilizes a kind of distributed ledger technology minus the blocks. IOTA is a permissionless distributed ledger that utilizes a cutting-edge technology, known as Tangle. Tangle is a new data structure based on a Directed Acyclic Graph (DAG). As opposed to blockchain, it has no blocks, no chain, and no miners. This unique new architecture enables IOTA to work differently compared to blockchains and other Distributed Ledger Technologies.

7.1.3 The Core Principles

IOTA uses a DAG instead of a blockchain to store its ledger. The main objective is to solve the scalability issue. As we all know, a blockchain has an inherent transaction rate limit, due to the conflict between block sizes and block issuance rates. If blocks are issued too frequently, or are too large, forks will occur often. When a fork happens, several new blocks are added to the chain simultaneously, and the network needs to decide between them, thus slowing down the validation process.

In a DAG, forks can still occur but unlike in a blockchain, a fork is not final. In the DAG system, diverging branches can still be merged back together, if they are consistent with each other. The transaction rate is therefore bounded only by the latency between the nodes. A DAG favors availability over consistency.

7.1.4 The Tangle Structure

Tangle is a Directed Acyclic Graph (DAG). In computer science, a directed graph is a collection of vertices (squares), which are connected to each other by edges (arrows). In the IOTA Tangle data structure, the vertices represent transactions, and the edges represent approvals. It retains the blockchain features that include distributed ledgers, immutability, and secure transactions, but it does not utilize the blocks. The Tangle structure is shown in Figure 7.1.

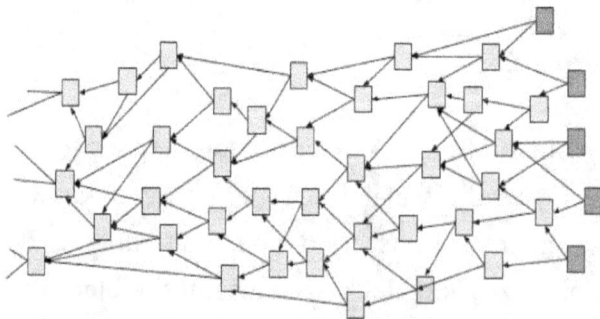

Figure 7.1 The Tangle Structure

With reference to Figure 7.2, if there is an edge (arrow) directing node (vertex) 100 to node 99, it means that node 100 approves the transaction at node 99. When a node issues a new transaction, it must choose 2 previous ones to approve, thereby adding 2 new edges (arrows) to the graph. Notice that each node must be connected to two previous nodes.

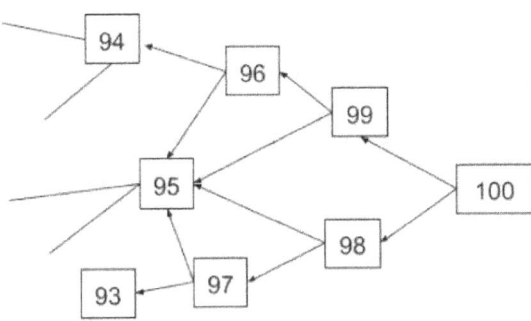

Figure 7.2

The first transaction in the Tangle is referred to as the genesis. All the IOTA tokens were created in the genesis, and no new ones will ever be created. All transactions in the tangle reference the genesis directly or indirectly.

Transactions with no approvers are called tips. In the figure above, node 100 is a tip because no one has approved its transaction yet. All the nodes must choose tips to approve, rather than older transactions, because this helps move the network consensus forwards. The method for choosing which two tips one should approve is one of the key innovations of IOTA.

Now, let us examine how tips are selected. We shall also discuss transaction rates and the concept of random walk. In IOTA tangle, transactions do not occur uniformly but rather randomly. At a certain period, there may be m transactions while in another period there may be only n transactions, where m>n or m<n. The transaction rate can be determined by a mathematical process known as the Poisson Point Process. The Poisson Point Process model is used to analyze random events, such as the arrival of customers at a store, phone calls at a call center or occurrence of earthquakes, distributed in time

The transaction rate may be calculated based on the simplified Poisson Point Process formula as follows:

$N = \lambda t$

N is the number of transactions and t is the time unit. λ is a constant. For example, if we set $\lambda = 5$, and time unit = 10 (the unit could be in milliseconds or seconds etc.), the number of transactions occurring in a 10-unit time interval is 5×10 = 50.

Setting a suitable value of λ is crucial to maintaining the coherence of the Tangle structure. If we set the value of λ to be exceedingly small, let us say 0.1, and the number of transactions remains at 50, the time interval will be 50 ÷ 0.1 = 500. In this case, it means that transactions will come in so slowly that it will form a chain instead of a Tangle, such that only one single tip can be approved at any given time, instead of approving two previous transactions. The scenario is illustrated in Figure 7.3.

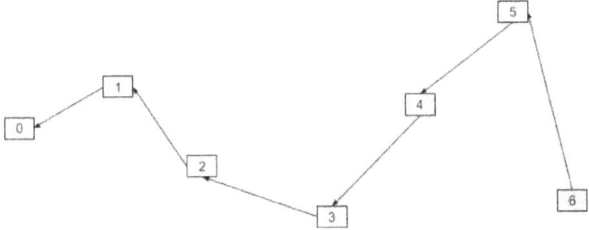

Figure 7.3

What will happen if we set the value of λ too high? For example, if λ = 10000 and N = 50, the time interval t is 0.0005. It means that transactions will be occurring so fast that the only tip they can view is the genesis node, as illustrated in Figure 7.4.

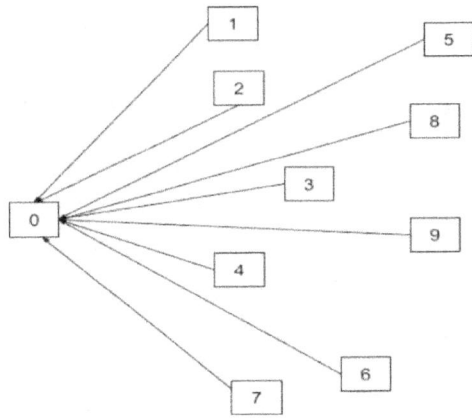

Figure 7.4

In both cases, the Tangle structure will crumble.

7.1.5 Unweighted Random Walk Algorithm

The tips selection algorithm we have discussed so far is a random selection process. This kind of selection process might not be suitable for real use cases. Therefore, we need to choose a more advanced tip selection algorithm. One of the algorithms is known as the unweighted random walk.

What is it? In programming, a walker is a variable used to move through an array or other data structure, often heading towards a fixed value and stepping through elements in an array. In Tangle, we can program a walker on the genesis transaction, and make it walk towards the tips.

On each step, it walks to one of the transactions which directly approves the one we are currently on. It chooses which transaction to walk with equal probability, therefore it is called unweighted random walk.

Though unweighted random walk (URW) is quite useful, it has its weakness that could crash the IOTA ecosystem. Fortunately, there is a better tips selection method known as the weighted random walk (WRW).

7.1.6 The Lazy Tips

The main issue of using the URW algorithm is the occurrence of lazy tips. Lazy tips are tips that choose to approve some old transactions rather than actively looking to approve new transactions. We label them lazy tips because they could not be bothered to update the latest state of the IOTA Tangle network. Instead, they choose to broadcast its transactions based on old data. Let us examine figure 7.5.

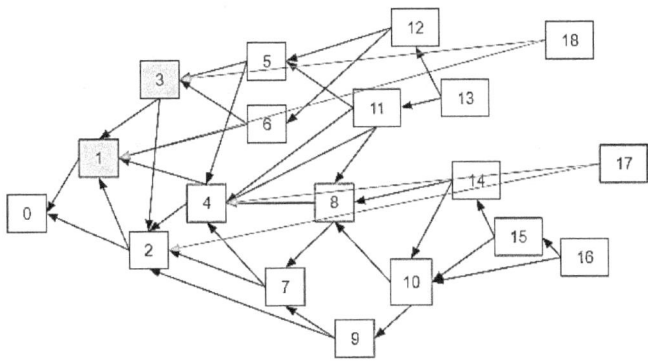

Figure 7.5

With reference to the diagram above, transaction 17 and transaction 18 are lazy tips as they only approved some old transactions, as shown clearly in the diagram. If we employ the unweighted random walk selection method, these two tips have equal chances to get approved as other tips. Their behaviors would not even be penalized by the IOTA system. If too many lazy tips exist in the system, the Tangle will become stagnant or simply fail, as illustrated in Figure 7.6.

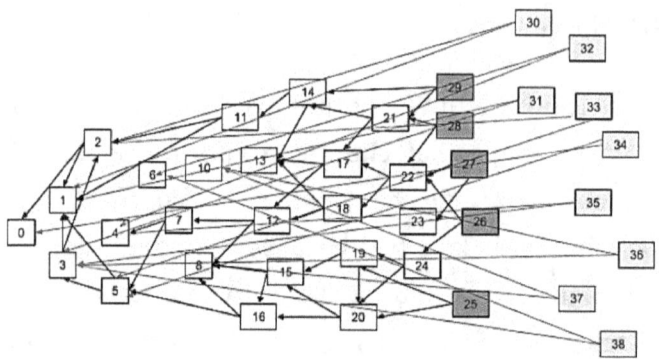

Figure 7.6

In the diagram above, we notice that transactions 30 to 38 chose to approve incredibly old transactions, leaving transactions 25 to 29 unapproved or orphaned. In such a situation, the Tangle structure will just stop propagating and eventually crumble.

7.1.7 Weighted Random Walk

How should we overcome the 'Lazy Tips' phenomenon? We might impose a rule that requires all incoming transactions to approve recent transactions. However, this coercive way is against the principles of decentralization and democracy, the core of decentralized ledger technologies. Therefore, IOTA opted for the persuasion method. It implements a built-in incentives system that rewards the participants for approving recent transactions. This method is called the weighted random walk (WRW).

Weighted random walk uses the bias strategy to select the path towards a tip. The bias strategy involves choosing a path that has the highest approved transactions over the path that has very few approved transactions. Here we introduce a term called cumulative weight to denote the number of approvers of the transactions. It means that the higher the number of approvers, the higher the cumulative weight and vice versa. The approvers could both be direct or indirect approvers. Let us examine the following diagram.

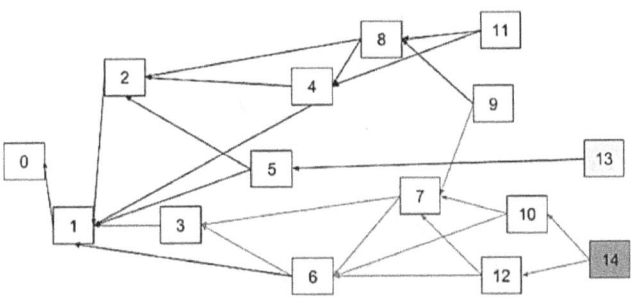

Figure 7.7

To approve tip number 13, the walker needs to walk to transaction number 5. However, transaction 5 only has a cumulative weight of 1, therefore the walker will not continue this path. Instead, it will look for the path that has the highest cumulative weight. In our example, transaction 3 has a weight of 6, therefore the walker will choose this path and eventually reach transaction 14 and approve it.

7.1.8 The Parameter Alpha

However, even the weighted random walk method has its own weakness. If we insist that every approval of the transactions must follow the rule strictly, we will do away with randomness completely and many tips will be left unapproved. The Tangle system will end up having many unapproved transactions, or orphans. (I introduced my own term, orphan, which may not be in accordance with the IOTA concepts. You can read the IOTA academic paper here. https://www.iota.org/research/academic-papers)

To overcome those issues, IOTA introduced a parameter α to control the 'weight' of the weighted random walk. If $\alpha = 0$, it becomes unweighted random walk and creates the issue of approving too many lazy tips. On the other hand, if we set the value of α too high, it will end up as a super weighted random walk which will leave many orphans in the Tangle.

Therefore, it is important to find a good balance between approving too many lazy tips and not leaving too many orphaned tips behind. To sum up, finding an ideal value for α is important to maintain the coherence of the Tangle ecosystem championed by IOTA.

Therefore, it is important to find a good balance between approving too many lazy tips and not leaving too many orphaned tips behind. To sum up, finding an ideal value for α is important to maintain the coherence of the Tangle ecosystem championed by IOTA.

7.2 R3 Corda

Corda is another enterprise-ready blockless DLT platform other than IOTA. It was developed and launched by R3 in 2016. R3 is an enterprise software firm which focuses on distributed ledger technology. Though Corda was only launched in 2016, the R3 story began in 2015 when it partnered with nine financial institutions to form a consortium. Today, it collaborates with more than 300 members and partners across multiple industries from both the private and public sectors to work on the Corda project.

Besides that, R3 has assembled a global team of over 180 professionals in 13 countries and over 2,000 technology, financial, and legal experts drawn from its global member base. (www.r3.com)

7.2.1 Key Concepts of Corda

Corda is an open source blockchain project, designed for business from the start. It allows businesses to build interoperable blockchain networks that transact in strict privacy. Like Ethereum, Corda also features smart contracts that facilitate direct transactions among the businesses. However, its smart contracts are written in Java and other JVM languages instead of Solidity. Also, it enables the development and deployment of distributed apps called CorDapps.

In addition, the Corda platform implements the flow framework to manage communication and negotiation between participants in the network. The Corda network is made up of a peer-to-peer network of nodes. One of the key concepts of Corda is its network service known as the notary. The notary service provides uniqueness consensus for verification of transactions.

7.2.2 The Corda Architecture

Although we often refer to Corda as a blockchain platform, strictly speaking, it is not a blockchain-based ecosystem. It is a kind of decentralized ledger technology network system that is not built by blocks. Instead, it looks a bit like the Tangle system in IOTA.

7.2.3 The Corda Network

The Corda network is an authenticated peer-to-peer network of nodes. Each node is a JVM runtime environment hosting Corda services and executing applications known as CorDapps. We can visualize the Corda network as a fully connected graph. The nodes on the graph can communicate with other nodes, as shown in figure 7.8.

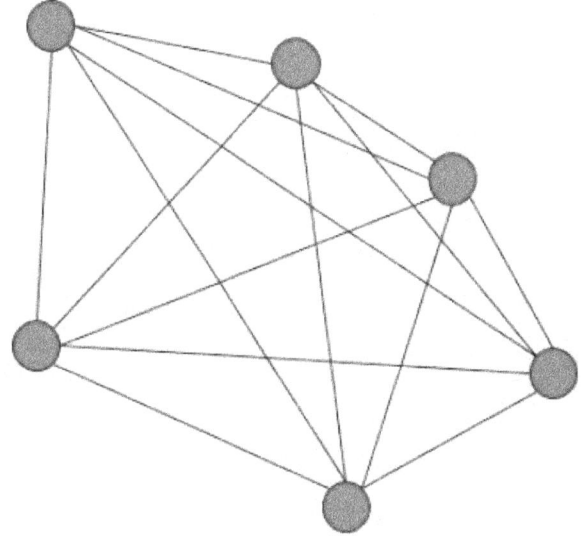

Figure 7.8

7.2.4 How does Corda differ from other DLT Platforms?

The Corda platform is different from other DLT platforms because the structure is blockless. Also, the way it propagates data is different. Other DLT platforms use global broadcast and gossip networks to propagate data. However, Corda does not employ the global broadcast method. Instead, it uses point to point messaging to transmit data.

According to the Corda white paper, all communication between nodes is direct, with TLS-encrypted messages sent over the AMQP. This means that data is shared only on a need-to-know basis. (TLS stands for Transport Layer Security. AMQP stands for Advanced

Message Queuing Protocol, an open standard application layer protocol for message-oriented middleware.)

Corda nodes discover each other via the Network Map Service. The network map service publishes the IP addresses through which every node on the network can be reached. Also, it broadcasts the identity certificates of those nodes and the services they provide. You can imagine the service as a phone book, which publishes a list of peer nodes containing information.

7.2.5 The Doorman

Corda networks are semi-private, which means it needs to impose a kind of gateway control before a node can join a network. This control is called doorman. Each network has a doorman service that enforces rules regarding the information that nodes must provide. These nodes need to go through the know-your-customer (KYC) process before being admitted to the network.

To join the network, a node must contact the doorman and provide the required information. If the doorman is satisfied, the node will receive a root-authority-signed TLS certificate from the network's permissioning service. This certificate certifies the node's identity when communicating with other participants on the network.

Chapter 8

Blockchain-Powered Financial Services

Though cryptocurrency was the first application of blockchain, blockchain can be applied in virtually any business and industry, particularly in financial services.

8.1 Cross-Border Money Transfer

Cross-border money transfer is a huge market. According to World Bank statistics, the scale of global cross-border payments has grown at an average annual rate of 5%. In 2016, it reached US $601 billion, and in 2017 it reached US $613 billion. Global remittances are expected to grow by 4.6% to $642 billion in 2018. However, due to the large number of intermediate links (as shown in Figure 8.1), the cost of cross-border remittances is high, and the average commission rate per remitter is as high as 7.68%. In addition, the remittance cycle is long, from a few days to weeks or even months. Cross-border remittances are also susceptible to fraud.

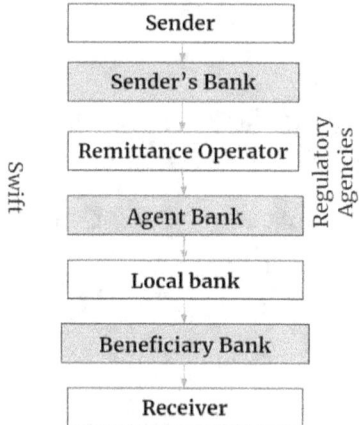

Figure 8.1 The Process of Cross-Border Money Transfer

The high cost of remittances comes mainly from fees levied by Swift, the global Interbank Financial Telecommunication Association. It is responsible for providing financial messaging service (FTS) to the global banking and financial industry. At present, 11000 financial institutions are in use, covering more than 200 countries.

The Swift system was established in the 1970s. It was efficient and fast for that year, but it will inevitably fall behind after the Internet information revolution. Credit Suisse said in a report that the old Swift has many security risks, and 6.1 billion financial messages are sent out every year, which is costly with an average rate of 10%.

To solve the pain point of high cost and delay of cross-border remittance, blockchain operators have launched new cross-border remittance schemes based on blockchain technology. McKinsey's data shows that "globally, the application of blockchain technology in B2B cross-border payment and settlement services will reduce the cost per transaction from approximately US $26 to US $15, of which approximately 75% are paid by intermediary banks. Network maintenance costs, 25% for compliance, error investigation and foreign exchange costs".

One of the blockchain pioneers in the cross-border transfer industry is Ripple. Ripple has created an open source software that enables peer-to-peer financial transactions between banks around the world. Ripple focuses on cross-border international bank clearing and has cooperated with 12 top 50 banks. Another player Okcoin, a Chinese blockchain company, has also set up Oklink, a Hong Kong Branch, to do cross-border remittance and clearing. Oklink is now completely free, and the future business model is to share the service fee with the merchant, which is about 0.1% of the settlement fee. Circle also claims that its exchange settlement costs are between 0.2% and 0.3% and are currently free. On the other hand, the R3 community-led bank cross-border clearing alliance has included more than 60 of the world's top banks, including Barclays Bank, Goldman Sachs Group and JPMorgan Chase, and recently Ping An Bank.

In terms of the speed of arrival, the blockchain companies have been able to transfer funds in real time. The Ripple Blockchain helps the world's first blockchain international interbank remittances to be completed in a total of 20 seconds. And Oklink's arrival speed is between 5 seconds and 10 minutes. In short, blockchain-based cross-border money transfer has the following advantages:

- Reduce costs and expenses
- The fee charged by the intermediary bank is exempted
- Cross-border payment and settlement more secure
- Speed up the transaction
- Provide peer-to-peer payment methods, eliminating intermediaries and enabling real-time payment

8.2 Blockchain-Based P2P Lending

Traditional P2P lending models are facing many issues. For example, the cost of onboarding customers remains high, so investors are wary of this kind of investment model. Besides that, this area is heavily regulated by the securities commission in most countries. While a handful of P2P companies have been approved to operate their businesses, many more P2P operators who failed to obtain a license are facing the nightmare of shutting down.

Conventional P2P lending cannot allow borrowers and investors to directly match financing, but rather needs to be handled as a credit intermediary through the P2P lending platform. The financing cost is increased because of the need to pay the agency fee. Other issues include the limited scalability of P2P lending services on an international scale. This is due to the problems of loan repayment guarantees, as well as regulatory issues (rules and regulations vary from country to country). There is also an urgent need to accelerate the process of granting loans.

Although P2P lending platforms are supposed to be operating in a decentralized manner, they are still largely operating in a centralized model. Data is usually stored and maintained on a central database, which might lead to human errors and manipulation of data.

On the contrary, data stored on a blockchain are stored on the decentralized and distributed network, where every stakeholder has access to a copy of the same ledger. Furthermore, data on the blockchain is immutable, so no party can alter and manipulate the stored data. These characteristics of the blockchain will greatly enhance data security, increase transparency, and instill trust amongst stakeholders. Therefore, blockchain is the perfect solution to solve the woes of current P2P lending models. Indeed, a dozen companies have started to deploy blockchain-based P2P lending platforms.

Blockchain-based P2P businesses are broadly divided into two models, the hybrid model, and the pure cryptocurrency model. The hybrid model involves using cryptocurrency and fiat money while the pure cryptocurrency model uses only cryptocurrencies.

8.2.1 The Hybrid P2P Lending Model

This model uses a combination of fiat currency and cryptocurrency to provide P2P lending services. Let us examine a few companies that implement this model.

SALT

SALT (Secure Automated Lending Technology) is a leader in the blockchain-based P2P lending industry. SALT's model allows borrowers to use their crypto assets as collateral to secure loans from an extensive network of lenders on the platform. It means SALT does not bother to check the credit score of borrowers, but grants eligibility based on the amount of crypto assets they are willing to put up as collateral. The main advantage for SALT borrowers is the ability to borrow fiat money against the security of their crypto assets, which is considered more practical to ordinary people than the pure cryptocurrency lending model.

To sign up as a member of SALT, a borrower needs to purchase SALT tokens, the cryptocurrency of the SALT platform. SALT is minted using an ERC20 smart contract. After signing up, borrowers must deposit a certain amount of crypto assets (cryptocurrency) as collateral into the platform's unique, multi-signature wallet address created by SALT. After the terms of the loan are agreed and approved, the lender will make a deposit in fiat money into the borrower's bank account. The borrower will be obligated to make repayments in fiat money or stable coins (currently accepting USDC, TUSD, and PAX) on a regular basis before the 15th of the month. In the event of a default, his or her crypto assets will be transferred to the lender.

For an asset to qualify as collateral on the SALT Platform, it must meet certain eligibility requirements. First and foremost, it must be a blockchain asset. This means that the ownership of the asset must be recorded on a public or permissioned blockchain. Digital assets will be onboarded based off community demand.

Examples of currently eligible collateral include Bitcoin (BTC), Bitcoin Cash (BCH), Ether (ETH), Litecoin (LTE), Dogecoin (DOGE), Dash (DASH), TruUSD (TUSD), USD Coin (USDC), Paxos Standard Token (PAX), and PAX Gold (PXG).

NEXO

The NEXO P2P model is somewhat like the SALT model. It also possesses a cryptocurrency known as the NEXO. According to the NEXO website, the NEXO Token is the world's first US SEC-compliant asset-backed token and is backed by the underlying assets of NEXO's loan portfolio. It can be used for discounted interest rates and loan repayments, as well as collateral. One incentive for holding the NEXO token is that it pays dividends to holders. Thirty percent of the profits generated from NEXO loans go to a dividend pool that is then distributed to NEXO holders. Currently, dividend payments are being made in Ethereum (ETH), but there's a good chance that this will expand to other cryptocurrencies in the future.

The loan approval process is fully automated. A credit line becomes instantly available to the borrower once the application is approved and there is no credit check. The borrower can spend money instantly with a card or withdraw money to a bank account. Spending on the credit line will incur an APR from 5.9% of what the borrower uses. Some advantages of NEXO compared to SALT is there is no minimum repayment, no hidden fees, and the interest is debited from the available limit. Besides that, the borrower can make repayments at any time. On top of that, the NEXO website states that it is the only insured account that lets you borrow instantly in 45+ fiat currencies and earn daily interest on your idle assets. Furthermore, NEXO makes its loans available worldwide. Anyone who holds cryptocurrency can take advantage of a NEXO loan. And since the loans are fully collateralized there is no need for borrowers to worry about credit history or approvals.

Though the use cases for NEXO loans will be somewhat limited since they're collateral-backed, the use of cryptocurrencies as collateral makes for an attractive alternative for those who hold cryptocurrencies and don't want to sell yet and give up future gains, but still need fiat currency for immediate use.

Now, more than twenty cryptocurrencies including BTC, ETH, NEXO, XRP, TRON and more can be accepted as the collateral. Any loans taken can be repaid using cryptocurrency, fiat currency, or the NEXO token. They have made it as easy as possible to repay any loans. In contrast, SALT only accepts loan repayment in fiat currency, which is an inconvenience for the borrowers.

8.2.2. Pure Cryptocurrency P2P Lending Model

ETHLend

ETHLend is a decentralized cryptocurrency credit platform and the world's first crypto lending marketplace. Unlike SALT and NEXO, it operates exclusively through Ethereum smart contracts. ETHLend also has a token known as the LEND token. It is the native ERC20 token of the ETHLend platform. Its token can be stored in any Ethereum wallet in a similar way as other ERC20 tokens.

The lending process at ETHLend is quite simple. When creating a smart contract, ETHLend requires borrowers to send ERC-20 tokens as collateral for ETH loans in the event of a borrower's default. Currently ETH, BTC, LEND and more than 150 ERC20 tokens are accepted as collateral.

There is no limit in the loan value, as the amount you can borrow depends on the value of your collateral. Borrowers can borrow up to 50% of their collateral value and up to 55% if LEND is used as collateral. This means the borrower needs to send to the smart contract 200% of the value of the loan in crypto assets.

To become a lender, you will need to register on the platform and send to your in-app wallet some Ether or any of the currencies accepted in order to fund a loan or create a loan offer. The accepted currencies are ETH, LEND, DAI and TUSD. This also means borrowers will receive the cryptocurrencies as loans.

The borrower needs to repay the loan in accordance with the contract, plus interest on the loan, and send them to a smart contract. The lender receives their ETH and interest from the smart contract, and the pledged tokens are unlocked and sent back to the borrower. If the borrower cannot repay the loan, the lender will get the payments plus a liquidation fee from the collateral.

Elix

Elix is an Ethereum-based platform for lending, crowdfunding, and payments. The Elix team primarily focused on mobile platforms and usability to attract as large a user base as possible from the start. I will not discuss the payment and crowdfunding component of this platform, but rather concentrate only on its P2P lending component.

The uniqueness of this system lies in the fact that Elix offers a peer-to-peer lending program based on mutual incentives for the lender and the borrower. In Elix, both the lender and the borrower are incentivized by the system to meet the terms of the loan. When applying for a loan, participants can choose a mining period to receive system rewards in the form of a new token, "Token P".

If the borrower pays the loan on time, the reward is divided between the lender receiving 65% and the borrower who receives 35%. If the borrower has late payments, the lender receives 100% of this fee. Token P will have a fixed maximum supply that the team expects to achieve in only a few decades.

8.3 Crypto Fund Management

Cryptocurrency is a new asset class derived from nascent blockchain technology. The phenomenal growth of cryptocurrencies in recent years has attracted many investors who used to invest in traditional financial products to start investing in crypto assets. Reports have shown that there is a significant amount of capital flowing into the crypto market. This capital flow has created an increasing demand for new financial products that cater to the needs of the crypto market.

Indeed, cryptocurrencies are rapidly gaining traction with the public. According to CoinMarketCap, the total market cap for all cryptocurrencies reached an amazing $739 billion in January 2018. Though the market cap dropped to a low $113 billion in December 2018 due to the bear market, it rebounded strongly in 2019 to a figure between $250 billion to $350 billion. Though much of this value has been generated by individual traders, it is also largely the result of large investment funds. These crypto fund management companies, which hold crypto assets worth as much as $1 billion or more, are the whales of the cryptocurrency community.

Generally, the trading of crypto assets is performed on exchanges. Most crypto investors keep and manage their crypto assets on exchanges, cold storage, mobile wallets, desktop wallets, hardware wallets, and more. The complex management process that requires sophisticated skills makes it extremely difficult for individuals to manage a diverse crypto portfolio.

Fortunately, a dozen crypto fund management companies have emerged with products and services that could help ease the tedious investment process in crypto investment. One of the most popular ones is the use of index funds to automate the process of investing in crypto assets for individuals, using AI algorithms. Another crypto financial product on the rise is the crypto hedge fund which caters only to high net worth individuals.

Indeed, crypto investment tools and products such as crypto index funds, automated trading with rebalancing, and tracking are becoming ubiquitous. Crypto index funds provide an opportunity for investors to build their own portfolio or track an index and reap profits from this new and volatile asset class.

Despite the potential issues, it is encouraging that crypto hedge funds seem to have performed reasonably well even during bear markets. And with most crypto funds in the index now employing external auditors, custodian services and fund administrators, the industry is becoming less risky. Although the crypto fund industry is still very much in a nascent stage, crypto funds could present institutions and individuals with an attractive way to invest in this sector. Let us examine some index funds in the crypto market.

8.3.1 Bitwise 10 Private Index Fund

The Bitwise 10 Private Index Fund is the world's first crypto asset index fund. It seeks to track the Bitwise 10 Large Cap Crypto Index ("Bitwise 10 Index"), which selects the 10 largest crypto assets based on criteria including 5-year diluted market capitalization, trade volume minimums, concentration limits, and compliance. The portfolio is rebalanced monthly. Assets are held in 100% cold storage, audited annually, and purchased across several liquidity providers to seek best execution. Bitwise actively evaluates network opportunities including hard forks, airdrops, emissions, staking rewards, super- and master-node rewards, and captures available benefits for fund investors where appropriate.

Bitwise is a crypto asset manager founded in 2017. The firm has a large software team, with backgrounds across Google, Facebook, Wealthfront, and military software security, which we believe is essential for navigating the space. Bitwise has been covered by CNBC, Forbes, Bloomberg, Barron's, WSJ, Coindesk, and others, and is active in the crypto asset community.

Table 8.1 Bitwise 10 Index Components

Coin Name	Symbol	Percentage
Bitcoin	BTC	77.8%
Ethereum	ETH	8.5%
Ripple	XRP	6.0%
Bitcoin Cash	BCH	2.4%
Stellar Lumens	XLM	0.6%
Litecoin	LTC	1.9%
EOS	EOS	1.4%
Monero	XMR	0.5%
Cardano	ADA	0.4%
DASH	DASH	0.4%

8.3.2 Crypto20

Crypto20 claims to be the first tokenized index crypto index fund in the world. Their motto is autonomous 'token-as-a-fund'.

In 2017, their team successfully pioneered the first tokenized crypto-only index fund, which used seed funding to buy the underlying crypto assets. There are no broker fees, no exit fees, no minimum investment, and full control over your assets.

Crypto20 provides a way to track the performance of the crypto markets by holding a single crypto asset. They claimed that their index funds have consistently beaten the average managed fund since their inception.

Learn more about Crypto20 from their whitepaper: https://cdn.crypto20.com/pdf/c20-whitepaper.pdf?.

Alternatively, you can investigate more accessible funds that don't require heavy investment. Let us look at the following funds.

8.3.3 Coinbase

The Coinbase Bundle offers a one-click purchase for the first five cryptocurrencies that were listed on Coinbase, which are weighted by market cap at the time of purchase.

- Bitcoin — 76.59%

- Ethereum — 15.84%
- Litecoin — 3.94%
- Bitcoin Cash — 3.11%
- Ethereum Classic — 0.52%

This retail-aimed product allows users to invest as little as $25 in the basket of crypto assets.

8.3.4 Hodlbot

HodlBot is a customizable cryptocurrency trading bot that enables users to index the market, create custom portfolios, and automatically rebalance their cryptocurrency portfolios.

HodlBot allows you to grow your portfolio like the world's most sophisticated investors. They are making institutional portfolio management software available to everyone. Best of all, HodlBot is free forever for account values under $500. Otherwise, it is $10/month with a 7-day free trial.

In short, crypto index funds are a fast-growing alternative financial product that is currently outperforming the stock markets and other traditional financial products. Though it is still riskier than traditional investments, it is worth venturing into this market to grow your capital.

Chapter 9 Transaction and Provenance Tracking

9.1 Transaction Tracking

The blockchain has a reconciled tracking and record-keeping mechanism that makes it easier for individuals, organizations, enterprises, or governments to track and manage transaction or event information. Cross-border payment is a good use case. The blockchain can track and store transaction records throughout the process. Another use case is that the Ministry of Transport can use blockchain technology to record and track the complete data of road users 'violations of traffic regulations, so that the offenders have nowhere to go and can easily process fines.

Blockchain technology allows us to track all types of transactions throughout the supply chain more safely and transparently. Every time a product changes hands, it can record transactions and store permanent data from manufacturing to sales. This can greatly reduce the time delays, high costs and human errors that plague current transactions.

Wal-Mart and nine other companies have partnered with IBM to release a blockchain through their supply chain to track global food to ensure food safety. The Food Trust 's goal is to improve the company's ability to identify issues related to food recalls, such as tracking outbreaks more quickly to reduce customer risk.

Frank Yiannas, vice president of food safety at Wal-Mart, called the Food Trust blockchain "the equivalent of FedEx food tracking."

9.2 Provenance tracking and record keeping

Blockchain can be used in provenance tracking and record keeping. The Diamond Time-Lapse plan was formulated in 2017. The plan is basically to record the historical ledger of diamond transfers, containing real-time data on the origin of the diamond, processes including cutting and polishing, mastering the work and certification of craftsmen.

Diamond Time-Lapse is a diamond and jewelry industry platform built on blockchain, the purpose is to let all industry participants understand the diamond information from the origin to the end customer.

Starting in 2015, Everledger first began using the best emerging technology in the global digital ledger to securely track and trace proven diamond sources. Everledger has collaborated with a series of stakeholders in the diamond supply chain (including diamond manufacturers and downstream retailers) to encrypt the source of more than 2 million diamonds in just three years.

In this era of counterfeit goods, fake documents, fake diplomas, and copyright infringement, it is difficult for us to identify the authenticity of materials. So, it often happens that when buying fake goods, the company invites the wrong person and the government asks for a fake doctor. Block-based tamper resistance, transparency and permanent preservation features have become saviors for anti-counterfeiting and can also protect intellectual property rights. The diamond tracking system discussed earlier is one of the use cases.

Another use case is https://stamp.io. This system allows you to upload files or data and provide them with digital certificates.

LuxTag in Malaysia is a blockchain source tracking and record keeping platform. LuxTag provides digital certificates by using blockchain technology to enable companies and their customers to protect the authenticity and ownership of their valuable assets. Currently focused projects are:

- Fashion industry
- Provenance tracking
- Blockchain Diploma

LuxTag has partnered with the Ministry of Education of Malaysia to launch the e-Scroll Blockchain Diploma Certification System to prevent this fake diploma. Each diploma contains a QR code, which can be scanned to prove its authenticity

Chapter 10

Blockchain-Powered Supply Chain Management

Traditional supply chain management is facing a lot of issues and pain points, such as tracking and tracing difficulties, counterfeit products, fraud, theft, lack of real time information and more. These issues add extra cost to the products and services. Fortunately, the blockchain technology may provide a viable solution to the issues. Let us delve into the following two case studies.

Case 1 Blockchain-Powered Smart Supply Chain Management - Auto Parts Business Case Study

The automotive supply chain is an overly complex and broad ecosystem, involving a wide range of participants such as parts suppliers, manufacturers, sellers, and aftermarket suppliers. Counterfeit product is a significant issue for automotive manufacturers and suppliers. The counterfeit spare parts market is currently estimated at several billion dollars.

10.1 Automotive Supply Chain Issues

Parts supply and management is key to an auto parts business. However, current auto parts supply chain faces many issues including:

- Difficulty in tracking of parts
- Theft of parts
- Data fraud.
- Counterfeit products

Maintaining a level of consistency and error-proofing, to ensure that the right part gets to the right location just in time, is a huge challenge for any automotive supplier.

Counterfeit products are a significant issue for automotive manufacturers/suppliers and the counterfeit spare parts market is currently estimated at several billion dollars. Counterfeit spare parts are often of low quality and thus more likely to fail. This leads to dissatisfied customers and trust in the brand is impacted. Especially in the case of vintage cars, a counterfeit spare part can significantly impact the car value.

Faced with thousands of spare parts, hundreds of parameters, and the number of manufacturers distributed regionally or globally, the SCM team needs to deal with a huge amount of data.

Two most common challenges are:

- The need to keep inventories well-stocked but not overstocked.
- The need to deal with the sheer amount of recalls

10.2 Possible Benefits of Blockchain Usage in Automotive SCM

Disruptive potential of blockchain technology for solving the pain points in automotive SCM could be immense.

Blockchain technology provides increased transparency across the supply chain and could significantly reduce the cost and complexity of doing business with multiple parties. For automakers and suppliers, blockchain technology offers unique benefits starting with protecting their brands from counterfeit products to enhance their brand experience by creating customer-centric business models. Let us examine the following potential benefits of blockchain-powered SCM in the auto parts industry.

10.2.1 Identification and Tracking of Automotive Spare Parts

Counterfeit Protection – Verifying Authenticity and Origin

Counterfeit products are a significant issue for automotive manufacturers/suppliers and the counterfeit spare parts market is currently estimated at several billion dollars. Counterfeit spare parts are often of low quality and thus more likely to fail. This leads to dissatisfied customers and trust in the brand.

A mutual collaboration is facilitated between the parties, ensuring that sensitive business information remains confidential. Confidentiality is enforced through blockchain cryptographic methods, not only from manipulators within the business network but also externally from attackers.

A spare parts service center for instance can accurately verify the authenticity of a part during replacement. The immutability of blockchain provides for a tamper proof solution and offers a single source of truth. Customers ultimately benefit through fewer disruptions and the trust relationship with the manufacturer is enhanced.

Protection of Aftermarket Business

The global aftermarket business was valued at over 800 billion USD in 2018 and is expected to grow to over a trillion USD over the next 10 years. Over 50% of this market consists of the sale of vehicle spare parts and business is split across OEM (Original Equipment Manufacturer) and IAM (Independent Aftermarket) Suppliers.

As each product or part is uniquely represented on the blockchain, the technology can be applied to enforce business terms related to the exact production volume and timing. This level of enforcement can also be applied for manufacturers working with more than one supplier as part of their dual sourcing strategy.

Spare Parts Liability Resolution

In case a spare part needs to be replaced due to failure, liability needs to be established and this requires tracing the part back to the manufacturer. If parts are identified and digitally represented on the blockchain, it offers an accurate way to trace the origin. Liability is thus clearly established and is transparent to all parties in the blockchain. Any liability disputes can be resolved much faster and resources can be focused on customer engagement.

Vehicle Recall Optimization

Many of the recalls involve product defects that are life-threatening, and automakers are exposed to a huge liability. With blockchain technology the car and the individual assembled parts can be uniquely represented on the blockchain. If automakers have accurate visibility on which defective parts were installed in which cars, then the scope of the recall can be precisely executed. This will result in massive cost savings for the manufacturer.

10.2.2 Optimizing the Supply Chain Process

Inbound Logistics and Smart Manufacturing

The efficient planning of production capacity requires the manufacturing plant to coordinate between multi-tier suppliers, third party logistics and transportation companies. Tracking and tracing individual parts across the inbound supply chain is complex and error prone. Accurate, real-time information is not available, and information is spread across individual databases.

By using a distributed immutable blockchain ledger across all parties, an accurate view of the status, quantity and location of the individual parts can be established. This granular visibility can improve real-time logistics and plant production capacity.

Outbound Logistics Planning

The outbound supply chain in the automotive sector consists of a complex network of manufacturers, distributors, importers, and dealers. Like the inbound supply chain, participants in the outbound supply chain do not have a common data sharing Model.

Having a shared blockchain-based system across the different participants will offer transparency and visibility. This will ensure faster transactions by lowering settlement periods.

10.2.3 Business Model Innovation

Car Personalization and Customer Engagement

Driver profile along with car customization preferences can be saved in a personal blockchain wallet. Shared or leased cars will authenticate the driver using the wallet and the car settings are personalized based on the driver profile. Automakers and mobility operators can thus create new business models focusing on individual preferences.

Dynamic Pricing Models in Automotive Insurance and Leasing

A driver profile including miles covered, economical usage of vehicle and accident history is securely stored on the blockchain.

Users share this data with providers offering insurance and leasing products based on their personal driving profile. The advantage that blockchain technology brings here is that the driver profile and historic events are immutably stored on the blockchain providing a single source of truth.

Providers can rely on this single source of truth for offering personalized products with dynamic pricing. Users have access to better priced products and get incentivized for good driving behavior

Digital Car Wallet

Ownership history, maintenance and repairs can be transparently and verifiably stored in a blockchain-based car wallet. Ownership record and fair price assessment of second-hand cars can be quickly established and transferring ownership can be done faster.

As vehicles are uniquely identified on the blockchain, stolen cars can be easily tracked and traced. Lack of trust and business friction arising in the transfer of ownership is hugely reduced. If repairs and parts replacements are verifiably tracked on the blockchain, warranty claims will be transparent for all parties.

Car-to-Infrastructure Transactions

Blockchain technology offers a unique way to automate transactions between machines and enable the future of M2M commerce. Cars in the future will be equipped with blockchain-based wallets, and transactions with toll booths, park stations and electric charging outlets will be automated without manual intervention.

10.2 Current Auto Parts SCM Model

The current auto parts SCM model is complex and inefficient as the channel members work in silos and do not have access to shared databased, as shown in Figure 10.1.

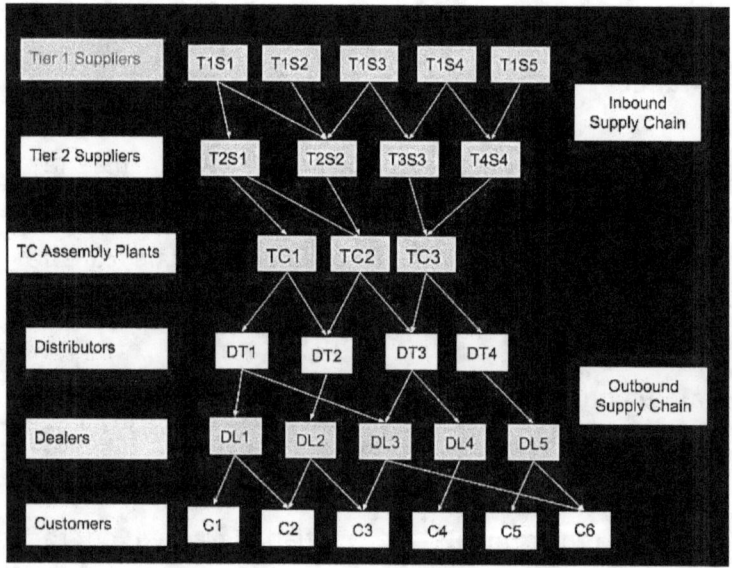

Figure 10.1

10.3 The Proposed Blockchain SSCM Model

The proposed blockchain smart supply chain model is based on the Hyperledger Fabric Framework. The channel members will be more interconnected and have better access to shared common ledger. The model is illustrated in Figure 10.2

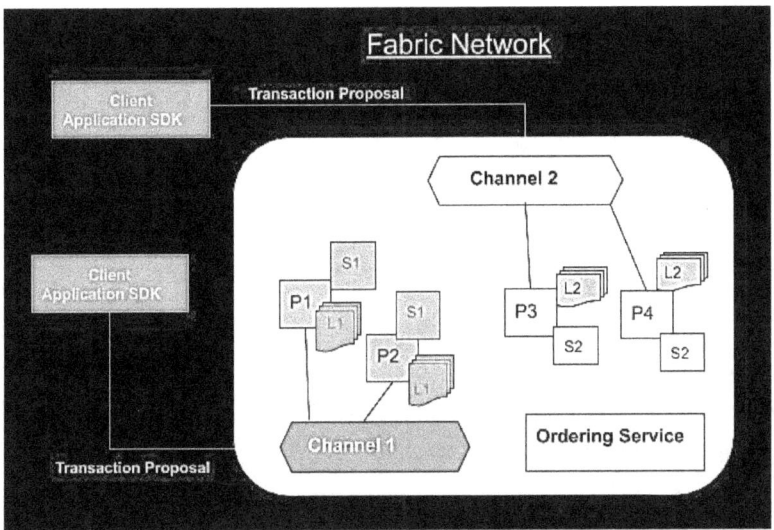

Figure 10.2

The diagram above shows two channels, channel 1 and channel 2. Each channel has its own application, peers, ledger, and smart contract (chaincode). In this example, channel 1 has two peers, P1 and P2 and channel 2 also has two peers, P3 and P4. Ordering service is the same across any network and channel.

Application 1 will send transaction proposals to channel 1. P1 and P2 will then simulate and commit transactions to ledger L1 based on chaincode S1. On the other hand, Application 2 will send transaction proposals to channel 2. P3 and P4 will simulate and commit transactions to ledger L2 based on chaincode S2. Further illustration of channels can be found in Figure 10.3

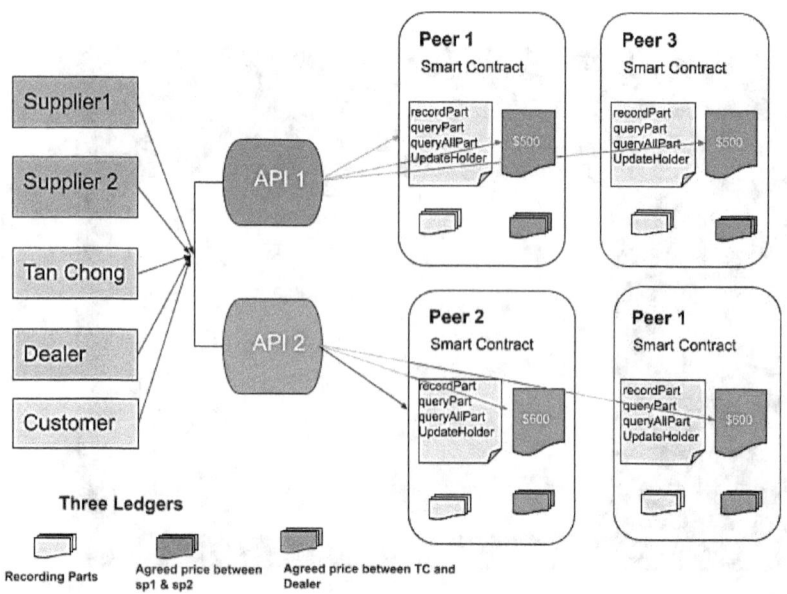

Figure 10.3

The SSCM blockchain network can be hosted on a secure server like AWS, as illustrated in Figure 10.4

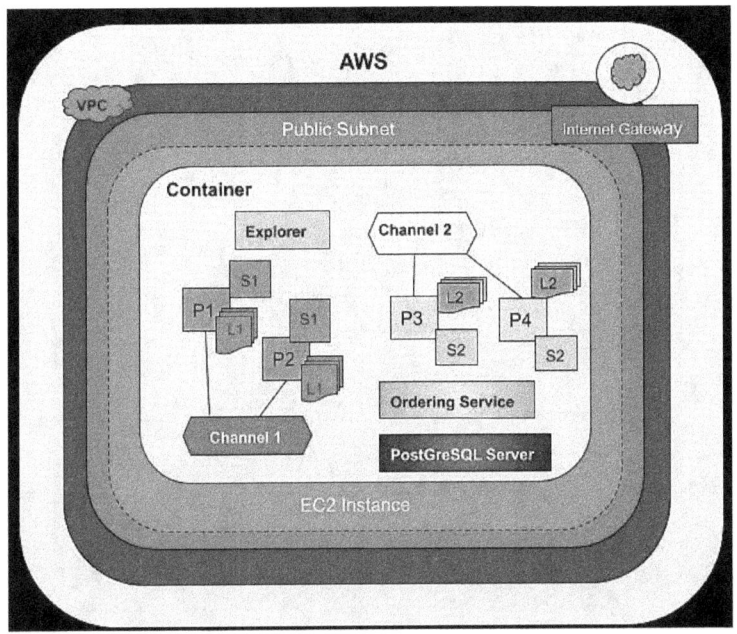

Figure 10.4

Case 2 Blockchain-Powered Smart Supply Chain Management - Textile Industry

This case study examines the issues faced by the Bangladesh textile industry and provides a possible solution based on blockchain.

The following figure outlines the complexity of the textile supply chain in Bangladesh.

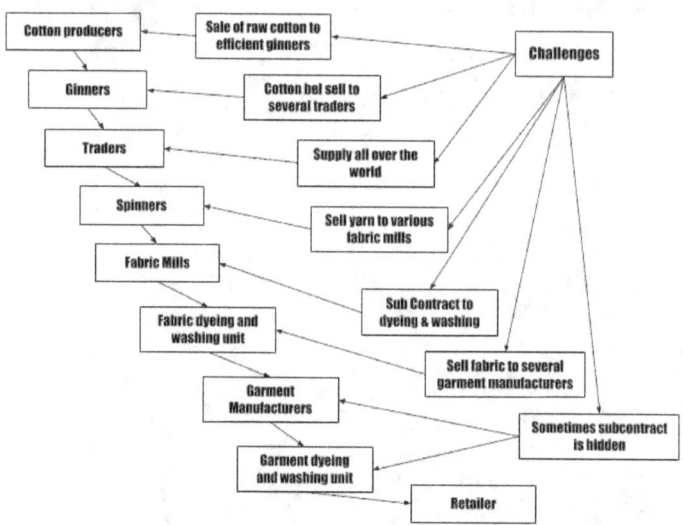

Figure 10.5 Textile Supply Chain

The above supply chain shows the traceability of cotton from firm holder to retailer. Cotton is the key input to the apparel industry. For just one T-shirt made from conventional cotton, you need to use 2700 liters of water. Now, sustainability is becoming an important parameter and apparel brands do not have the time or resources to monitor all aspects of the supply chain, whether crop production or retail. But the problem is, they do not know where the cotton comes from.

The textile supply chain from the raw product to the retailer trade remains overly complex. It is almost impossible to retrace a textile to its place of origin as supply structures in the textile and clothing industry are kept secret. Cotton traceability is becoming an important part for sustainability. Using technology for traceability, it is possible to retrace each production step at each level of the production chain.

Cotton Producers: Small firm holder cultivates and harvests the cotton crops, which are delivered to ginners. For traceability, cotton producers can give a unique code or tag to their raw cotton.

Ginners: Cotton bales are classed according to fiber strength, length, color, non-fiber content and fineness. Ginners sell cotton bale to various cotton traders.

Traders: Traders usually buy cotton bale from various sources and sell it to spinning mills all over the world. So, traceability is difficult for textile industry. For traceability, cotton bales need a bar code or tag.

Spinners: Spinning mills buy cotton bales from several traders. Using a traceability system, they can get information about their cotton bales.

Fabric Mills: Fabric mills buy yarn from various sources. Sometimes, it can come from foreign spinning mills. So, traceability can be more complex.

Dyeing & Washing Unit: Sometimes fulfils fabric demand. Fabric mills may have a subcontract with another unit or engage in outsourcing.

Garment Manufacturers: Every garment manufacturer buys fabric from various sources. And sometimes they have a hidden subcontract with other units.

Retailers: Retailers are the final seller to consumers. Due to sustainability issues, they want to trace their whole supply chain. Every product could have a unique code or barcode that gives customers all the information about that product, from cotton production to retailer.

The traditional SCM is overly complex as the channel members are working in silos and do not have access to shared database. The SCM model is as shown in Figure 10.6

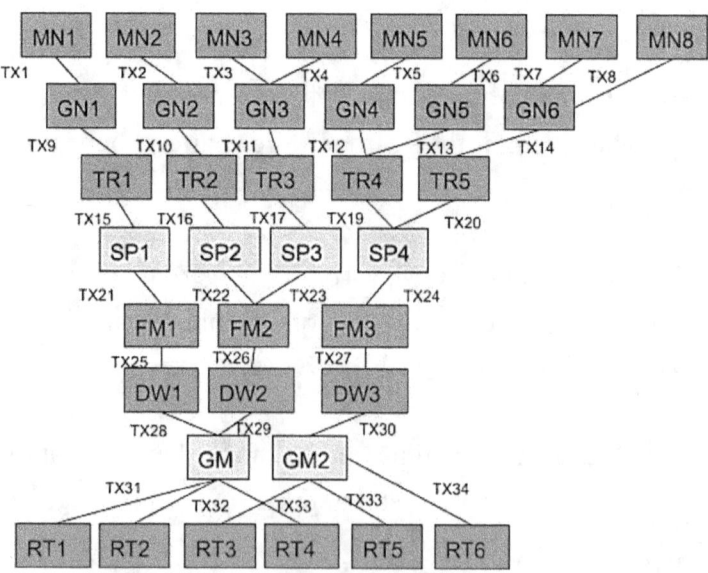

Figure 10.6 Transaction Flow of Traditional SCM

CP Cotton Producer   TX-Transaction

GN-Ginners   TR-Traders

SP-Spinners   FM-Fabrics Mills

DW-Dyeing and Washing   GM-Garment Manufacturers

RT-Retailers

10.4 The Blockchain Solution

The solution is to develop a textile blockchain network hosted on a cloud server, as shown in Figure 10.7. The blockchain network architecture is based on Hyperledger Fabric Framework.

All the transactions between channel members will be recorded through **channel APIs** by the **peer nodes**. The peer nodes will then submit the data to the blockchain platform hosted on a cloud server to be validated by the validator nodes and recorded permanently on the blockchain. **Smart contracts (chaincode)** will be executed in between. The updated blockchain will be broadcasted to the whole Textile Blockchain Network. Every channel member will be able to trace and track their **product ID** by scanning the **QR code** that is connected to the network via the **UI** that is connected to the channel APIs.

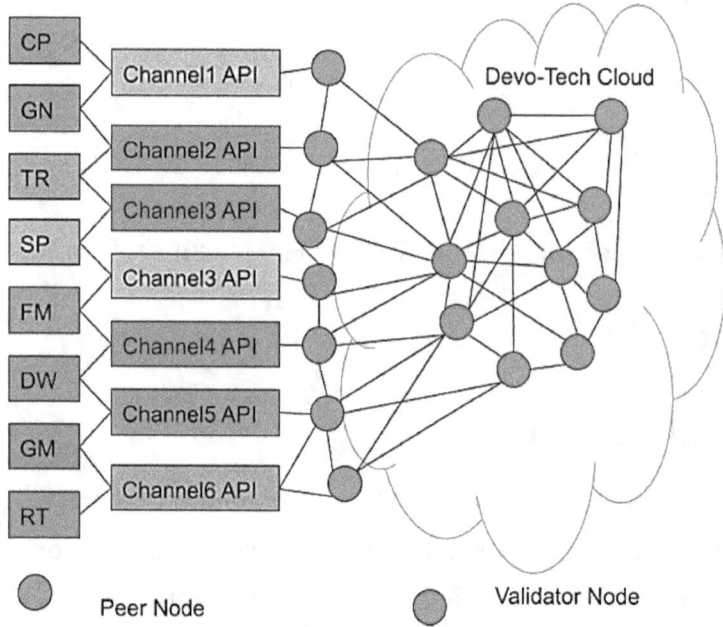

Figure 10.7

The transaction details are saved in the world state as a key/value pair based on the specifications of a chaincode contract, allowing Ali's API to effectively create a transaction on the ledger.

```
$ var cotton_bale = { id: '0001', Ginner: 'Ali', location: { Street: 'Gulshan Rd', City: 'Dhaka'}, when: '20190607123546', weight: '100kg' }
```

This solution will ensure trust, transparency, traceability and trackability in textile supply chain management.

Chapter 11

Building a Digital Government Powered by Blockchain

Digital government is a state-of-the-art concept from public administration science, a successor of the e-government paradigm. The former model simply indicated the digitalization of the public administration. Digital government refers to the creation of new public services and service delivery models that leverage digital technologies as well as governmental and citizen information assets. The new paradigm focuses on the provision of user-centric, agile, and innovative public services. Blockchain is one of the most innovative digital technologies that must be considered under the new paradigm of governmental policy making and service delivery.

Estonia started testing blockchain technology in 2008, even before the Bitcoin whitepaper that first coined the term "blockchain" was published. Since 2012, blockchain has been in production use in Estonia to protect national data, e-services, and smart devices both in the public and private sectors. Estonia has built a decentralized network system known as the X-Road (Numa, 2019), as shown in Figure 11.1.

The X-Road Public Internet helps store information in a distributed way while securely communicating through a data exchange layer. Besides that, the system ensures interoperability, confidentiality and integrity between institutions and platforms. The exchange authentication includes multi-level authorization and processing logs. Moreover, all data is encrypted and signed, and all the included parties are strongly identifiable.

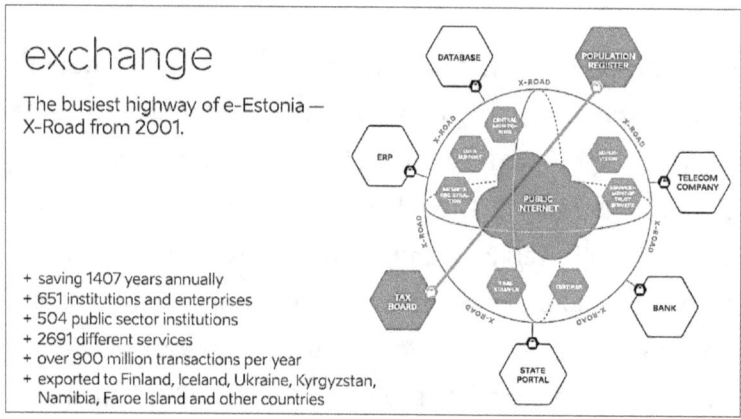

Figure 11.1 X-Road-The Decentralised Public Internet (Source: https://e-estonia.com/)

On the other hand, the Dubai Blockchain strategy will help Dubai achieve the vision of H. H. Sheikh Mohammed bin Rashid Al Maktoum by making "Dubai the first city fully powered by Blockchain by 2020" and make Dubai the happiest city on earth. The strategy will be using three strategic pillars: Government Efficiency, Industry Creation, and International Leadership.

The Proposed Model of a Digital Government Powered by Blockchain

11.1 National Digital Id Blockchain Net

The first step in creating a digital government is to create a National Digital ID Blockchain Net. I propose a National Digital ID Blockchain Net that implements Ethereum Parity's Proof of Authority (PoA) Consensus Protocol, hosted on the National Registration Department (NRD) cloud server. This should be a private permissioned blockchain.

11.2 A Short History of POA

The Ropsten test network that used PoW was brought down in February of 2017 by people taking advantage of the network's low PoW by increasing the block gas limit by almost 2000% while sending huge transactions through the network. Ropsten has since disallowed super high gas limits, but the issue with low PoW remains for the next exploit. This PoW vulnerability led to the next test network known as Rinkeby that uses a PoA (Proof of Authority) called Clique where authorized signers mint the blocks. The POA protocol can also be implemented using Ethereum Parity.

Proof of Authority (PoA) is a reputation-based consensus algorithm that introduces a practical and efficient solution for blockchain networks (especially the private ones). The term was proposed in 2017 by Ethereum co-founder and former CTO Gavin Wood.

Proof-of-Authority (PoA) is a new consensus algorithms family that provides high performance and fault tolerance. In PoA, rights to generate new blocks are awarded to nodes that have proven their authority to do so. To gain this authority and a right to generate new blocks, a node must pass a preliminary authentication.

11.3 Advantages of POA Consensus Protocol

The POA consensus protocol has the following advantages:

- High-performance hardware is not required. Compared to PoW consensus, PoA consensus does not require nodes to spend computational resources for solving complex mathematical tasks.
- The interval of time at which new blocks are generated is predictable. For PoW and PoS consensuses, this time varies.
- High transaction rate. Blocks are generated in a sequence at an appointed time interval by authorized network nodes. This increases the speed at which transactions are validated.
- Tolerance to compromised and malicious nodes, if 51% of nodes are not compromised. PoA implements a ban mechanism for nodes and means of revoking block generation right.

11.4 The National Digital ID Blockchain Net Notary Nodes

The first step in building the National Digital ID Blockchain Net is to select the Notary Nodes (Validator Nodes). They must be chosen from people who can be trusted and have high reputation.

Examples: high level public servants like NRD director, chief judge, minister, lawyer, central bank governor, NGO president etc.

11.5 The Role of Notary Nodes

A notary node (validator) is an independent individual who stakes their identity and is entrusted to maintain a node on the network that validates transactions and commits new blocks to the blockchain. In the case of National Digital ID Blockchain Net, their role is to validate data submitted to them and send them back to the registration nodes to complete the application process and issue the ID, birth certificate, or other documents.

11.6 Responsibilities of Notary Nodes

A notary node (validator) has both technical and social responsibilities, both of which are important for the health, performance, and security of the network.

Technical Responsibilities:

- Ensure node is secure by practicing safe key management
- Maintain node requisite software version
- Monitor node to ensure its availability and participation in consensus
- Monitor network in general and communicate with other validators and network entities if problems arise

Social Responsibilities:

- Participate in on-chain governance of the network
- Adding new validators
- Removing validators, i.e. for compromising security of network, malicious behavior, non-participation in governance
- Monitor node to ensure its availability and participation in consensus
- Changing the approve ballot threshold
- Changing consensus contract

11.7 The Role of Registration Nodes

Registration nodes comprise directors of NRD branches throughout the country. Their role is to accept and process IDs, passports, birth certificates, and other documents and applications. They can only submit the data to the National Digital ID Blockchain Net to be validated by notary nodes.

11.8 Government Agency Nodes

The National Digital ID Blockchain Net should be connected to all the ministries, government departments, local councils, government agencies and institutions to improve connectivity. They should be given permission to access certain data on the shared database, like tax records, health data, criminal records, financial status etc, without involving any paperwork, thus creating a paperless environmentally friendly e-government.

11.9 Storing Biometric Data

Storing biometric data on a blockchain is not advised. Any personally identifiable information should be stored in off-chain storage as a verifiable claim with a cryptographic reference to the data placed on a blockchain for integrity and provenance.

11.10 Data Storage in National Digital ID Blockchain Net

Citizen data are stored in the Blockchain as key/value pairs (eg: JSON file) based on the type of document.

```
$   var   IC  =  {  id:  '0001',  name:   'Ali',
date_of_birth:'20070928', address: { No: '108', street:
'Avenue 10', City:'New York City", district: Manhattan ',
state:'New York'},date: '20190610' ,time:'1235', place :
PJ01', ,biometric_ref:'0012abvned'}
```

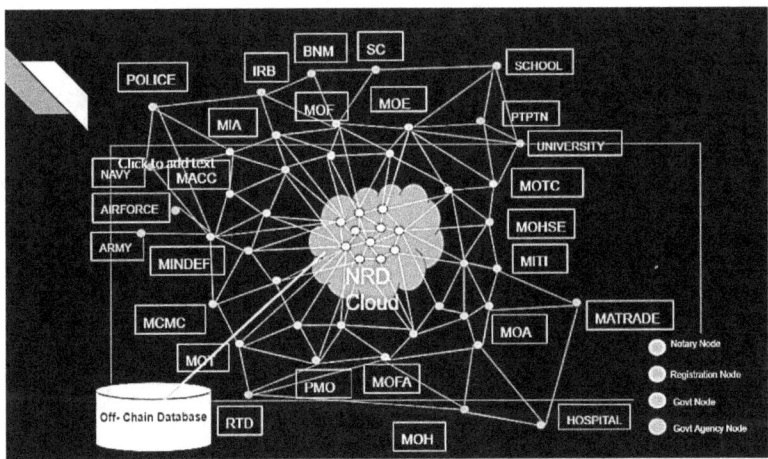

Figure 11.2 National Blockchain Net

Chapter 12

HR Digital Transformation-powered by Blockchain

Human resource management has undergone tremendous changes in recent years particularly with regards to digitalization of human resource. The emergence of blockchain technology could further transform the world of HR.

According to Griffiths(cited in Gale, 2018), blockchain has the potential to streamline a lot of inefficient work related to employee data verification. Blockchain can store a candidate education, certifications, and work history in a single ledger, therefore it would take just minutes rather than days to verify the data. Besides that, the data cannot be modified or hacked once they are stored in the blockchain, thus guarantee data security and trustworthiness.

In addition, blockchain has the potential impact on HR by allowing personal data to be owned by the individual rather than the organization(Mike, cited in Gale 2018). Consequently, every employee could maintain control over their entire employment data, including educational background, training, and work history. It also means that an individual work identity is more portable, it moves with the individual rather than stuck inside the former organization when an employee changes job.

Besides that, blockchain could disrupt conventional HR processes with respect to financial transactions. Blockchain could streamline payroll function significantly by allowing automated and direct payment based on smart contracts, without the need of a third party such as a bank or other intermediaries.

Recently, PWC (2018)has identified a few areas where we can apply the blockchain technology in HR. The areas include talent sourcing and management, targeting productivity gains, cross-border payment and mobility and Fraud prevention, and cybersecurity and data protection.

12.1 Talent sourcing and management

Blockchain could have a major impact on talent sourcing and management. It allows employees to maintain and control access to a comprehensive, trustworthy blockchain-based record of their education, skills, training, and workplace performance. By providing potential employers with access to their blockchain-based employment data, companies would be able to match individuals to roles much more accurately and effectively.

12.2 Targeting productivity gains

Blockchain can better match people's skills and performance to jobs. Finding and recruiting the right talent is always problematic for business organizations, therefore by helping them do this more effectively and efficiently will surely boost their productivity. Besides that, blockchain can help to reduce the burden of data-intensive processes like payroll and VAT, allowing companies to focus more on their core businesses.

12.3 Cross-border payments and mobility

Multinational companies could create their own blockchain-based corporate cryptocurrencies that they can use for cross-border payment across their global supply chains, without the need of third parties for settlement and reconciliation. In the future, central banks may legalize this type of cryptocurrency and support convertibility into fiat currencies. In addition, blockchain could facilitate employee's mobility across the border with respect to payroll adjustment, international expenses, and taxes.

12.4 Fraud prevention, cybersecurity, and data protection

HR department usually needs to handle high-volume financial transactions and sensitive personal data; therefore, it is utmost important to prevent frauds as well as to safeguard the data. This is the area where blockchain could be extremely useful. Blockchain's use of consensus to authenticate data can help to eliminate frauds.

Another issue that blockchain can help to overcome is cyber threats. Many SMEs are ill-prepared for cyber-attacks and the results could be detrimental to their businesses. Blockchain could help ensure cybersecurity as the data are immutable and tamper-proof because it uses SHA-256 hashing cryptography.

12.5 HR Blockchain Use Cases

HR Blockchain use cases have started to emerge and have the potential to disrupt traditional HR systems. Among them are ChronoBank.io, PEACOUNTS, and bitWAGE. Let us examine each one of them.

12.5.1 ChronoBank.io

This is an HR blockchain platform designed to improve the recruitment process as well as payroll. It claimed that it will disrupt the HR industry like how Uber has disrupted the taxi industry.

ChronoBank ecosystem comprises a hiring platform(LaborX), a decentralized exchange(TimeX), a multi-signature wallet(Chronowallet) and a cryptocurrency that is pegged to labor hours(Labor Hour token).

LaborX is their flagship global hiring platform that connects candidates to the companies. It features an industry first immutable reputation system and a crypto payment system based on smart contract. The reputation system allows faster screening of candidates therefore save time and cost in hiring the right candidates. In addition, the crypto payment system enables candidates to get paid on time.

Furthermore, it plans to use a stable coin as the crypto payment to eliminate volatility common in most cryptocurrencies. This coin is known as Labour-Hour tokens. These tokens are linked to average hourly wages in the host country and are backed by a real labor force from big recruitment and labor-hire companies. Labor is considered a tradeable resource so ChronoBank will tokenise this resource into the LH-Tokens.

12.5.2 PeaCounts

PeaCounts is a blockchain-based payroll system. PeaCounts claimed that their payroll system will revolutionize the way employees are paid by using blockchain to remove the trust-based elements of the payroll process. It ensures the employees will get paid as soon as the work is completed. On the other hand, the employer will pay just for the work completed.

It features a smart contract that can track an employee location and time spent on certain tasks. It also holds the PEA Tokens and release them to the employee upon completion of the tasks. This system ensures that the employee gets paid efficiently and fairly.

The PeaCount payroll system is a private blockchain created as a fork off the Bitcoin. It also implements the zk-Snarks protocol and a multi-access wallet to ensure security in payroll transactions.

12.5.3 bitWage

bitWage is a payroll and HR services platform designed for the digital age. Basically, it is a global outsourcing platform that serves the freelancers who wish to seek jobs worldwide and employers who wish to hire remote workers .

The bitWage payroll system allows employers to pay their remote employees rapidly with low transactions. The employees have the option to receive their wages and salaries in any of twenty-four fiat currencies, four cryptocurrencies , and four precious metals.

Chapter 13

Decentralized Finance

Decentralized finance, popularly known as DeFi which means operating financial applications on a decentralized platform such as blockchain. It is the new financial architecture that leverages decentralized networks and decentralized technologies such as smart contracts to transform old financial products into trustless and transparent protocols that run without intermediaries.

In contrast, centralized finance means a single organization like a bank controls and manages the funds of the clients. This kind of centralized control has many weaknesses, including the abuse of funds and manipulation of personal data, frauds, single point of failure due to hacking, and more.

Decentralized finance has many advantages as it is aligned with the characteristics that blockchain technology possesses.

13.1 The Advantages of DeFi

13.1.1 Maintain Full Control of Your Own Digital Assets

The digital assets that you own on a DeFi platform solely belong to you alone and you have the freedom to use it in whatever ways you like, without the interference of an intermediary. There is no centralized authority, such as a bank, with the ability to freeze your account, seize your assets, or block your transactions.

13.1.2 Increased Accessibility

According to the World Bank, globally there are still approximately 1.7 billion unbanked adults. These people are at a disadvantage when it comes to pursuing many financial opportunities that could improve their socioeconomic status and lift them out of poverty.

Unfortunately, centralized financial institutions do not have an incentive to target this population. The revenue they would receive from providing services to the currently unbanked simply does not justify the costs of reaching them. In contrast, DeFi providers operate without expensive intermediaries hence they are more willing to serve the underprivileged people. Furthermore, DeFi is borderless and 'permissionless' hence everyone on earth particularly the unbanked population can access this form of affordable financial services. Therefore, DeFi has the potential to reduce the world's poverty.

13.1.3 Opportunity to Own a Portion of An Expensive Asset

Another DeFi application is tokenized assets. Tokenizing assets is creating digital tokens to represent the ownership of real assets that can be traded like securities such as shares. By creating tokenized assets that represent, say, a portion of a real estate investment, you open the investment for people who previously could not afford it, to having access from anywhere in the world. Almost anyone can trade tokenized assets as he or she is not required to commit to an entire high-value investment at once. Instead, he or she has the option to buy or sell just a portion of the asset.

13.1.4 Transparency

DeFi data is publicly available, enabling you to keep service providers honest. For instance, you can easily check the reserves of a DeFi bank, shop around for accurate loan rates, or even track the transactions of public figures. Let us examine a well-known use case of DeFi, the Maker DAO

13.2 Types of DeFi Products

Popular DeFi products include decentralized exchanges, loan and savings markets, tokenized physical assets such as gold, derivatives, forecasting/betting markets, payment, insurance, asset management and more.

The complete list of DeFi products are as shown in Figure 13.1.

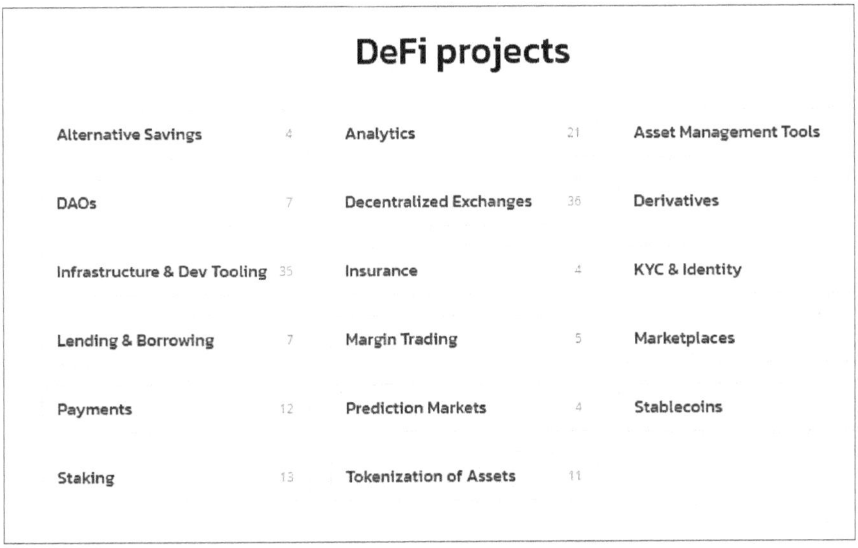

DeFi projects

Alternative Savings	4	Analytics	21	Asset Management Tools	
DAOs	7	Decentralized Exchanges	36	Derivatives	
Infrastructure & Dev Tooling	35	Insurance	4	KYC & Identity	
Lending & Borrowing	7	Margin Trading	5	Marketplaces	
Payments	12	Prediction Markets	4	Stablecoins	
Staking	13	Tokenization of Assets	11		

Figure 13.1 Source: DeFiprime(https://defiprime.com/)

DeFi loan and savings markets allow you to lend, borrow, or deposit money in a platform. Among the popular loan and savings platforms are Compound, Aave, MakerDAO, Fulcrum, dYdX, and more. If you lend out your digital assets by depositing them in a liquidity pool, you will earn interest over a period. On the other hand, you can borrow a digital asset by giving another digital asset as a collateral. The collateral is usually ETH but can be other cryptoassets. The debt has an accruing interest which is to be paid off along with the principal.

Decentralized exchanges or DEXs are like stock exchanges but run by smart contracts on the Ethereum blockchain. While both allow you to trade assets, decentralized exchanges only trade cryptoassets and do not require centralized authorities to manage the trading. They run on autopilot 24/7. Therefore, it offers fantastic opportunity to anyone in the world to have access to invest in digital assets, particularly the unbanked and underserved.

In a nutshell, DeFi products allows you to use your digital assets to secure a loan and use that loan to invest in some other digital assets that you expect to gain higher returns. You may also leverage on your collateral to secure more loans to purchase more assets with the expectation that the value of the assets will appreciate, not unlike real estate investment. Besides, you can lend your assets in a lending and borrowing market to earn more attractive interest than banks.

In addition, you may contribute your assets to liquidity pools in the DeFi money market to earn rewards. If your risk appetite is high, you may trade with margin in many different types of Decentralized exchanges. You can even expose yourself to higher risk by leveraging. The list goes on, so do not miss the opportunities!

Let us explore several popular DeFi platforms.

13.2.1 Maker DAO

MakerDAO is an open-source project on the Ethereum blockchain and a Decentralized Autonomous Organization created in 2014.

The project is managed by people around the world who hold its governance token, MKR.

MakerDAO is a decentralized credit platform on Ethereum that supports Dai, a decentralized, unbiased, collateral backed stablecoin whose value is pegged to USD. The Maker Protocol which is known as Multi collateral Dai (MSD) allows users to mint Dai by leveraging collateral assets approved by the Maker Governance. Maker Governance is a community organized and operated process of managing various digital assets of the Maker Protocol.

The Maker Protocol is one of the largest dApps on the Ethereum blockchain. It was the first DeFi application to gain significant adoption among the crypto communities. Since the release of Single Collateral Dai in 2017, user adoption of this stablecoin has increased dramatically. Indeed, it has become a driving force in the DeFi movement. The Maker Protocol is designed by a diverse group of individuals that include developers, external partners, other persons, and entities. It is managed and governed by people who hold the governance token MKR through a system of scientific governance involving executing voting and governance polling.

Anyone can use the Maker Protocol to open a Collateralized Debt Position (CDP), lock ETH as collateral, and generate Dai as a debt against that collateral. Dai debt incurs a stability fee (i.e., continuously accruing interest), which is paid (in MKR) upon repayment of borrowed Dai.

The MKR is burned, along with the repaid Dai. Users can borrow Dai up to 66% of their collateral value (150% collateralization ratio). CDPs that fall below that rate is subject to a 13% penalty and liquidation (by anyone) to bring the CDP out of default. Liquidated collateral is sold on an open market at a 3% discount.

Holders of Maker's other token (MKR) govern the system by voting on, e.g., risk parameters such as the stability fee level. MKR holders also act as the last line of defense in case of a black swan event. If the systemwide collateral value falls too low too fast, MKR is minted and sold on the open market to raise more collateral, diluting MKR holders.

To use MakerDAO services, you can access the Oasis App using the following link:

https://oasis.app/

13.2.3 AAVE-The Decentralized Lending and Borrowing Platform

Aave is a decentralized non-custodial money market protocol in which users can participate as depositors and borrowers. Depositors provide liquidity to the market to earn passive income, while borrowers can borrow in an overcollateralized or undercollateralized manner.

In layman terms, Aave enables users to lend and borrow a range of Ethereum-based cryptoassets. Borrowers can select from either stable or variable interest rates, and lenders can collect interest.

Aave began as ETHLend in 2017 after it successfully raised $16.2 million in an ICO to create a decentralized lending platform. ETHLend is a decentralized cryptocurrency credit platform and the world's first crypto lending marketplace that operates exclusively through Ethereum smart contracts. ETHLend also has a token known as the LEND token. It is the native ERC20 token of the ETHLend platform. Its token can be stored in any Ethereum wallet in a similar way as other ERC20 tokens.

However, after the recent approval in 2020 of the Aave Improvement Proposal, the protocol is requesting LEND token holders to migrate to the new AAVE token. At the time of writing, 89.65% of LEND tokens have been migrated to AAVE.

To use the service, you must deposit a certain amount of your preferred cryptocurrency. After depositing, you will earn passive income based on the market borrowing demand. Additionally, depositing digital assets allows you to borrow by using your deposited assets as a collateral. Any interest you earn by depositing funds helps offset the interest rate you pay by borrowing.

You can access the Aave App via the following link:

https://app.aave.com/markets

13.2.3 Compound-A DeFi Money Market

Compound is a protocol on the Ethereum blockchain that features a money market comprising a group of assets with algorithmically generated interest rates, based on supply and demand for those assets. The asset provider (lender) and borrower interact directly with the protocol, earning and paying floating interest rates, without having to negotiate conditions such as maturity, interest rates, or collateral with peers or business partners. In addition, Compound features its native utility token COMP that allows holders to govern its protocol.

Anyone can supply assets to Compound's liquidity pools and immediately begin earning perpetually compounding interest that varies with respect to supply and demand. Supplied asset balances are represented by cTokens: representations of the underlying asset that earn interest and serve as collateral. Each cToken can be convertible into an underlying asset, as interest accrues in the market. For example, if you supply DAI (a type of stable coin) to the protocol, you will earn cDAI and you can convert it back to DAI any time.

Users could borrow up to 50-75% of their cTokens' value, depending on the quality of the underlying asset. Users can add or remove funds at any time, but if their debt becomes undercollateralized, anyone can liquidate; a 5% discount on liquidated assets serves as incentive for liquidators. The

Compound protocol sets aside 10% of interest paid as reserves; the rest goes to suppliers.

The protocol currently supports BAT, DAI, ETH, COMP, USDC, USDT, UNI, WBTC, and ZRX. Compound has been audited and formally verified. As of May 2020, Compound has transitioned to community governance; COMP token-holders and their delegates debate, propose, and vote on all changes to Compound. To use Compound, you must access its website via the following link:

https://compound.finance/

13.2.4 dYdX, a Lending, Borrowing and Trading Platform

dYdX is a decentralized platform that supports margin trading, spot trading, lending, and borrowing. The dYdX platform allows users to lend, borrow, or margin trade any supported asset like ETH, DAI, USDC, and more. Interest rates vary by asset and adjust with respect to supply and demand. Interest continuously accrues and is paid to lenders, minus 5% which is set aside for dYdX's insurance fund. In addition, dYdX allows users to borrow, lend and make bets on the future prices of popular cryptocurrencies. We shall focus on the lending and borrowing component of dYdX in this section and will discuss the trading component in another chapter.

On the dYdX platform, both lenders and borrowers interact with global lending pools via smart contracts (Hu, Getting Started With dYdX — Borrowing, n.d.). There is one global lending pool for each supported asset. When you deposit an asset on dYdX, your asset will be deposited into its corresponding lending pool, where borrowers can then borrow the same asset. This model allows borrowers and lenders on dYdX to deposit and withdraw assets at any time they wish.

To access dYdX platform, you can use the following link:

https://trade.dydx.exchange/margin/ETH-DAI

To learn more about DeFi and how to invest in DeFi products to gain attractive returns, please check out my DeFi books using the following links:

"DeFi Handbook: A Comprehensive Guide to Decentralized Finance" using the following links:

Paperback: https://www.amazon.com/dp/B08P4SPHGX

Kindle Version: https://www.amazon.com/dp/B08P9S9K68

"DEFI Investment Made Easy: A Beginner's Guide to Investing in Decentralized Finance" using the following links:

Paperback: https://www.amazon.com/dp/B08S2Y5GRS

Kindle Edition: https://www.amazon.com/dp/B08RZCYBX1

Chapter 14

Building Blockchain for Business

Blockchain is the underlying technology for Bitcoin, Ethereum, and other cryptocurrencies. However, cryptocurrency is far from the only application of blockchain for businesses. One of the most popular business applications of blockchain is fundraising, especially for startups. Apart from conventional ways of funding, blockchain enables alternative methods of fundraising such as ICO or STO.

In the past few years, many companies have raised an incredible amount of money via ICO. Some of the biggest and most successful ICO projects include NEO, Ethereum, Spectrecoin, and Lisk. More info about ICO can be found on the Investopedia website.

That said, I am not going to discuss ICO in this article. Instead, we shall explore blockchain applications in businesses. Though we can use blockchain for all kinds of business applications, whether blockchain is suitable for a business depends on the nature of the business, the business model, the requirements, and many other factors.

Before implementing blockchain, the C-level management team of a business organization should conduct a feasibility study to determine whether it is necessary and plausible to adopt blockchain technology. You should ask the following questions:

- Can blockchain add value to the current business?
- Can blockchain increase the organization's competitiveness?
- Do you need to deal with many trustless parties?
- Do you need a decentralized and distributed database system?
- Can blockchain improve workflow efficiency?
- Can blockchain increase revenue and profit?
- Do you have enough financial resources to implement blockchain?
- Can blockchain technology integrate with existing systems?
- Do you have enough talents to manage the blockchain system?

Once you have decided that implementing blockchain would benefit your company, you need to carry out the following steps:

1. Identify a suitable use case.
2. Assemble your team.
3. Design the blockchain architecture.

14.1 Identify a suitable use case

To embark on a blockchain project, you need to identify the most suitable use case for your business. The best way is to examine use cases in an industry that is like your business. Generally, there are three areas in which blockchains can perform very well.

14.1.1 Data Authentication & Verification

This includes immutable storage, digital signatures, and encryption. Data in almost any format can be stored in the blockchain. Blockchains can create public-private key pairs and be used for generating and verifying digital signatures. Therefore, it can be used for data authentication & verification.

One of the best usages is counterfeiting prevention. For example, Luxtag, a Malaysia-based blockchain company, has patented an anti-counterfeit technology. This technology enables businesses and their customers to protect the authenticity and ownership of their valuable assets by providing digitized certificates using blockchain technology. They have rolled out their first product, known as e-Scroll, for a consortium of Malaysian public universities to verify and validate certificates using a blockchain-powered web application.

Another area related to authentication and verification is data provenance. One of the most successful companies in this area is Everledger. This company has built the Diamond Time-Lapse Protocol, a traceability initiative built on a blockchain-based platform for the diamond and jewelry industry. The system is to ensure that there is transparency along the entire diamond's lifetime journey, instilling consumer confidence and driving industry growth.

Supply chain management is another sector where blockchain could be useful. The most notable is the initiative by Walmart using blockchain technology to ensure food safety. Walmart has been working with IBM on a food safety blockchain solution requiring all suppliers of leafy green vegetables for Sam's and Walmart to upload their data to the blockchain by September 2019. By placing a supply chain on the blockchain, it makes the process more traceable, transparent, and fully digital.

Other business applications could be medical records management, insurance, KYC management for banks, and more.

14.1.2 Digital Asset Management

Any asset that can be digitized is considered a digital asset. Digital assets include eBooks, digital art, images, video, music, journals, newspapers, audio books, online training courses, recipes, and more. With the invention of blockchain technology, digital assets also include crypto assets. Crypto assets can be cryptocurrencies like Bitcoin, Ethereum, and other altcoins, or the tokenized version of a real-world asset such as gold, silver, oil, land titles, property, paintings, etc.

Currently, most digital assets are traded over the Internet via the centralized e-commerce marketplace. However, digital assets can be traded more efficiently over the decentralized peer-to-peer blockchain platforms.

Some real-world use cases for digital assets management in blockchain include:

- AlphaPoint. Provides enterprise-grade software that enables institutions to convert assets to securities tokens and trade those assets on an e14.xchange.
- Polymath. Enables trillions of dollars of securities to migrate to the blockchain.
- Harbor. Offers a digital securities platform for compliant fundraising, investor management, and liquidity.
- Powerledger. Provides a platform for peer-to-peer energy trading.

14.1.3 Smart Contracts

A smart contract is a programmable contract that enables auto execution of a contract the moment it fulfills certain terms and conditions. It is akin to a vending machine – you get your product by inserting some coins or banknotes.

According to Investopedia, smart contracts are:

> "self-executing contracts with the terms of the agreement between buyer and seller being directly written into lines of code. The code and the agreements contained therein exist across a distributed, decentralized blockchain network. Smart contracts permit trusted transactions and agreements to be carried out among disparate, anonymous parties without the need for a central authority, legal system, or external enforcement mechanism. They render transactions traceable, transparent, and irreversible."

Almost any blockchain business application involves the use of a smart contract. A famous use case is Cryptokitties. A smart contract is executed when a user acquires a unique virtual kitty from the Cryptokitties collectible marketplace via a bidding process. The highest bidder gets to own the digital asset. Other dapp transactions also make use of smart contracts.

Blockchain-powered supply chain management makes use of smart contracts to handle transactions between manufacturer, suppliers, wholesalers, and retailers.

In the insurance industry, the client who wishes to buy insurance can provide personal information including sensitive data like medical records via a smart contract to the insurance company. In the health care industry, a patient can get faster and more accurate diagnoses and treatment via a smart contract that allows them to share medical records.

14.2 Assemble your Team

After conceptualizing a business use case that is suitable for your business, you need to assemble your team to kick-start the blockchain project. Getting the right people in your team is crucial to success. Your team should comprise people with business skills and people with technical skills. People with business skills should be able to see the overall picture of your business model and know how to execute it. They must also have good interpersonal skills, strategic thinking, good networks, and financial knowledge. The people with business skills should be assigned the posts of CEO,

CFO, marketing manager, business development manager, and so on.

People with good IT skill in general and blockchain are equally important. The CTO must have many years of experience in the IT and software industry and have a good grasp of blockchain concepts and knowledge. He or she must be assisted by a technical lead who has good practical experience in setting up the blockchain platform, know how to program the smart contract, sound knowledge of programming languages including Solidity, JavaScript, Goland, C++, Java, Python, and so fort.

In addition, if you plan to raise funds via ICO, you need to employ a compliance officer, preferably a lawyer who understands the guidelines provided by the security commission and the central bank.

14.3 Designing the Blockchain Architecture

You need to decide whether to build the blockchain network from scratch or use a third party blockchain solution like Azure blockchain, Oracle, or AWS blockchain. The former is time-consuming, whereas the latter could be up in as little as 30 minutes.

Each of the enterprise blockchains offer their own functionalities and features as well as cost advantages. Both AWS and Azure offers solutions for Ethereum, Hyperledger Fabric, Corda, and

Quorum, while Oracle only caters for Hyperledger Fabric. We can compare their features in Table 14.1.

Table 14.1

	AWS	Azure	Oracle
Framework	Ethereum, Hyperledger Fabric, Corda and Quorum	Ethereum, Hyperledger Fabric, Corda and Chain	Hyperledger Fabric
Price	Varies according to the plan, pay per use	Varies according to the plan, pay per use	$0.75 pay as you go
Major Partners	Cisco, BlockApps, GuildOne, Intel, Kaleido, Mainfold Technology, Corda R3 and several other consulting partners.	BlockApps, Corda and 23 partners	
Major Clients	T Mobile and Guideware	Xbox, 3M and Insurware	

The cost of setting up Azure Blockchain Workbench is roughly $400-$500 depending on your region and usage. The main costs are three VMs and one app service. Two VMs are for the default blockchain network, and one VM is for the microservices on Workbench. For AWS Blockchain pricing, refer to

https://aws.amazon.com/managed-blockchain/pricing/

Chapter 15 Storing Data on Blockchain

Despite the hype and its promising future, blockchain still has its shortcomings, the issue of data storage is one of them. The transactions based on the POW consensus for bitcoin, Ethereum, and other cryptocurrencies are extremely slow and therefore not suitable for storage of large data. For example, the deployment of dApp Cryptokitties nearly crippled the Ethereum network

The main problem of storing data on a blockchain is the limitation of the amount of data we can store because of its protocol and the high transaction costs. As a matter of fact, a block in blockchain can store data from a few kilobytes to maybe a few megabytes. For example, the block size of the Bitcoin is only 1Mb. The block size limitation has a serious impact on the scalability of most cryptocurrencies and the bitcoin community is debating whether to increase the block size.

Another issue is the high cost of the transactions. Why is storing data on the blockchain so expensive? It is because the data must be stored by every full node on the blockchain network. When storing data on the blockchain, we do pay the base price for the transaction itself plus an amount per byte we want to store. If smart contracts are involved, we also pay for the execution time of the smart contract. Even storing kilobytes of data on the blockchain can cost you a fortune.

Therefore, it is not viable to store large data files like images and videos on the blockchain. Is there a possible solution to solve the storage issue? Yes, there are quite a few solutions but the most promising one is IPFS.

15.1 What is IPFS?

IPFS or Interplanetary File System is an innovative open-source project created by the developers at Protocol Labs. It is a peer-to-peer filesharing system that aims to change the way information is distributed across a wide area network. IPFS has innovated some communication protocols and distributed systems and combine them to produce a unique file-sharing system.

The current HTTP client-server protocol is location-based addressing which faces some serious drawbacks. First, location-based addressing consumes a huge amount of bandwidth, and thus costs us a lot of money and time. On top of that, HTTP downloads a file from a single server at a time, which can be slow if the file is big. In addition, it faces single point of failure. If the webserver is down or being hacked, you will encounter **404 Not Found error**. Besides that, it also allows for powerful entities like the governments to block access to certain locations.

On the contrary, IPFS is a content-based addressing system. It is a decentralized way of storing files, like BitTorrent. In the IPFS network, every node stores a collection of hashed files. The user can refer to the files by their hashes. The process of storing a file on IPFS is by uploading the file to IPFS, store the file in the working directory, generate a hash for the file and his file will be available on the IPFS network. A user who wants to retrieve any of those files simply needs to call the hash of the file he or she wants. IPFS then search all the nodes in the network and deliver the file to the user when it is found.

IPFS will overcome the HTTP weaknesses. As files are stored on the decentralized IPFS network, if a node is down, the files are still available on other nodes, therefore there is no single point of failure. Data transfer will be cheaper and faster as you can get the files from the nearest node. On top of that, it is almost impossible for the powerful entities to block access to the files as the network is decentralized.

15.2 Blockchain and IPFS

IPFS is the perfect match for the blockchain. As I have mentioned, the blockchain is inefficient in storing large amounts of data in a block because all the hashes need to be calculated and verified to preserve the integrity of the blockchain. Therefore, instead of storing data on the blockchain, we simply store the hash of the IPFS file. In this way, we only need to store a small amount of data that is required on the blockchain but get to enjoy the file storage and decentralized peer-to-peer properties of IPFS.

One of the real-world use cases of blockchain and IPFS is Nebulis. It is a new project exploring the concept of a distributed DNS that supposedly never fails under an overwhelming access request. Nebulis uses the Ethereum blockchain and the Interplanetary File

System (IPFS), a distributed alternative to HTTP, to register and resolve domain names. We shall see more integration of Blockchain and IPFS in the future.

Chapter 16 Plasma-The Solution for Security and Scalability

16.1 The Scalability Issue

Blockchain always faces the trade-off issue between security and scalability. Though their PoW consensus protocol guarantees near perfect security, it also slows down the processing speed significantly. Currently, the Ethereum processing speed is 15 transactions per second while Bitcoin is 7 transactions per second. Both platform's processing capacities are nowhere near Visa's processing speed of 45,000 transactions per second.

Furthermore, the increase in the number of dApps deployed on the main Ethereum main chain has caused congestion and slows down transactions tremendously. One of the most famous cases is Cryptokitties, it clogged up the Ethereum network in just a few weeks of deployment due to its unprecedented popularity.

In seeking a viable solution to the scalability issue, Vitalik Buterin and Joseph Poon have joined hands in conceptualizing and developing Plasma, a framework that can scale Ethereum processing power. Joseph is also the co-founder of the Lightning network, a framework that has greatly increase Bitcoin processing speed. Both plasma and Lightning network are trustless multilayered blockchain networks.

16.2 Plasma

Plasma is a system that comprises the main blockchain and the 'child blockchains' that branch out from the main blockchain(aka parent blockchain or root blockchain). The child blockchains can co-exist but function independently from the parent chain and each other.

The Plasma system allows anyone to create their own child blockchains a.k.a plasma chains with their own smart contracts. Therefore, the Plasma system enables the creation of all kinds of use cases based on different business logic in their smart contracts. To ensure security, the root chain monitor and enforces the state in all the plasma chains and penalize the bad actors if there is proof of frauds. In this way, the Plasma system makes off-chain transactions possible while relying on the Ethereum main blockchain to maintain its security.

16.3 The Plasma Structure

The Plasma architecture is like a tree structure with the main Ethereum blockchain as the root. The child blockchains then branch out from the root blockchain, like branches grown out from the root of a tree. Every child chain, in turn, can spawn new child chains, the process can go on. Therefore, the plasma structure constitutes a hierarchy of blockchains, as shown in Figure 16.1

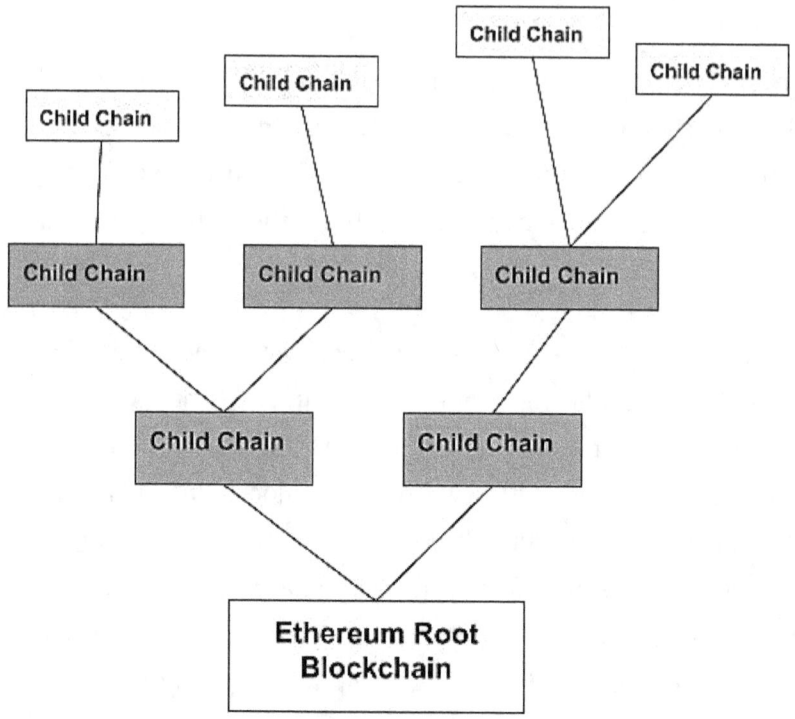

Figure 16.1

16.4 How does Plasma Works?

Plasma can greatly increase processing speed and throughput on the Ethereum blockchain because it allows off-chain transactions, like the payment channels of the Lightning network and other off-chain technologies. All the off-chain techniques take operations away from the main Ethereum blockchain.

16.5 State Channels

The concept of Plasma was derived from State Channels but improved on the latter. State channel works by creating an off-chain communication channel (a.k.a state channel)where transactions are not sent to the smart contract on the main chain, instead, they are sent through the Internet without touching the main blockchain. It is only after all the transactions have been completed (for example, a crypto game has finished) that the final state is sent to the smart contract on the main chain, closing the channel in the process. The smart contract will check the legitimacy of the transactions and release the asset (such as some ETH or a prize) to the recipient.

The state channel technique can improve scalability because it can reduce the number of transactions on the main blockchain. For example, a crypto chess game played between two players may involve hundreds of moves, which means hundreds of transactions will be executed on the Ethereum blockchain. However, if we use the state channel, we need to execute only 3 transactions that include registration of the players to initiate the game, submission of the final state to the blockchain and closing the channel.

16.6 Steps in Implementing Plasma

Plasma works in a similar way but with a different approach. Instead of creating the channels, it creates the child blockchains, as illustrated earlier. Smart contracts are created on the main Ethereum blockchain(The root chain) and they define the rules in the child blockchains. In other words, the smart contract serves as the root of the child blockchains. The child blockchains can employ their own consensus algorithm, such as proof of stake. The blocks validator will submit the state of the child chain to the Root Chain smart contract periodically. The smart contract will register the state of each Child Chain in the form of block hashes of the Child Chain.

We can illustrate how Plasma works by examining a crypto game such as Crytant Crab or Cryptokitties. The smart contract on the main chain will set the rules of the game, then deploy the actual game application smart contracts on the child-chain, which contains all the game logic and rules. The game assets such as characters or collectibles are created on the Ethereum main chain and then transferred onto the child-chain using the plasma root. When the players play the games, all the executions are confined to the child chain, without interacting with the root chain.

16.7 Plasma Exits

Plasma Exits is a security mechanism behind Plasma that allows users in a Plasma Chain to stop participating in the chain and move their funds or assets back to the root chain. When a user wishes to exit a child chain, he or she needs to submit an exit application. The application is not immediately approved because a proof is required. This waiting period is called the challenge period, which means anyone can challenge the user's claim by submitting a fraud proof. If the challenge is not valid or there is no challenge, the application will be approved, and the user can exit and collect back his assets or funds. Plasma is still evolving and now the Plasma team has come out with the improved version of Plasma known as Plasma cash.

TECHNICAL SECTION

I have minimized technical jargons in this section so that even readers who are not technical savvy could understand the basics. For the technical guys, I hope these articles could benefit you and motivate you to build more complex blockchain stuff. Happy reading.

Chapter 17 Solidity and Smart Contracts

Solidity is a high-level programming language that is used to create and implement smart contracts in Ethereum. The smart contracts created using Solidity can be used for financial transactions, crowdfunding, voting, intelligent supply chain management, improvement of IoT workflow, ride sharing automation, smart city administration and more.

It has Python, C++ and JavaScript influences and is used for Ethereum Virtual Machine (EVM). As a result, it is convenient and easy to grasp for those that are already familiar with the Python, C++, or JavaScript.

17.1 Choosing the IDE to Develop Smart Contracts

The best tool to write, compile, test and deploy smart contracts is the **Remix**. Remix is a browser-based IDE that provides an inbuilt compiler as a well as run-time environment without server-side components.

We can also use other code editors for Solidity . I suggest we use Visual Studio Code or Solidity Plugin for Visual Studio. For Solidity plugin, you need to download it from

https://marketplace.visualstudio.com/items?itemName=ConsenSys.Solidity.

Besides that, you might need to install Visual Studio 2019.

17.2 Writing Your First Smart Contract in Solidity

A smart contract is a data, that can be referred to as its state, and code, which can be referred to as its functions, collection, that resides on a specific address in the Ethereum blockchain.

The first line of the smart contract is always:

```
pragma solidity >=0.4.22 <0.7.0;
```

pragma is a keyword, which is used to instruct the compiler how the source code should be treated. In this example, the pragma specified that the source code is written for the Solidity Library version 0.4.22 or a newer version of the language up to, but not including version 0.7.0.

To define a contract, we use the statement

```
contract  contractName {

    }
```

You can use any name for the contract, but any meaningful name will be better. For example,

```
Contract  NewCoin{
}
```

indicates you intend to create a contract for a new cryptocurrency.

17.2.1 Assigning variables

Next, we would like to introduce some variables into the contract. First, let us assign some string variables and some integer variables.

To assign a string variable, the syntax is

`string myName;`

In Solidity, there are two types of integers, the **signed integer,** and the **unsigned integer.**

A signed integer means it can store positive or negative values while an unsigned integer can only store positive values.

To specify that it will be an unsigned integer, we use the keyword `uint` before the name of the new variable.

To assign an unsigned integer, the syntax is as follows.

`uint MyAge;`

17.2.2 Access Modifier

You may want to add the access modifier(or visibility modifier) **private** or **public** to the variable. Most programming languages put access modifier in front of the datatype specifier like `private string name` but in Solidity, we put access modifier between datatype specifier and the variable name, as follows:

string private myName;

String public myName

uint private MyAge;

uint public MyAge;

17.3 The Remix IDE

One of the best tools to write, compile, test and deploy smart contracts is Remix. Remix is a browser-based IDE that provides an inbuilt compiler as a well as run-time environment without server-side components. You can access Remix from the following link:

https://remix.ethereum.org

We can also use other code editors for Solidity . I suggest we use Visual Studio Code or Solidity Plugin for Visual Studio. For Solidity plugin, you need to download it from

https://marketplace.visualstudio.com/items?itemName=ConsenSys.Solidity

Now launch Remix IDE. You can add your own smart contract by clicking on the little + button on the far-left corner of the Remix IDE. A new dialog will appear, and you can create a new Solidity file.

After creating the new file, a new window will appear on a new tab displaying your new file. The file will also be show on the left pane of the IDE under the browser.

Now, let us create a new contract by entering the following code into the Remix IDE.

```
pragma solidity >=0.4.22 <0.7.0;
contract myContract {
    string private name;
    uint private age;
}
```

The first line inside the contract itself declares string name name and an unsigned integer variable called age. We have already created a simple smart contract though it does not do anything yet. You can compile and deploy it if you want to. Now let us add some functions to the smart contract

```
pragma solidity >=0.4.22 <0.7.0;
contract myContract {
    string private name;
    uint private age;
    function setName(string memory newName) public{
```

```
        name = newName;
    }
    function getName() public view returns (string memory){
        return name;
    }
    function setAge(uint newAge) public{
        age=newAge;
    }
    function getAge() public view returns (uint){
        return age;
    }
}
```

We create the function `setName` to allow the user inputs a string value. Set the modifier to `public` as we want to permit everyone to see it. Otherwise when you deploy the contract you will not be able to view the function on the Remix IDE.

To return the value of name entered by a user, we create the function getName

The view keyword in public view returns is the replacement for constant. It indicates that the function will not alter the storage state in any way.

Next, we create the function setAge by declaring a parameter newAge as an unsigned integer. The setAge function will allow the user input an integer value when you deploy the contract.

To return the value of age entered by the user, we create the function getAge.

Now compile and deploy the Remix IDE, the output is shown in Figure 17.1

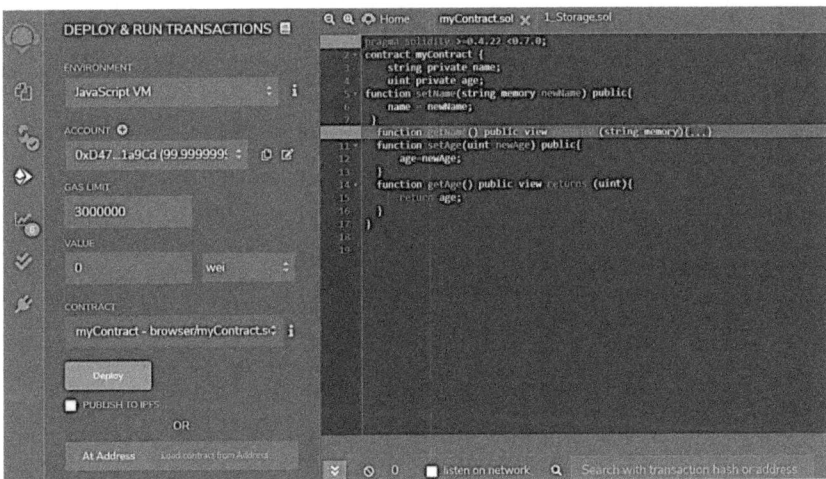

Figure 17.1

When you deploy the contract, a transaction is executed from your wallet address to the contract. A gas fee is charged in the process. You can view the transaction on Etherscan, as shown below:

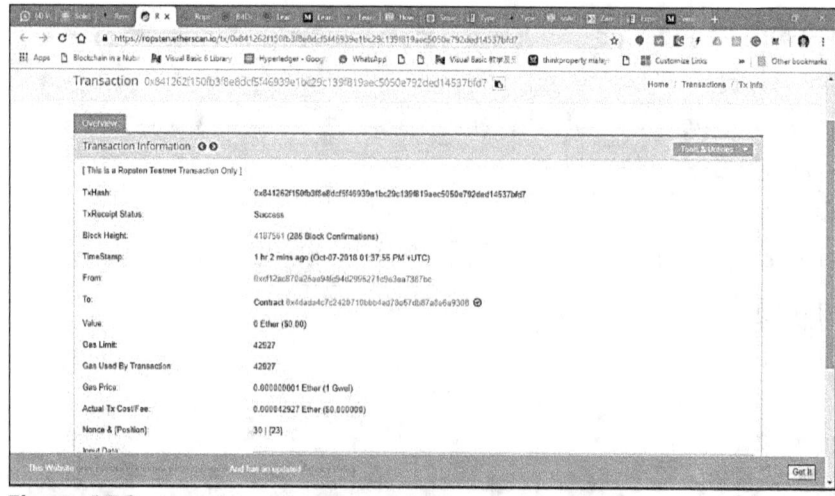

Figure 17.2

When you click on the setName function, a transaction will also occur. You need to wait for the transaction to complete before you click on the getName function. You can see that whatever you entered in the setName box will appear on the getName box. You can do the same for the setAge and getAge functions. The output is as shown in Figure 17.3

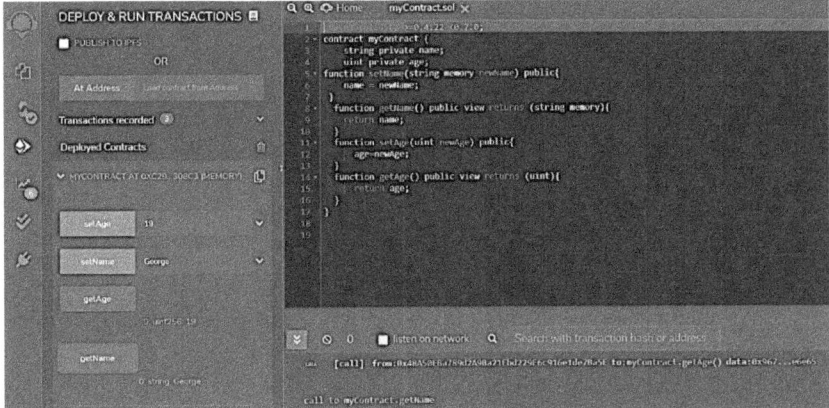

Figure 17.3

17.4 Creating a cryptocurrency using Solidity

It is completely possible to create coins out of thin air. Furthermore, anyone can send coins to each other without any need for registering with username and password - all you need is an Ethereum keypair.

In this section, we shall show you how to create a cryptocurrency using a smart contract.

Here is the code:

pragma solidity >=0.4.22 <0.7.0;

contract Mycurrency {

```
// The "public" keyword allows external accounts to read
the variable

    address public minter;

    mapping (address => uint) public coinBalances;


    // Light clients can react on changes efficiently thanks
to events.

    event Sent(address from, address to, uint sum);

    // The code of this constructor is run only once the
contract is created.

    function myCoin() public {

        minter = msg.sender;

    }

    function mint(address receiver, uint sum) public{

        if (msg.sender != minter) return;

        coinBalances[receiver] += sum;

    }

    function send(address receiver, uint sum) public{

        if (coinBalances[msg.sender] < sum) return;

        coinBalances[msg.sender] -= sum;

        coinBalances[receiver] += sum;
```

```
        emit Sent (msg.sender, receiver, sum);

    }

}
```

The line `address public minter;` declares a state variable of type address that is publicly accessible. The address type is a 160-bit value that does not allow any arithmetic operations. It is suitable for storing addresses of contracts or keypairs belonging to external persons. The keyword `public` automatically generates a function that allows you to access the current value of the state variable from outside of the contract. Without this keyword, other contracts have no way to access the variable.

The next line, `mapping (address => uint) public balances;` also creates a public state variable, but it is a more complex datatype. The type maps address to unsigned integers. Mappings can be seen as hash tables which are virtually initialized such that every possible key exists and is mapped to a value whose byte-representation is all zeros. This analogy does not go too far, though, as it is neither possible to obtain a list of all keys of a mapping, nor a list of all values. The type mapping is used for mapping address variables to unsigned integers.

The line `event Sent(address from, address to, uint amount);` declares an event which is emitted in the last line of the function send. User interfaces (as well as server applications of course) can listen for those events being emitted on the blockchain without much cost. As soon as it is emitted, the listener will also receive the arguments from, to and amount, which makes it easy to track transactions

The special function Coin is the constructor which is run during creation of the contract and cannot be called afterwards. It permanently stores the address of the person creating the contract: msg is a magic global variable that contains some properties which allow access to the blockchain. msg.sender is always the address where the current (external) function call came from.

Finally, the functions that will end up with the contract and can be called by users and contracts alike are mint and send. If mint is called by anyone except the account that created the contract, nothing will happen. On the other hand, send can be used by anyone (who already has some of these coins) to send coins to anyone else. Compile and run the cryptocurrency contract, output is as shown in Figure 17.4.

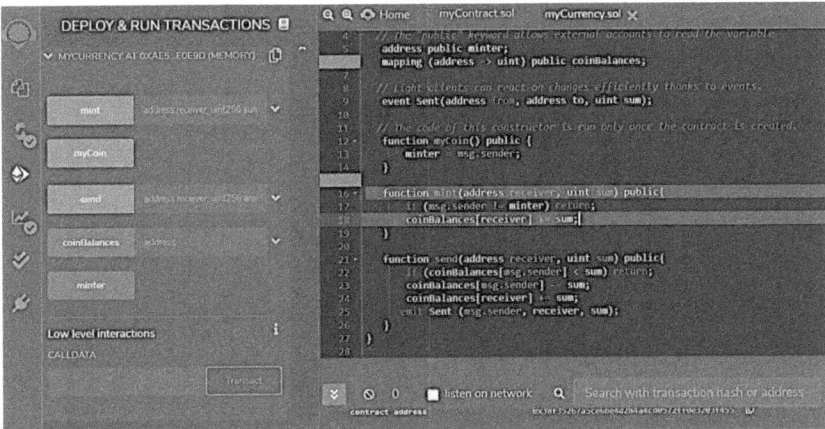

Figure 17.4

Chapter 18

Decentralized Applications (DApps)

DApp is an abbreviation for *decentralized application*.

A DApp has its backend code running on a decentralized peer-to-peer blockchain or DLT network. Contrast this with an app where the backend code is running on centralized servers.

A DApp can have a frontend code and a user interface written in any language that can make calls to its backend. Furthermore, its frontend can be hosted on decentralized storage such as Swarm or IPFS.

A DApp can be programmed using a smart contract that can be written in any language but for Ethereum platform it is preferable to use Solidity. A DApp is always a combination of a frontend and a smart contract.

I will discuss a conceptual model on how to develop a DApp and a simple guide on how to develop a DApp in the following section.

18.1 Event Management and Ticketing DApp

The event management and ticketing industry is a huge market, particularly the event management software market. Markets Insider reported that the event management software market is projected to grow from 5.7 billion USD in 2019 to 11.4 billion USD by 2024, at a CAGR of 15% from 2019 to 2024.

However, despite the great potential of the event and ticketing industry, there are numerous problems and issues plaguing the current centralized event ticketing industry. The main issues include ticket counterfeiting, ticket scalpers, instant sell-outs, and overpriced resale tickets on secondary markets (EventChain, 2017).

The good news is that the blockchain could fix the issues. A blockchain is a distributed digital ledger that can be used to record transactions and other data across a decentralized peer-to-peer network made up of a cluster of computing devices.

Using blockchain technology, every ticket sale can be publicly verified, and thus the authenticity of the ticket can be guaranteed. It is also able to prevent fraudulent sales and counterfeiting. It sets rules (using smart contracts) preventing secondary ticket websites from hoarding tickets and charging inflated prices for premium events. If the rules are broken, the fraudulent accounts are frozen, and the tickets are made invalid.

In a nutshell, a blockchain-based event and ticketing system has the following benefits:

- Elimination of ticket duplication and counterfeit tickets
- Elimination of scalpers
- Elimination of ticket touts and purchasing bots

- Fully transparent ticketing aftermarket
- Automatic refund at the time of cancelation

18.2 Use Cases

18.2.1 BitTicket

The Edinburgh-based Citizen Ticket is an event ticketing platform backed by blockchain technology that uses the cryptocurrency Ethereum Classic. In May 2017, they deployed the blockchain-based ticketing system BitTicket and delivered the first live event using blockchain technology.

BitTicket is a ticket delivery service that event organizers, venues, and artists can use to secure their tickets with blockchain technology. BitTicket provides users with one wallet QR code that holds all their BitTickets securely, no matter which ticketing provider they bought them from. They simply present it along with proof of ID to gain entry. Due to the security of BitTicket identity, ticket transfer to friends and family can be done easily and with assurance. BitTickets are immutable, transferable, and verifiable.

BitTicket guarantees the following:

- Your purchased ticket is genuine
- Inherent protection against industrial-scale ticket touts and ticket purchasing bots
- Transfer your tickets securely and with ease between friends & family

- Provides one wallet for all your tickets – no more individual tickets

18.2.2 GUTS

GUTS uses blockchain technology to create a transparent ticketing ecosystem where inflated secondary market prices and ticket fraud are eliminated. Their motto is simple, transparent, and secure.

GUTS brings numerous benefits for different stakeholders:

- Artist and Managers
    - A fair chance for all the fans to attend the show
    - Expand the fan base with exact data
    - Direct communication with your fans - send them a message right before the show starts
- The Venue, Festival and Theatre Operators
    - No ticket fraud: fewer complaints and a stronger image
    - You know exactly who is present at any time (and who is not)
    - Automatic refund procedure at the time of cancelation or resale
    - Identification via mobile phones means shorter queues
- Ticket Providers
    - Complete control of the tickets in both the primary and secondary market
    - Easy to integrate with existing ticketing solutions

18.2.3 LAVA

LAVA is a blockchain-based ticketing system that guarantees fair and secure smart tickets for music lovers. The system prevents ticket touting and fraud ruining festivals for music lovers.

The LAVA ecosystem has the following features:

- 100% Safe
    - Using latest blockchain technology to eliminate ticket fraud
- Smart Tickets
    - Smart tickets to stop the exploitation of festival tickets using a unique digital footprint
- Lava Wallet – Eliminate printing completely by generating the ticket digitally and sending the digital ticket to the Lava wallet directly
- No booking fees

18.2.4 PouchNATION

PouchNATION is an event management software system that uses the blockchain technology to good effect. PouchNATION is the first platform to implement blockchain and new digital currency across all verticals in event management. Its components comprise guest registration, cashless payment, access control, activity tracking, social engagement and detailed analytics reporting.

This innovative platform could overcome issues that the ticket industry is currently facing with managing events, attendance tracking apps, eliminating duplicate tickets, and validating registration at the door.

They have executed over 100 events including cashless events in Indonesia, Philippines, Vietnam, Malaysia, Thailand, and Myanmar.

18.2.5 EventChain

EventChain is a global Smart Ticketing blockchain project that will allow events worldwide to sell SmartTickets through a peer-to-peer network, solving the issues of the centralized event ticketing industry.

It implements the EventChain token network for event management to ensure faster transactions, indisputable ticket vouchers, transparency from event hosts and fully flexible and programmable SmartTickets. With the use of the EVC token, smart contract code, and the Ethereum blockchain, EventChain's transaction network brings increased accountability, transparency, and security to event ticketing.

To fix excessive ticket fees, EventChain is distributing EVC tokens, a digital ERC20 token created for buying, selling, and programming SmartTickets on the Ethereum distributed network. EventChain claims that their transaction fees are much lower, and the transaction confirmation speed is near seconds.

18.2.6 Event Management and Ticketing Platform - A Conceptual Model

After examining the above use cases, I propose a conceptual model that utilizes a similar concept to develop a blockchain-based event management and ticketing platform. Below is a simple conceptual model of the Event Management and Ticketing Platform:

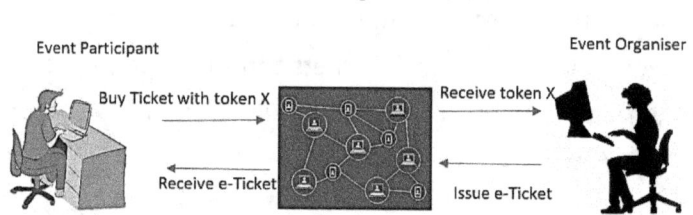

Figure 18.1

The platform allows an event organizer to create an event and broadcast it to the website as well as a mobile wallet. The event should comprise details such as event title, date, time, venue, and a ticketing ordering button. The participant can then order tickets by paying Token X. Once the organizer receives Token X, the e-ticket shall be automatically delivered to the participant's mobile wallet. To enter the event venue, the organizer just needs to scan the e-ticket of the participant.

To build the platform, we need to build a smart contract layer on top of the blockchain network to automate the buying and selling of event tickets. We shall use Solidity to write the contracts. There shall be at least three smart contracts - the ERC20 token contract (to generate Token X), the event contract, and the ERC721 ticket contract. The event contract will need to link to the ticket contract as it needs to use the data in the ticket contract. The keyword to access the data in another contract is import. For example, we can create an event contract event.sol that imports the ticket contract ticket.sol, using the syntax as follows:

```
Pragma Solidity ^0.5.0

import "./ticket.sol";
```

The event.sol file shall create an event contract that specifies event details such as total tickets, collected funds, start time, etc. The code could be as follows:

```
Contract Event {
  struct EventDetails {
  uint256 ticketAmount;
  uint256 SoldticketAmount;
  uint256 CollectedFunds;
  uint256 StartTime;
  }
```

The event contract shall also include a create event function, as follows:

```
function CreateEvent{
```

```
    uint256 _ticketAmount;

    uint256 _Startime

}
```

Apart from these, there are many more functions that can be included in smart contracts.

18.3 Developing a DApp - KittyChain Shop

In this project, we shall use Ganache (https://truffleframework.com/ganache)

to develop the KittyChain Shop DApp.

Ganache is a personal blockchain for Ethereum development you can use to deploy contracts, develop your applications, and run tests. It is available as both a desktop application as well as a command-line tool (formerly known as the TestRPC). Ganache is available for Windows, Mac, and Linux.

Truffle is a world-class development environment, testing framework and asset pipeline for blockchains using the Ethereum Virtual Machine (EVM), aiming to make life as a developer easier.

The KittyChain DApp is an adoption tracking system for a pet shop.

18.3.1 Steps to Build the Dapp

1. Setting up the development environment
2. Creating a Truffle project using a Truffle Box
3. Writing the smart contract
4. Compiling and migrating the smart contract
5. Testing the smart contract
    8Creating a user interface to interact with the smart contract
6. Interacting with the DApp in a browser

Step 1 Setting Up the Development Environment

Install the following:

1. Node.js
2. Git
3. Truffle

Having installed the aforementioned packages, we shall proceed to install Ganache. You can download Ganache by navigating to http://truffleframework.com/ganache and clicking the "Download" button.

Step 2 Creating the Project Using a Truffle Box

Truffle initializes in the current directory, so first create a directory in your development folder of choice and then move inside it.

mkdir pet-shop-tutorial

cd pet-shop-tutorial

Now you have created a Truffle Box called pet-shop, which includes the basic project structure as well as code for the user interface.

Next, use the truffle unbox command to unpack this Truffle Box.

truffle unbox pet-shop

The Output

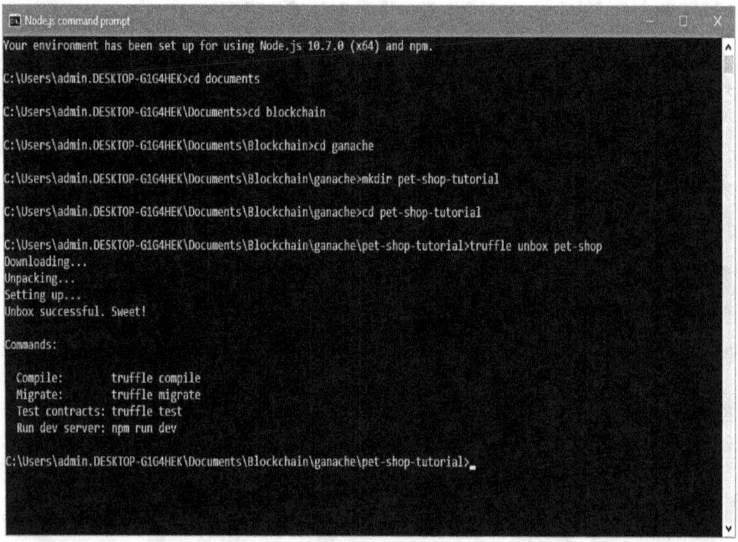
Node.js command prompt
Your environment has been set up for using Node.js 10.7.0 (x64) and npm.
C:\Users\admin.DESKTOP-G1G4HEK>cd documents
C:\Users\admin.DESKTOP-G1G4HEK\Documents>cd blockchain
C:\Users\admin.DESKTOP-G1G4HEK\Documents\Blockchain>cd ganache
C:\Users\admin.DESKTOP-G1G4HEK\Documents\Blockchain\ganache>mkdir pet-shop-tutorial
C:\Users\admin.DESKTOP-G1G4HEK\Documents\Blockchain\ganache>cd pet-shop-tutorial
C:\Users\admin.DESKTOP-G1G4HEK\Documents\Blockchain\ganache\pet-shop-tutorial>truffle unbox pet-shop
Downloading...
Unpacking...
Setting up...
Unbox successful. Sweet!
Commands:
Compile: truffle compile
Migrate: truffle migrate
Test contracts: truffle test
Run dev server: npm run dev
C:\Users\admin.DESKTOP-G1G4HEK\Documents\Blockchain\ganache\pet-shop-tutorial>

Figure 18.2

Directory Structure

The default Truffle directory structure contains the following folders and files:

- contracts/: Contains the Solidity source files for our smart contracts. There is an important contract in here called Migrations.sol, which we will discuss later.
- migrations/: Truffle uses a migration system to handle smart contract deployments. **Migration** is an additional special smart contract that keeps track of changes.
- test/: Contains both JavaScript and Solidity tests for our smart contracts.
- Truffle.Js: Truffle Configuration File.

Step 3 writing the smart contract

We shall write the smart contract that will act as the backend logic and storage.

Create a new file named Adoption.sol in the contracts/ directory. To save time, please download the file from:

http://javascript-tutor.net/blockchain/download/contracts/Adoption.sol

Adoption.sol

```
pragma solidity ^0.4.24;

  contract Adoption {
```

```solidity
    //array of 16 addresses, 20 bytes
    address[16] public adopters;
// Adopting a pet
    function adopt(uint petId) public returns (uint) {
    require(petId >= 0 && petId <= 15);
adopters[petId] = msg.sender;
    return petId;
    }
// Retrieving the adopters
    function getAdopters() public view returns (address[16]) {
        return adopters;
    }
}
```

Step 4 Compiling and Migrating the Smart Contract

Now that we have the smart contract, we shall proceed to compile and migrate it.

Truffle has a built-in developer console known as Truffle Develop, which generates a development blockchain that we can use to test and deploy the smart contract. It also can run Truffle commands directly from the console.

We need to compile the smart contract written in Solidity to bytecode for the Ethereum Virtual Machine (EVM) to execute. Think of it as translating our human-readable Solidity into something the EVM understands. In a terminal, make sure you are in the root of the directory that contains the DApp and type:

```
truffle compile
The output
Compiling ./contracts/Migrations.sol...
Compiling ./contracts/Adoption.sol...
Writing artifacts to ./build/contracts
```

Now that we have successfully compiled our contracts, it's time to migrate them to the blockchain! Migration is the deployment script meant to alter the state of the application's contracts, moving it from one state to the next. For the first migration, you might just be deploying new code, but over time, other migrations might move data around or replace a contract with a new one. By the way, there is one JavaScript file already in the migrations/ directory: **1_initial_migration.js**. This file handles deploying the **Migrations.sol** contract to observe subsequent smart contract migrations and ensures we do not double-migrate unchanged contracts in the future. Now let us create our own migration script.

Create a new file named 2_deploy_contracts.js in the migrations/directory. To save time, download the file from the following link:

http://javascript-tutor.net/blockchain/download/contracts/2_deploy_contracts.js

Before we can migrate our contract to the blockchain, we need to have a blockchain running. We shall use Ganache, a personal blockchain for Ethereum development you can use to deploy contracts, develop applications, and run tests. If you have not already, download Ganache and double click the icon to launch the application. This will generate a blockchain running locally on port 7545. Launch Ganache and you get the following output as shown in Figure 18.3

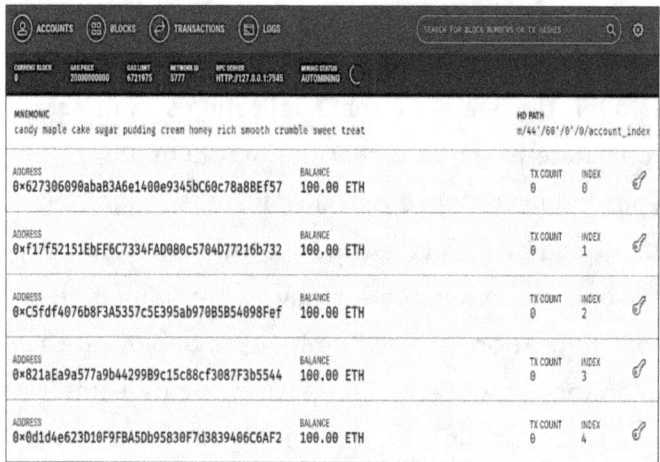

Figure 18.3 Ganache UI

Now back in your VS Code terminal, enter the following command:

`truffle migrate`

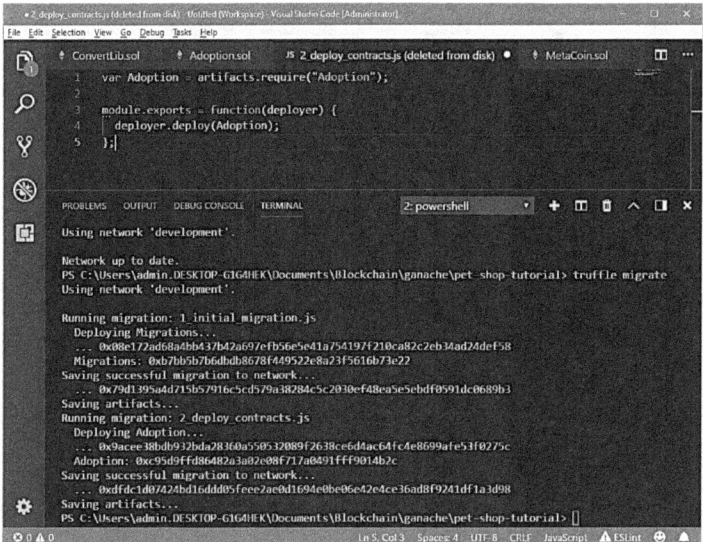

Figure 18.4

You can see the migrations being executed in order, followed by the blockchain address of each deployed contract.

In Ganache, note that the state of the blockchain has changed. The blockchain now shows that the current block, previously 0, is now 4. In addition, while the first account originally had 100 Ether, it is now lower at 99.94, due to the transaction costs of migration.

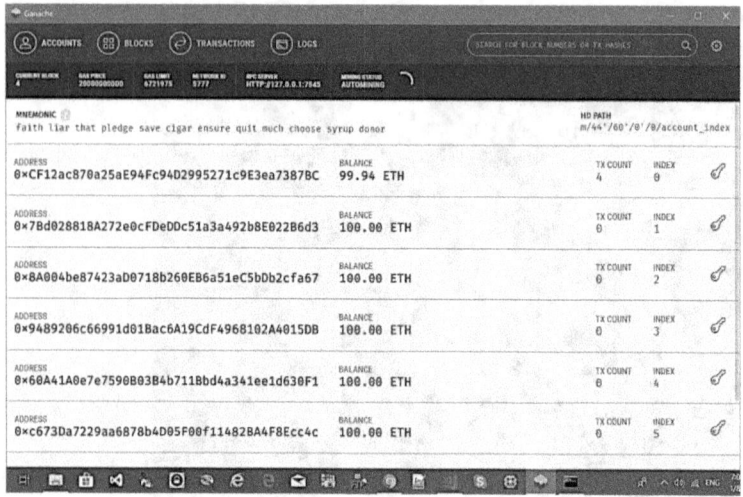

Figure 18.5

Step 5 Testing the smart contract

Truffle is very flexible when it comes to smart contract testing, in that tests can be written either in JavaScript or Solidity. In this tutorial, we will be writing our tests in Solidity.

Create a new file named TestAdoption.sol in the test/ directory. To save time, download a copy of the file from the following link:

http://javascript-tutor.net/blockchain/download/test/TestAdoption.sol

We start the contract off with three imports:

- Assert.sol: Gives us various assertions to use in our tests. In testing, an assertion checks for things like equality, inequality, or emptiness to return a pass/fail from our test.

- DeployedAddresses.sol: When running tests, Truffle will deploy a fresh instance of the contract being tested to the blockchain. This smart contract gets the address of the deployed contract.
- Adoption.sol: The smart contract we want to test.

To run the test, enter the following command:

Truffle test

The output is as shown in Figure 18.6.

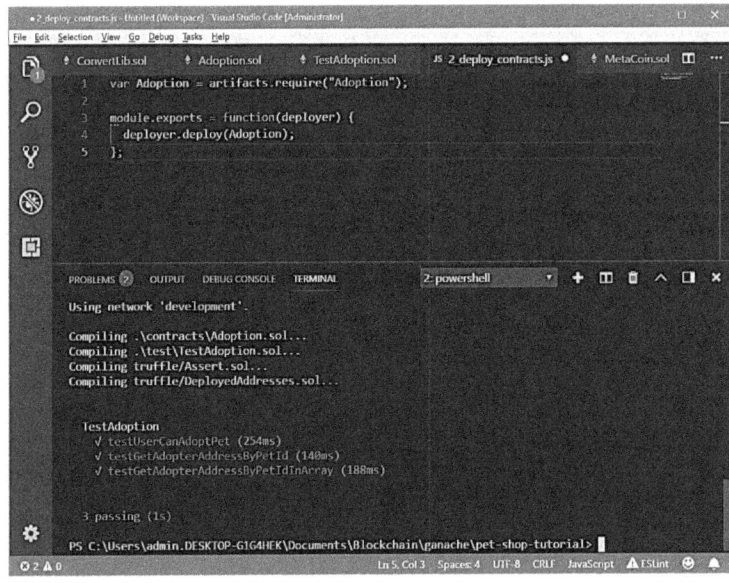

Figure 18.6

Step 6 Creating a User Interface to Interact with The Smart Contract

Now that we've created the smart contract, deployed it to our local test blockchain and confirmed we can interact with it via the console, it's time to create a UI so that the user can interact with the pet shop!

Included with the pet-shop Truffle Box is the code for the app's frontend. It is the JavaScript file app.js within the src/ directory. You can download the app.js file from the following link:

http://javascript-tutor.net/blockchain/download/src/js/app.js

We need to instantiate web3 to create the UI. The global App object is to manage our application, load in the pets data in init() and then call the function initWeb3(). The web3 JavaScript library interacts with the Ethereum blockchain. It can retrieve user accounts, send transactions, interact with smart contracts, and more.

First, we check if there is a web3 instance already active. (Ethereum browsers like Mist or Chrome with the MetaMask extension will inject their own web3 instances.) If an injected web3 instance is present, we get its provider and use it to create our web3 object.

If no injected web3 instance is present, we create our web3 object based on our local provider. (Here we fallback on http://localhost:7545 that points to Ganache.)

Step 7 Instantiating the Contract

We need to instantiate our smart contract so web3 knows where to find it and how it works. Truffle has a library to help with this called truffle-contract. It keeps information about the contract in sync with migrations, so you do not need to change the contract's deployed address manually.

First, we retrieve the artifact file for our smart contract. Artifacts are information about our contract such as its deployed address and Application Binary Interface (ABI). The ABI is a JavaScript object defining how to interact with the contract including its variables, functions, and parameters.

Once we have the artifacts in our callback, we pass them to **TruffleContract()**. This creates an instance of the contract we can interact with. With our contract instantiated, we set its web3 provider using the App.web3Provider value we stored earlier when setting up web3.

We then call the app's **markAdopted()** function in case any pets are already adopted from a previous visit. We have encapsulated this in a separate function since we'll need to update the UI any time, we make a change to the smart contract data.

Step 8 Getting the Adopted Pets and Updating The UI

We shall access the deployed Adoption contract, then call **getAdopters()** on that instance.

We first declare the variable **adoptionInstance** outside of the smart contract calls so we can access the instance after initially retrieving it.

Using **call()** allows us to read data from the blockchain without having to send a full transaction, meaning we will not have to spend any Ether.

After calling **getAdopters()**, we then loop through all of them, checking to see if an address is stored for each pet. Since the array contains address types, Ethereum initializes the array with 16 empty addresses. Therefore, we check for an empty address string rather than null or other false value.

Once a petId with a corresponding address is found, we disable its adopt button and change the button text to "Success", so the user gets some feedback. Any errors are logged to the console.

Step 9 Handling the Adopt() Function

We use web3 to get the user's accounts. In the callback after an error check, we select the first account.

From there, we get the deployed contract as we did above and store the instance in adoptionInstance. This time though, we are going to send a transaction instead of a call. Transactions require a "from" address and have an associated cost. This cost, paid in Ether, is called gas. The gas cost is the fee for performing computation and/or storing data in a smart contract. We send the transaction by executing the adopt() function with both the pet's ID and an object containing the account address, which we stored earlier in account.

The result of sending a transaction is the transaction object. If there are no errors, we proceed to call our markAdopted() function to sync the UI with our newly stored data.

Step 10 Interacting with The Dapp In A Browser

The easiest way to interact with our DApp in a browser is through MetaMask, a browser extension for both Chrome and Firefox.

Install MetaMask in your browser. Once installed, you will see the MetaMask fox icon next to your address bar. Click the icon and you will see this screen appear:

At the initial MetaMask screen, click Import Existing DEN. In the box marked Wallet Seed, enter the mnemonic that is displayed in Ganache, as shown in Figure 18.7.

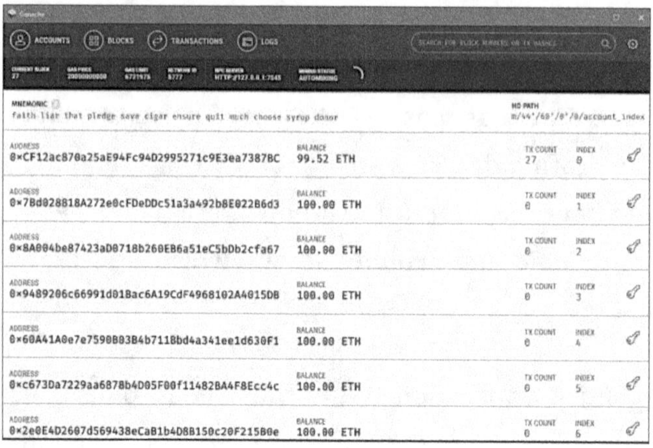

Figure 18.7

Enter a password below that and click OK.

Now we must connect MetaMask to the blockchain created by Ganache. Click the menu that shows "Main Network" and select Custom RPC.

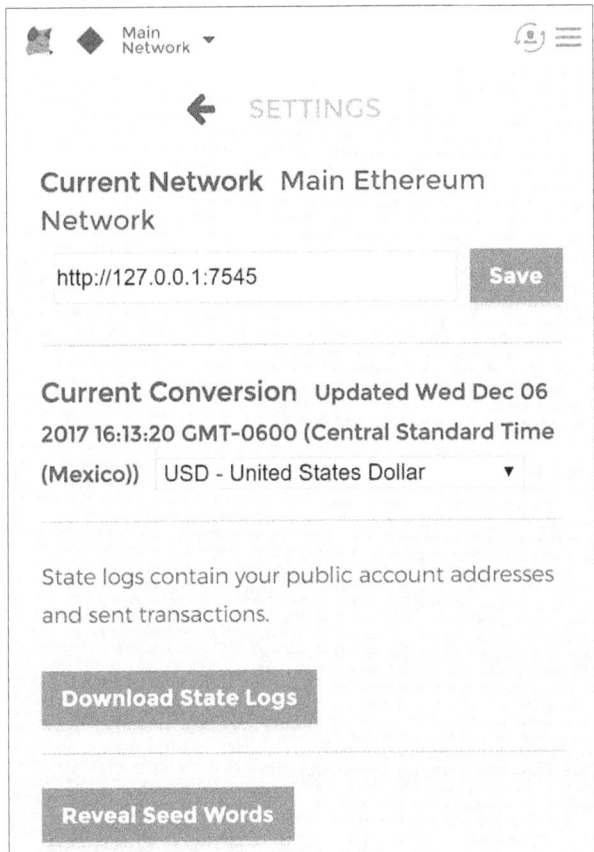

Figure 18.8

In the box titled "New RPC URL", enter http://127.0.0.1:7545 and click Save.

The network name at the top will switch to say, "**Private Network**".

Each account created by Ganache is given 100 Ether. You will notice it is slightly less on the first account because some gas was used when the contract itself was deployed and when the tests were run. (Make sure you are running Ganache as well.)

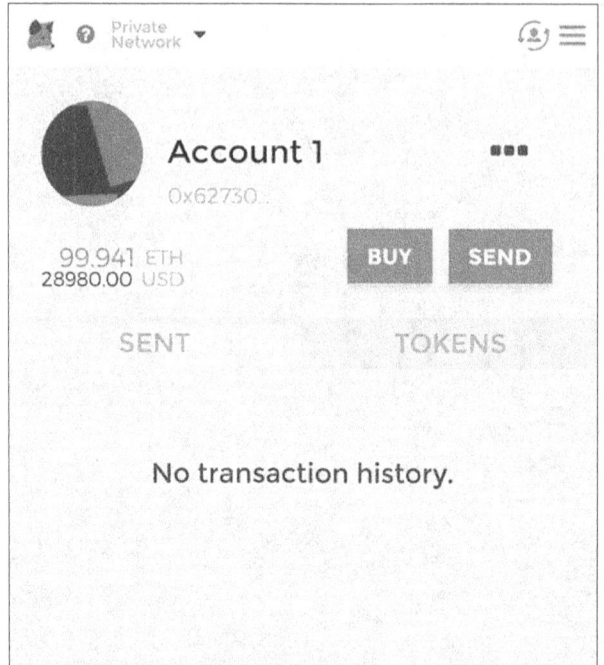

Figure 18.9

Step 11 Installing and Configuring Lite-Server

We can now start a local web server and use the DApp. We are using the lite-server library to serve our static files. This shipped with the pet-shop Truffle Box but let us look at how it works.

Let us examine bs-config.json:

```
{
  "port": 3000,
  "server": {
```

```
  "baseDir": ["./src", "./build/contracts"],
  "open": false
    },
  "browser": ["chrome"]
}
```

This tells lite-server which files to include in our base directory. We add the ./src directory for our website files and ./build/contracts directory for the contract artifacts.

I added "browser": ["chrome"]

So that the UI opens in the Chrome browser. We have also added a dev command to the scripts object in the package.json file in the project's root directory. The scripts object allows us to alias console commands to a single npm command.

244

To launch the app, enter the command in the VS Code Console.
npm run dev

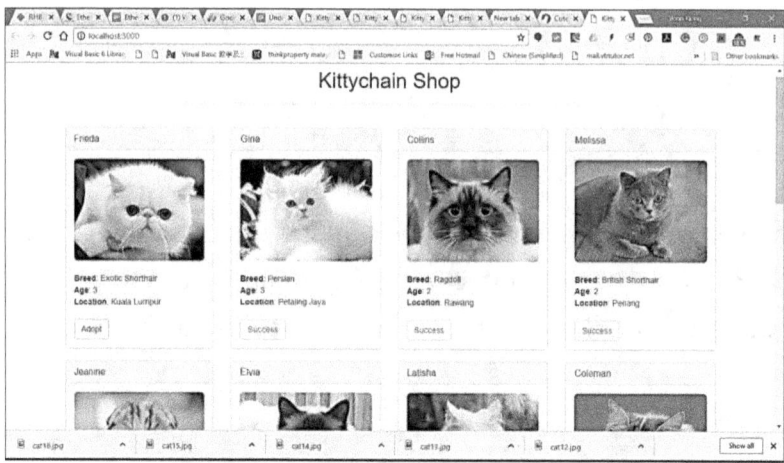

Figure 18.10 KittyChain Shop UI

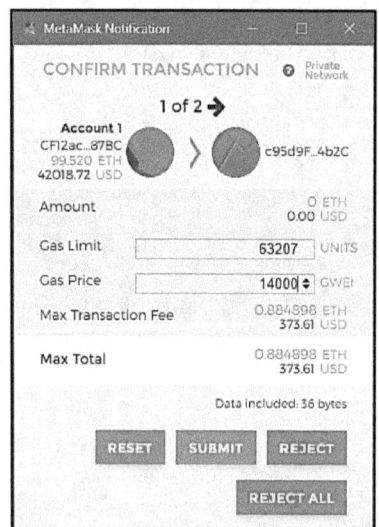

Figure 18.11

245

Metamask appears after clicking adopt.

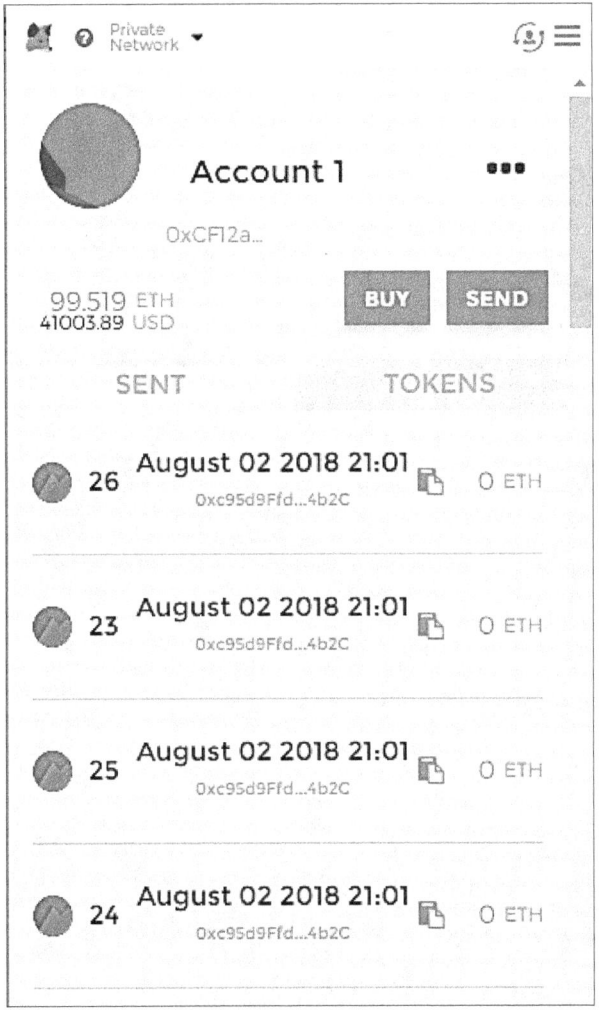

Figure 18.12 Transactions are shown on Metamask.

Transactions shown on Ganache:

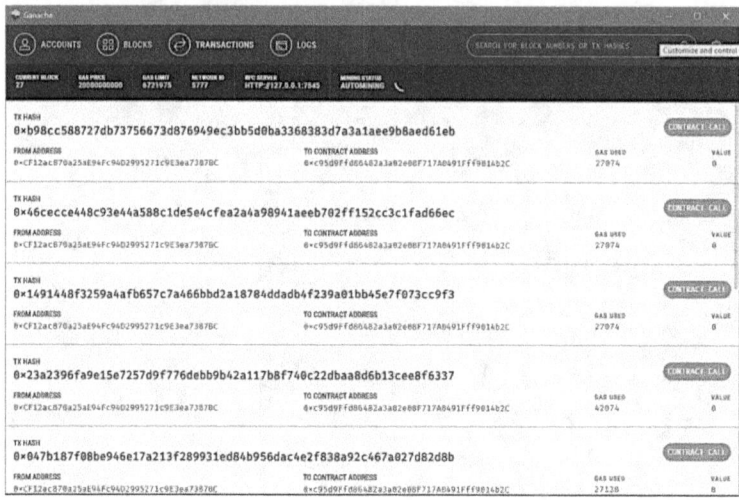

Figure 18.13

Chapter 19

Developing an Ethereum Cryptocurrency on Windows

You can develop your very own cryptocurrency using your laptop that runs Windows operating system. This article a step by step guide for newbies to easily developing and deploying a token using the sample code provided by the Truffle framework. Truffle is a world-class development environment, testing framework and asset pipeline for blockchains using the Ethereum Virtual Machine (EVM).

This is a step-by-step guide for developing an Ethereum-based cryptocurrency on Windows.

To start the project, we need to set up a development environment with the following requirements:

- A code editor
- Source control
- Unit tests
- Debugging

For code editor, we use Visual Studio code for the following reasons:

- VS Code integrates very well with Git for source control. Git is currently the best choice for source control.
- VS Code works well with Truffle framework that manages unit tests.
- VS Code works well with Truffle for debugging

Besides that, Visual Studio code is a great tool for editing Solidity smart contracts and is available on Windows, Mac & Linux.

I. Installation of the Packages

Step1: Install Chocolatey

Launch PowerShell as administrator. In PowerShell, enter the following command:

Set-ExecutionPolicy Bypass

The Set-ExecutionPolicy changes the user preference for the Windows PowerShell execution policy.

*Bypass-Nothing is blocked and there are no warnings or prompts. This execution policy is designed for configurations in which a Windows PowerShell script is built in to a a larger application or for configurations in which Windows PowerShell is the foundation for a program that has its own security model.
* Why Chocolatey-"You've never deployed software faster than you will with Chocolatey." -Rob Reynolds. Chocolatey is a software management automation.*

Install Chocolatey by entering the following code:

```
iex ((New-Object System.Net.WebClient).DownloadString('https://chocolatey.org/install.ps1'))
```

*https://chocolatey.org/docs/installation

*iex-invoke expression-The Invoke-Expression cmdlet evaluates or runs a specified string as a command and returns the results of the expression or command. Without Invoke-Expression, a string submitted at the command line would be returned (echoed) unchanged.

*A cmdlet (pronounced "command-let") is a lightweight Windows PowerShell script that performs a single function.

* https://chocolatey.org/install.ps1 downloads the Chocolatey installation zip file, unzips it and continues the installation by running a scripts in the tools section of the package.

After installation completed, close and reopen PowerShell as administrator again.

Step 2 Install Visual Studio Code, Git and Node.Js

Enter the following code in PowerShell:

```
choco install visualstudiocode -y

choco install git -y

choco install nodejs -y
```

*Git (/gɪt/[7]) is a version control system for tracking changes in computer files and coordinating work on those files among multiple people. It is primarily used for source code management in software development,[8] but it can be used to keep track of changes in any set of files. As a distributed revision control system, it is aimed at speed, data integrity] and support for distributed, non-linear workflows.

*Node.js is a JavaScript runtime built on Chrome's V8 JavaScript engine.

*As an asynchronous event driven JavaScript runtime, Node is designed to build scalable network applications. In programming, asynchronous events are those occurring independently of the main program flow. Asynchronous actions are actions executed in a non-blocking scheme, allowing the main program flow to continue processing

Close and reopen PowerShell before proceeding to the next step

Step 3 Install Truffle Framework

Truffle is a world class development environment, testing framework and asset pipeline for Ethereum, aiming to make life as an Ethereum developer easier. Truffle website is as follows:

(https://truffleframework.com/docs)

We use npm (Node Package Manager) to install Truffle Framework. Enter the following code:

```
npm install -g truffle
```

You can check the version of installed packages with the following code:

```
node -v

npm -v

truffle --version
```

The output is as shown in Figure 19.1.

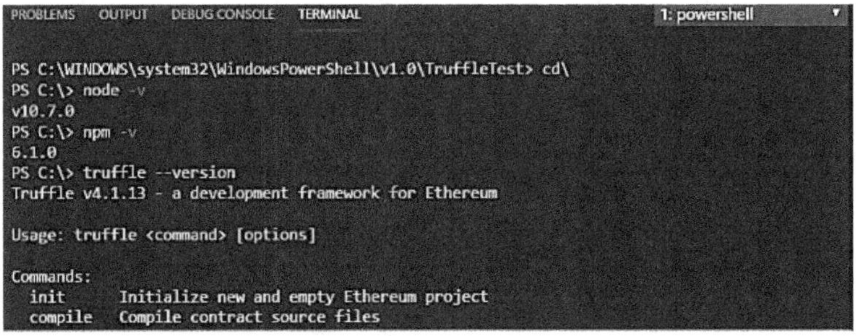

Figure 19.1

II. Configuring VS Code for Ethereum Blockchain Development

Step 1 Choose the Folder for Your Project

Choose a folder you prefer for your project and enter the following code:

```
mkdir TruffleTest; cd TruffleTest; code .
```

The final command in the chain is "Code .", which opens an instance of Visual Studio Code in the folder from which the command is executed.

Step 2 Install Solidity in The Vs Code IDE

In the VS Code IDE, search for Solidity and install it

Step 3 Install Material Icon Theme

In the VS Code , install Material Icon Theme.

Now you have the VS integrated with PowerShell IDE for Ethereum Blockchain development.

III. Creating a Blockchain Application

We will create a sample cryptocurrency and a smart contract using the built-in sample MetaCoin in Truffle. Now, download the files that can be compiled and deployed to a simulated blockchain using Truffle.

The code is

```
truffle unbox metacoin
```

The output should looks as shown in Figure 19.2.

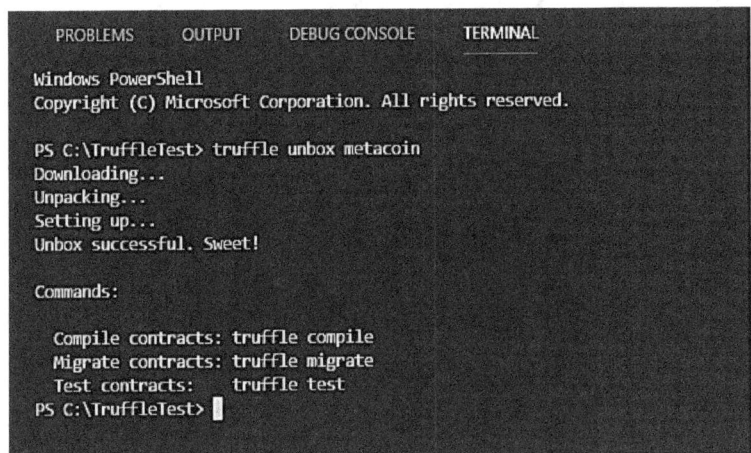

Figure 19.2

After downloading Truffle metacoin, we should be able to view two important application files written in Solidity:

MetaCoin.sol and ConvertLib.sol

As shown in Figure 19.3.

* Solidity is a contract-oriented, high-level language for implementing smart contracts. It was influenced by C++, Python and JavaScript and is designed to target the Ethereum Virtual Machine (EVM).

*the Ethereum Virtual Machine is designed to serve as a runtime environment for smart contracts based on Ethereum.

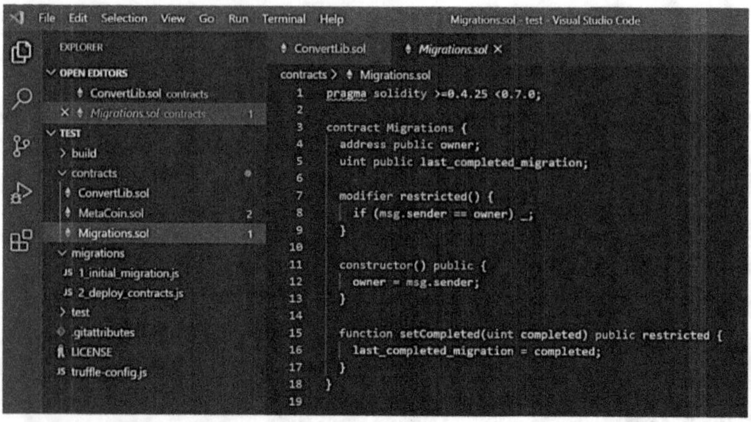

Figure 19.3

These two files can be compiled and deployed to a simulated blockchain using Truffle.

To compile the smart contract, using the following command

truffle compile

*Or use **truffle.cmd compile** if there is error as shown in Figure 19.4

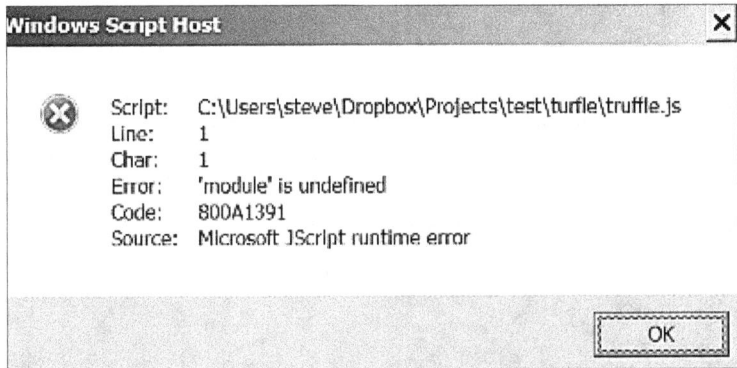

Figure 19.4

Source: https://ethereum.stackexchange.com/questions/21017/truffle-microsoft-jscript-runtime-error

After compilation completed, you will notice that a 'build' folder has been added to the list of files, which contains the compiled json files ConvertLib.json, MetaCoin.json, and Migrations.json, as shown in Figure 19.5.

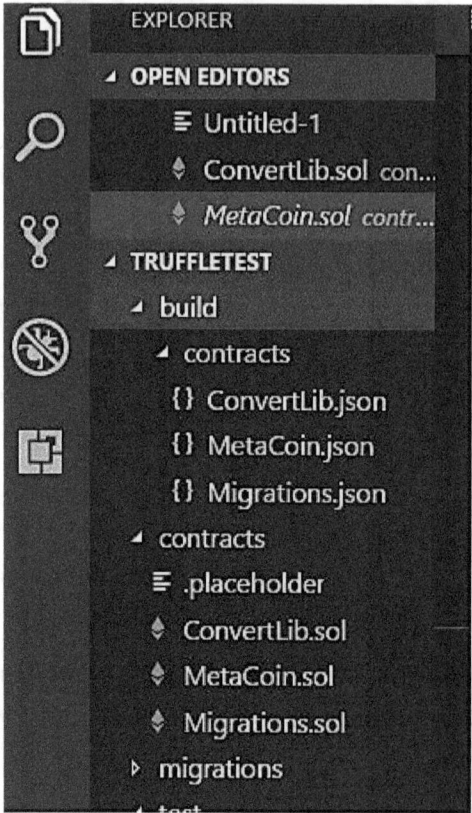

Figure 19.5

IV Deploying the Contract

To deploy the contract, we shall migrate the contract to a test network in truffle development environment.

The 'develop' command appears in the Truffle development console environment. This will set up a kind of dummy blockchain, that operates similarly to the real Ethereum blockchain, and allows us to test deployment and execution of the code without needing to interface with an actual blockchain.

To compile the contract, key in the following command

```
truffle develop
```

This command will launch the truffle development environment, automatically configured with 10 accounts and keys. The output is as shown in Figure 19.6.

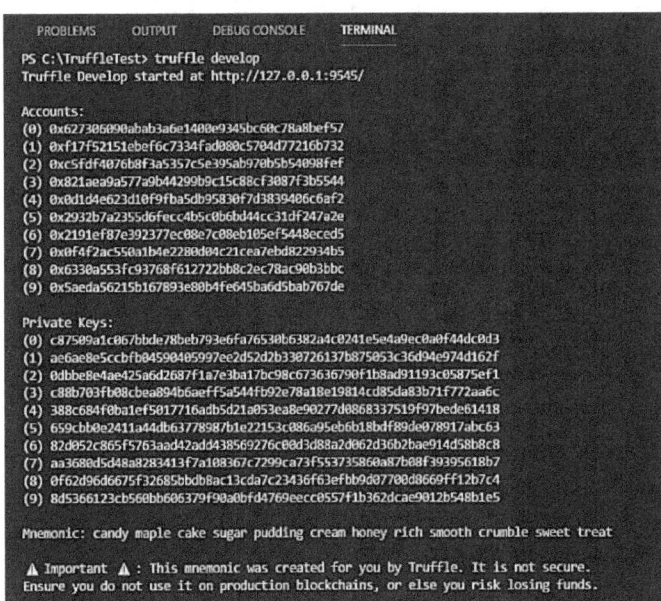

Figure 19.6

To deploy the compiled contract to the Truffle environment, enter the following command:

```
migrate
```

This will deploy the contracts to the test environment. The output is as shown in Figure 19.7.

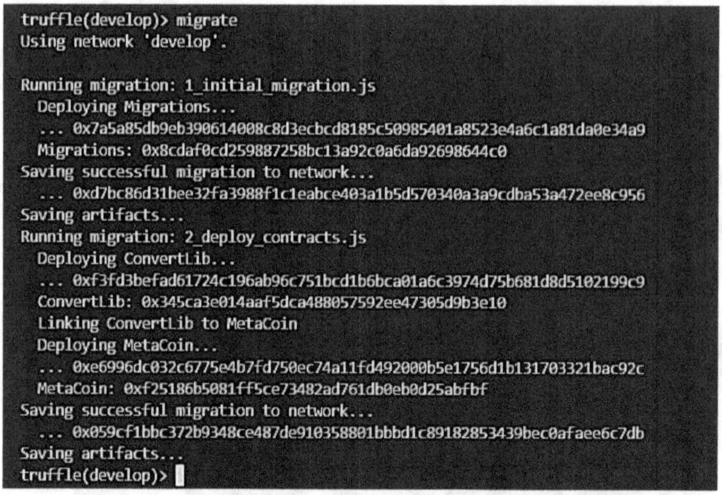

```
truffle(develop)> migrate
Using network 'develop'.

Running migration: 1_initial_migration.js
  Deploying Migrations...
  ... 0x7a5a85db9eb390614008c8d3ecbcd8185c50985401a8523e4a6c1a81da0e34a9
  Migrations: 0x8cdaf0cd259887258bc13a92c0a6da92698644c0
Saving successful migration to network...
  ... 0xd7bc86d31bee32fa3988f1c1eabce403a1b5d570340a3a9cdba53a472ee8c956
Saving artifacts...
Running migration: 2_deploy_contracts.js
  Deploying ConvertLib...
  ... 0xf3fd3befad61724c196ab96c751bcd1b6bca01a6c3974d75b681d8d5102199c9
  ConvertLib: 0x345ca3e014aaf5dca488057592ee47305d9b3e10
  Linking ConvertLib to MetaCoin
  Deploying MetaCoin...
  ... 0xe6996dc032c6775e4b7fd750ec74a11fd492000b5e1756d1b131703321bac92c
  MetaCoin: 0xf25186b5081ff5ce73482ad761db0eb0d25abfbf
Saving successful migration to network...
  ... 0x059cf1bbc372b9348ce487de910358801bbbd1c89182853439bec0afaee6c7db
Saving artifacts...
truffle(develop)>
```

Figure 19.7

To test the contract, enter the following command.

test

You will see the output as shown in Figure 19.8.

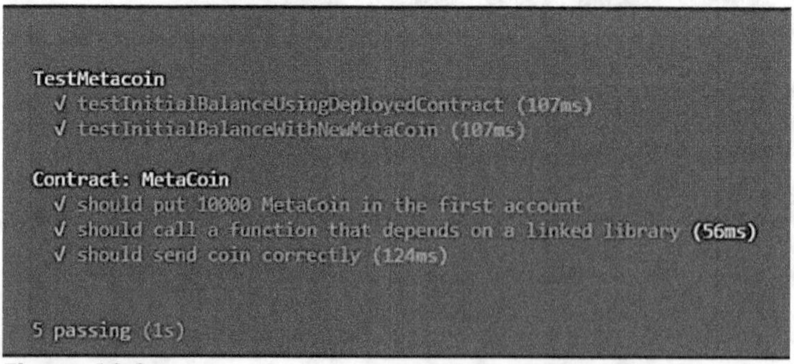

```
TestMetacoin
    ✓ testInitialBalanceUsingDeployedContract (107ms)
    ✓ testInitialBalanceWithNewMetaCoin (107ms)

Contract: MetaCoin
    ✓ should put 10000 MetaCoin in the first account
    ✓ should call a function that depends on a linked library (56ms)
    ✓ should send coin correctly (124ms)


5 passing (1s)
```

Figure 19.8

To exit the Truffle console, type ctrl+D

To reenter the Truffle console, enter the following code.

```
truffle develop
```

```
migrate --reset
```

```
test
```

V Interacting with the contract with Web3

We have deployed and test the contract, now let us do something with the contract. We will need to use the Web3 framework to interact with the smart contract on the Ethereum blockchain. Web3 is a JavaScript library which is bundled into the Truffle development console.

When the Truffle development console is started, it automatically configures 10 addresses, and assigns each of the addresses 100 Eth. You can check the ten available addresses by entering the following code:

```
web3.eth.accounts
```

The output is as shown in Figure 19.9.

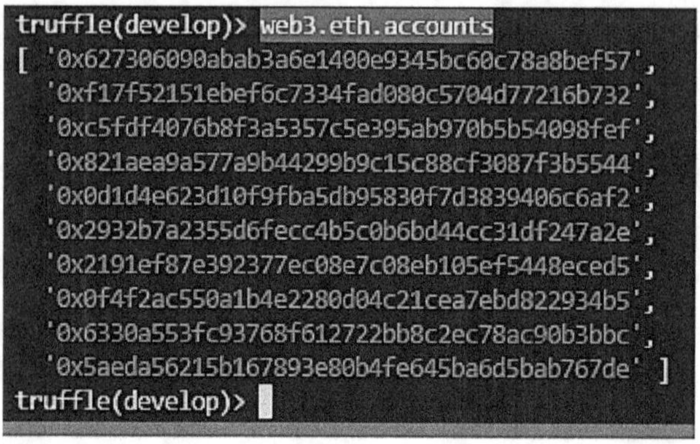
truffle(develop)> web3.eth.accounts
['0x627306090abab3a6e1400e9345bc60c78a8bef57',
'0xf17f52151ebef6c7334fad080c5704d77216b732',
'0xc5fdf4076b8f3a5357c5e395ab970b5b54098fef',
'0x821aea9a577a9b44299b9c15c88cf3087f3b5544',
'0x0d1d4e623d10f9fba5db95830f7d3839406c6af2',
'0x2932b7a2355d6fecc4b5c0b6bd44cc31df247a2e',
'0x2191ef87e392377ec08e7c08eb105ef5448eced5',
'0x0f4f2ac550a1b4e2280d04c21cea7ebd822934b5',
'0x6330a553fc93768f612722bb8c2ec78ac90b3bbc',
'0x5aeda56215b167893e80b4fe645ba6d5bab767de']
truffle(develop)>

Figure 19.9

You can display individual account using the following syntax

```
web3.eth.accounts[n]
```

For example, enter the following code to see the output

```
web3.eth.accounts[2]
```

The output is as shown in Figure 19.10.

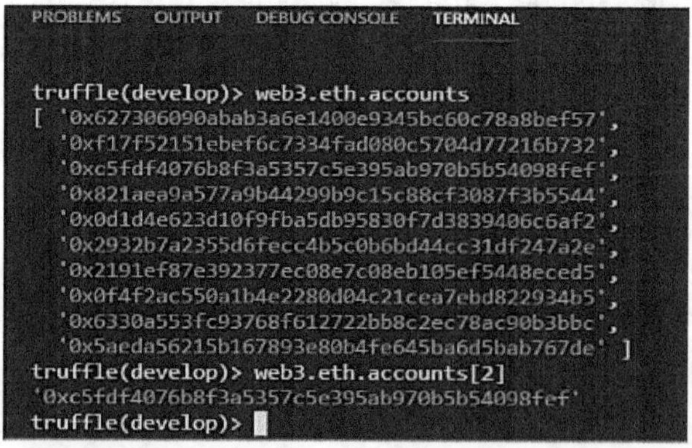
PROBLEMS
OUTPUT
DEBUG CONSOLE
TERMINAL
truffle(develop)> web3.eth.accounts
['0x627306090abab3a6e1400e9345bc60c78a8bef57',
'0xf17f52151ebef6c7334fad080c5704d77216b732',
'0xc5fdf4076b8f3a5357c5e395ab970b5b54098fef',
'0x821aea9a577a9b44299b9c15c88cf3087f3b5544',
'0x0d1d4e623d10f9fba5db95830f7d3839406c6af2',
'0x2932b7a2355d6fecc4b5c0b6bd44cc31df247a2e',
'0x2191ef87e392377ec08e7c08eb105ef5448eced5',
'0x0f4f2ac550a1b4e2280d04c21cea7ebd822934b5',
'0x6330a553fc93768f612722bb8c2ec78ac90b3bbc',
'0x5aeda56215b167893e80b4fe645ba6d5bab767de']
truffle(develop)> web3.eth.accounts[2]
'0xc5fdf4076b8f3a5357c5e395ab970b5b54098fef'
truffle(develop)>

Figure 19.10

There are four functions in the MetaCoin.sol file, as follows:

- MetaCoin, the constructor. It is called when the contract is deployed.
- sendCoin, for transferring coins between addresses.
- getBalanceInEth, to convert between MetaCoins, and Ethereum.
- getBalance, to show the balance in the requested address.

A constructor is a special method of a class or structure in object-oriented programming that initializes an object of that type. A constructor is an instance method that usually has the same name as the class and can be used to set the values of the members of an object, either to default or to user-defined values.

The constructor MetaCoin comprises only one line

```
balances[tx.origin] = 10000;
```

You can change this to any amount

This code initializes the transaction to 10000 MetaCoin(Not Eth)

The initial address is

Web3.eth.accounts[0]

Checking Balance with the getBalance() method

You can check the balance of any account using the following code

```
web3.eth.getBalance(web3.eth.accounts[n]).toNumber()
```

Will display the balance in wei. To convert it to ether, you need to divide it by 10^18. You can use:

web3.eth.getBalance(web3.eth.accounts[n]).toNumber()/1000000000000000000

Or

web3.fromWei(web3.eth.getBalance(web3.eth.accounts[n]),'ether').toNumber();

For example, to check the balance of account 0, enter the following code

web3.eth.getBalance(web3.eth.accounts[0]).toNumber()

**The cryptocurrency generated by the getBalance function is Wei

1 Ether = 1,000,000,000,000,000,000 Wei (10^{18}) or 1 Wei=10^{-18} Ether

The output is as shown in Figure 19.11.

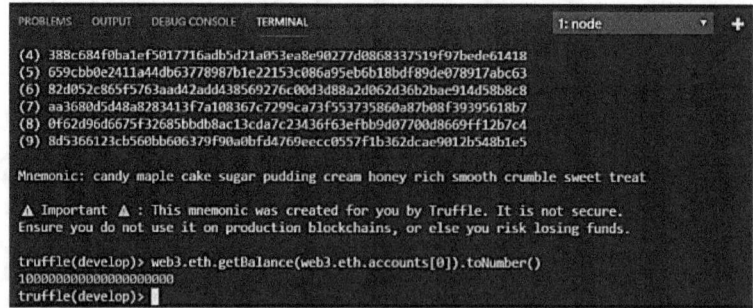

Figure 19.11

To check the balance in Ether for account 0, enter the following command:

```
web3.fromWei(web3.eth.getBalance(web3.eth.accounts[0]),'ether').toNumber();
```

The output is as shown in Figure 19.12.

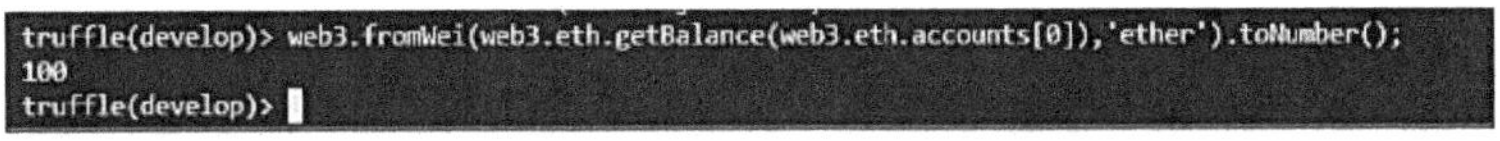

```
truffle(develop)> web3.fromWei(web3.eth.getBalance(web3.eth.accounts[0]),'ether').toNumber();
100
truffle(develop)>
```

Figure 19.12

To check the balance of Web3.eth.accounts[0] in MetaCoin(not ether), use the following command:

```
MetaCoin.deployed().then(function(instance){return instance.getBalance.call(web3.eth.accounts[0]);}).then(function(value){return value.toNumber()});
```

The output is as shown in Figure 19.13.

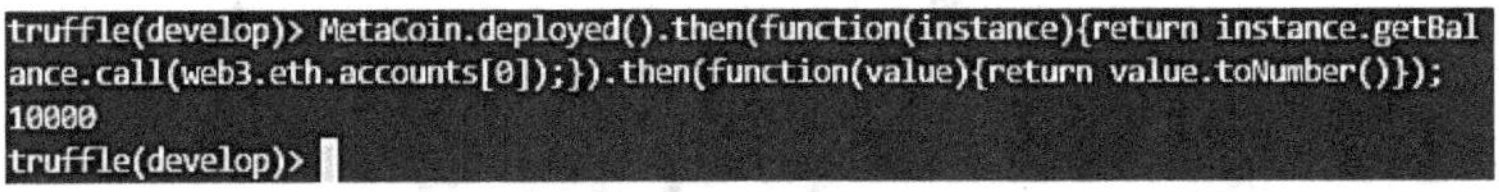

```
truffle(develop)> MetaCoin.deployed().then(function(instance){return instance.getBalance.call(web3.eth.accounts[0]);}).then(function(value){return value.toNumber()});
10000
truffle(develop)>
```

Figure 19.13

Send Coin with the sendCoin Function

To send metacoin from account[0] to account[1], use the following command

```
MetaCoin.deployed().then(function(instance){return instance.sendCoin(web3.eth.accounts[1], 100);});
```

To send metacoin from account[m] to account[n], use the following command

```
MetaCoin.deployed().then(function(instance)    {    return
instance.sendCoin(web3.eth.accounts[n],                10,
{from:web3.eth.accounts[m]});})
```

Example

```
MetaCoin.deployed().then(function(instance)    {    return
instance.sendCoin(web3.eth.accounts[1],    1000,    {from:
web3.eth.accounts[0]});})
```

The output is as shown in Figure 19.14.

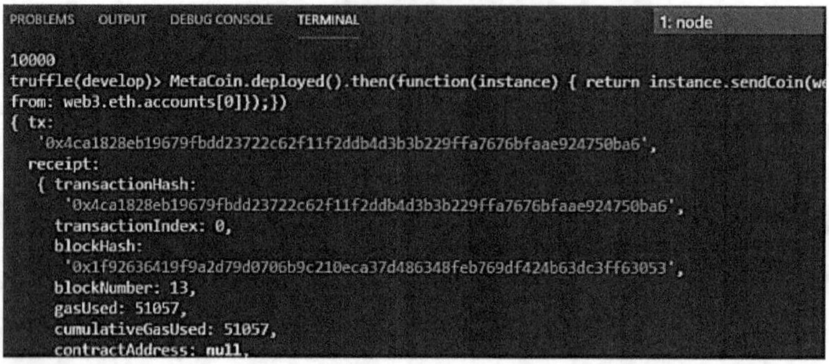

Figure 19.14

The check whether the transaction is successful, we can check the balance of both accounts. (Note that this is the MetaCoin balance, NOT the Eth balance)

```
MetaCoin.deployed().then(function(instance){return
instance.getBalance.call(web3.eth.accounts[0]);}).then(fu
nction(value){return value.toNumber()});
```

The output is as shown in Figure 19.15.

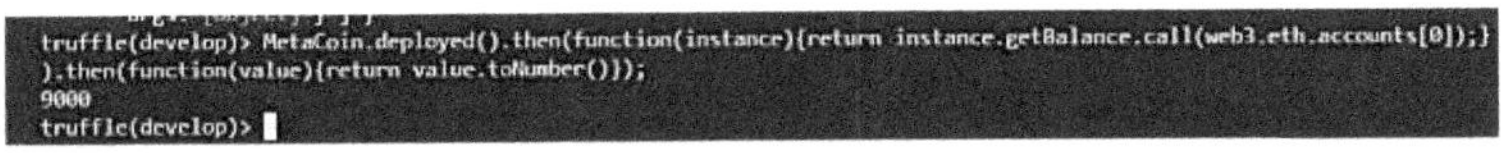

```
truffle(develop)> MetaCoin.deployed().then(function(instance){return instance.getBalance.call(web3.eth.accounts[0]);}
).then(function(value){return value.toNumber()});
9000
truffle(develop)>
```

Figure 19.15

To convert MetaCoin to Ether, use the following code:

```
MetaCoin.deployed().then(function(instance){return
instance.getBalanceInEth.call(web3.eth.accounts[n]);}).th
en(function(value){return value.toNumber()});
```

Example

```
MetaCoin.deployed().then(function(instance){return
instance.getBalanceInEth.call(web3.eth.accounts[0]);}).th
en(function(value){return value.toNumber()});
```

The output is as shown in Figure 19.16.

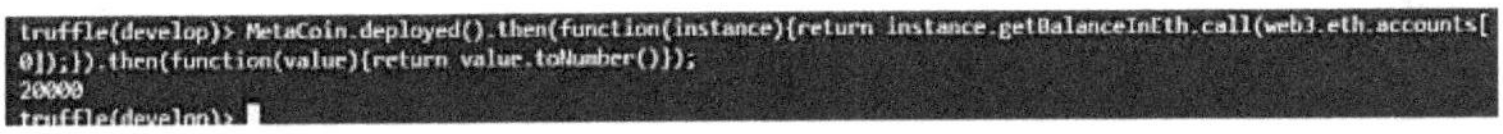

```
truffle(develop)> MetaCoin.deployed().then(function(instance){return instance.getBalanceInEth.call(web3.eth.accounts[
0]);}).then(function(value){return value.toNumber()});
20000
truffle(develop)>
```

Figure 19.16

Debugging the Transaction

In the sendCoin() example, a transaction has occurred on the blockchain. This transaction can be stepped through line by line, using the Truffle debugger. To do this, the Truffle debug command is used, passing in the transaction hash. This hash can be found in the console output following the sendCoin function call.

The command is

```
truffle(develop)>                                          debug
'0x4ca1828eb19679fbdd23722c62f11f2ddb4d3b3b229ffa7676bfaa
e924750ba6'
```

This will start the Truffle debugger. The instructions for interacting with the debugger are printed to the console, as shown in Figure 19.17.

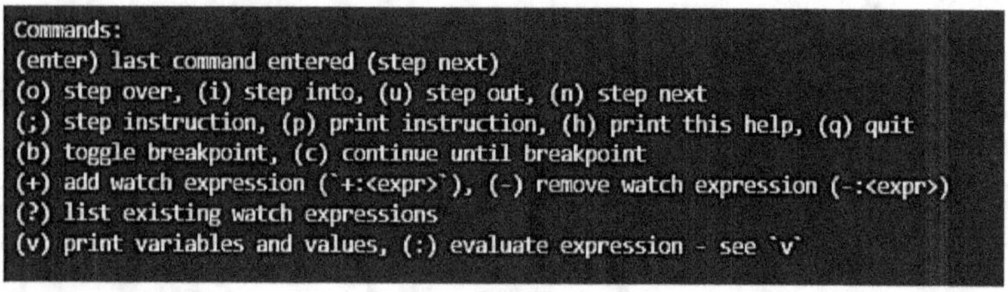

```
Commands:
(enter) last command entered (step next)
(o) step over, (i) step into, (u) step out, (n) step next
(;) step instruction, (p) print instruction, (h) print this help, (q) quit
(b) toggle breakpoint, (c) continue until breakpoint
(+) add watch expression (`+:<expr>`), (-) remove watch expression (-:<expr>)
(?) list existing watch expressions
(v) print variables and values, (:) evaluate expression - see `v`
```

Figure 19.17

You should start by adding a watch to the passed variables. do this by entering the following command:

```
+: receiver
```

```
+: amount
```

As you step through the code, the values passed into the function will be shown. Note, these are 'undefined' at the start of the function call.

You can press the enter key a few times to step through the code that was executed in this transaction. The output is as shown in Figure 19.18.

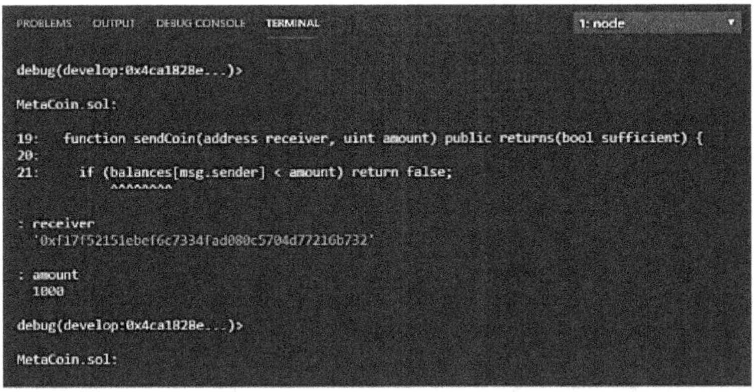

Figure 19.18

The debug commands can be used to inspect the variables, and add watched variables, as shown in Figure 19.19.

Figure 19.19

You can try to enter other commands.

Lastly, type quit to quit debugger

VI Deploying Your MetaCoin Contract with Truffle

Deploy to Ganache

Ganache is your personal Ethereum blockchain which is convenient for testing and interacting with your contracts during development. It ships with a helpful GUI that allows you to see available test accounts quickly, explore transactions, read logs, and see how much gas was consumed. Configure your truffle.js and truffle.config.js for the Ganache network:

```
module.exports = {

  networks: {

    ganache: {

      host: "127.0.0.1",

      port: 7545,

      network_id: "*" // matching any id

    }

  }

};
```

Launch Ganache

In the Truffle console, enter the following command:

```
truffle migrate --network ganache
```

The output is as shown in Figure 19.20.

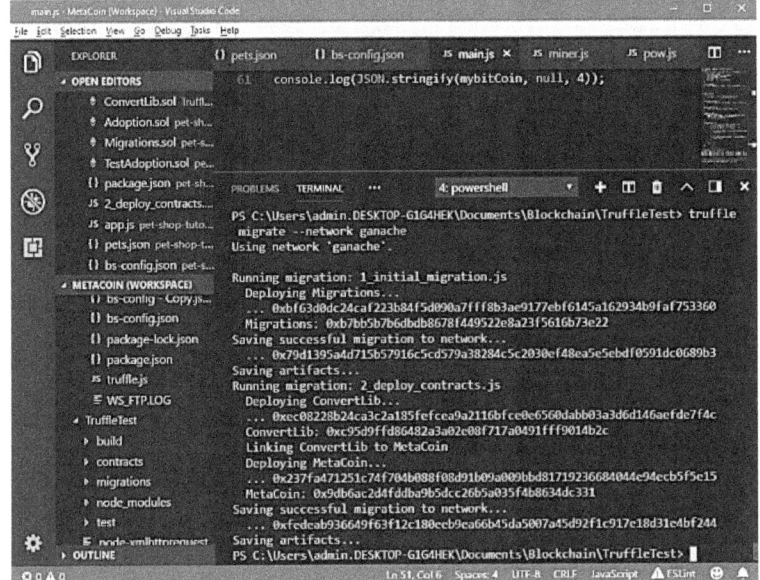

Figure 19.20

Ganache output is as shown in Figure 19. 21.

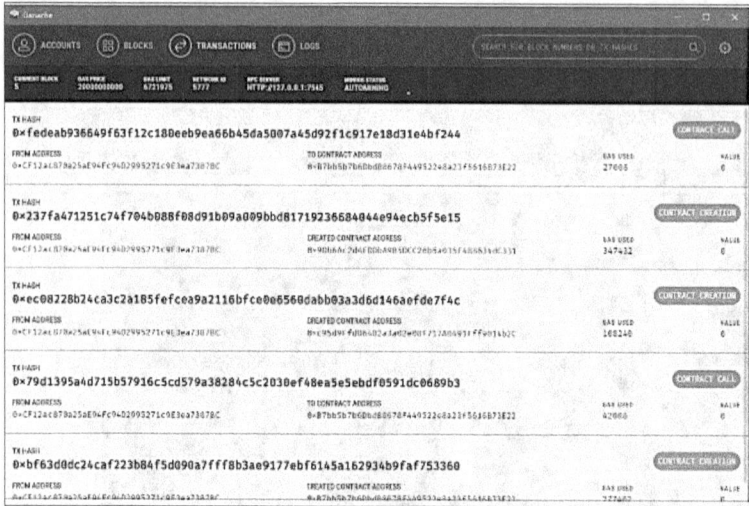

Figure 19.21

Click transaction and compare the transaction hash. They are the same.

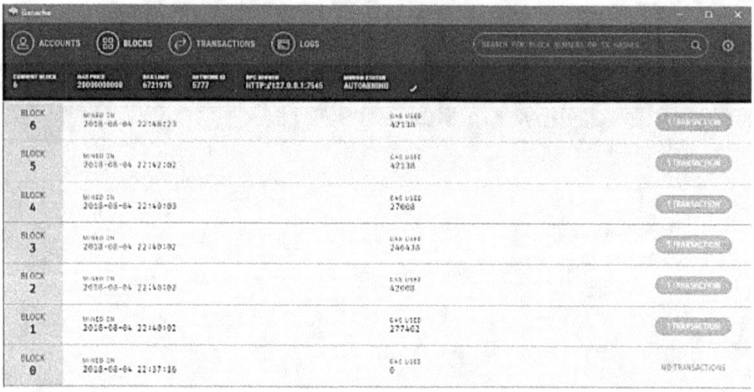

Figure 19.22

Deploy to Ropsten

Run a node connected to Ropsten and specify the address of the default (first) account to unlock. You will be prompted for a passphrase.

```
geth --unlock <account> --testnet --rpc --rpcapi eth,net,web3
```

Configuration for the Ropsten network:

```
module.exports = {

  networks: {

    ropsten: {

      host: "127.0.0.1",

      port: 8545,

      network_id: 3,

      gas: 4700000

    },

  }

};
```

Deploy to the Ropsten network:

```
truffle migrate --network ropsten
```

Deploy to Rinkeby

Rinkeby network is available only using geth client.

```
geth    --unlock    <account>    --rinkeby    --rpc    --rpcapi eth,net,web3
```

Configuration for the Rinkeby network:

```
module.exports = {
  networks: {
    rinkeby: {
      host: "127.0.0.1",
      port: 8545,
      network_id: 4
    },
  }
};
```

Deploy to the Rinkeby network:

```
truffle migrate --network rinkeby
```

Chapter 20

Creating Your Own Token for ICO

ICO is a hot topic in the crypto world today. In this article, I will attempt to explain how to create your own token for an ICO project.

First, you need to set up a private Ethereum network before you can proceed to create the token. After setting up the private network, you need to run it. (The detail steps for setting up a private Ethereum network is discussed in another article)

Next, you need to install the Ethereum wallet before you proceed. Follow the steps below to install the Ethereum Wallet.

1. Install Ethereum Mist Wallet for Windows 10.
2. Visit the link https://github.com/ethereum/mist/releases
3. Download Ethereum-Wallet-win64-0-11-0.zip
4. Create a folder Ethereum under the Program Files folder and extract the zip files there.

Launch the Ethereum wallet after successful installation. Also, create an account in the wallet, as shown in Figure 20.1

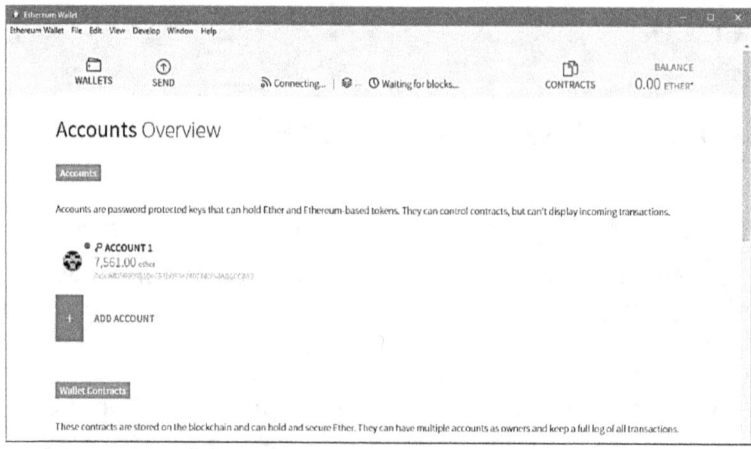

Figure 20.1

Next, Open the Wallet app and then go to the Contracts tab as shown in Figure 20.2

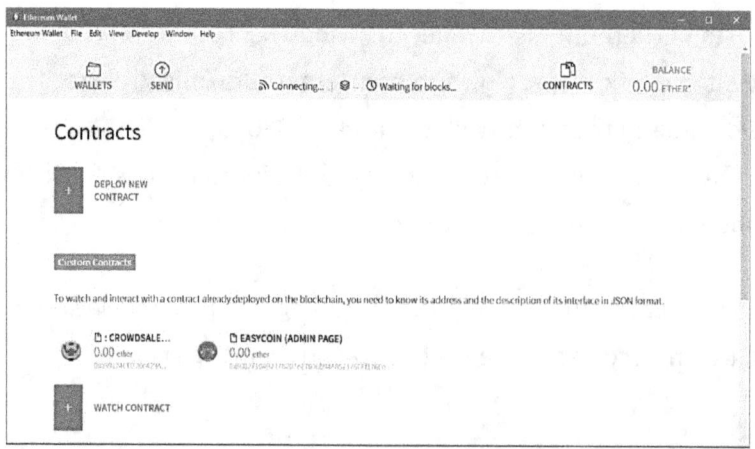

Figure 20.2

Click on DEPLOY NEW CONTRACT and bring up the Solidity Contract Source code text editor as shown the following Figure 20.3

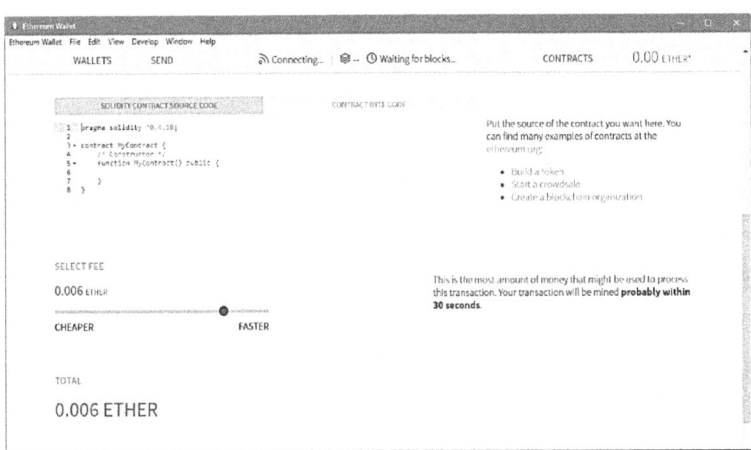

Figure 20.3

Now type the following smart contract code in the code editor.

pragma solidity ^0.4.24;

contract BestToken {

    /* This creates an array with all balances */

    mapping (address => uint256) public balanceOf;

    string public name;

    string public symbol;

    uint8 public decimals;

```
/* Initializes contract with initial supply tokens to the creator of the contract */
constructor(
    uint256 initialSupply,
    string tokenName,
    string tokenSymbol,
    uint8 decimalUnits
) public {
    balanceOf[msg.sender] = initialSupply;   // Give the creator all initial tokens
    name = tokenName;                        // Set the name for display purposes
    symbol = tokenSymbol;                    // Set the symbol for display purposes
    decimals = decimalUnits;                 // Amount of decimals for display purposes
}

/* Send coins */
function transfer(address _to, uint256 _value) public returns (bool success) {
    require(balanceOf[msg.sender] >= _value);    // Check if the sender has enough
    require(balanceOf[_to] + _value >= balanceOf[_to]); // Check for overflows
```

```
    balanceOf[msg.sender] -= _value;                //
Subtract from the sender

    balanceOf[_to] += _value;                       //
Add the same to the recipient

    return true;

  }

}
```

If the code compiles without any error, you should see a "pick a contract" drop-down list on the right, as shown Figure 20.4

Figure 20.4

Click Pick a contract button and select the "BestToken" contract. On the right column, you will see all the parameters you need to personalize your own token. You can tweak them as you like, I use the following parameters: 10,000 as the supply, BestCoin for the token name, "#" as the symbol and 2 decimal places. Your wallet should be looking like Figure 20.5

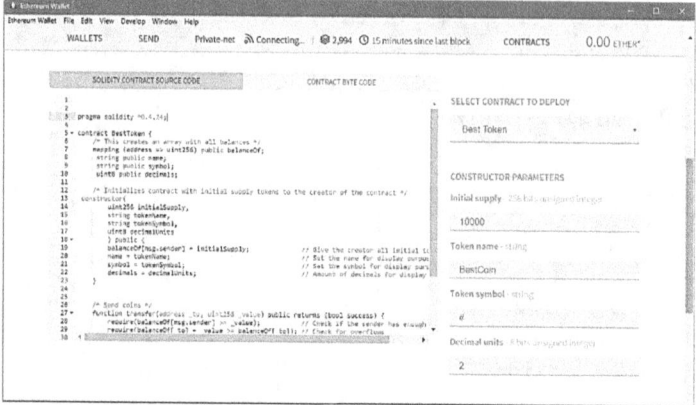

Figure 20.5

Scroll to the end of the page and you will see an estimate of the computation cost of that contract and you can select a fee on how much Ether you are willing to pay for it. Any excess Ether you do not spend will be returned to you so you can leave the default settings if you wish. Press "deploy", type your account password, and wait a few seconds for your transaction to be picked up.

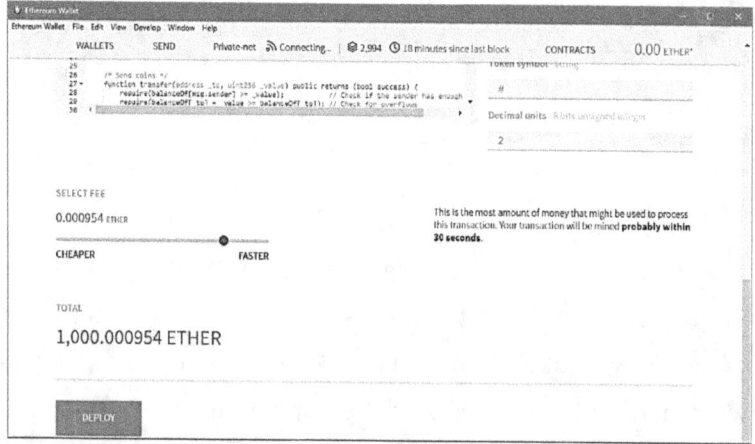

Figure 20.6

Now click the DEPLOY button to deploy the smart contract, the output dialog is as shown in Figure 20.7

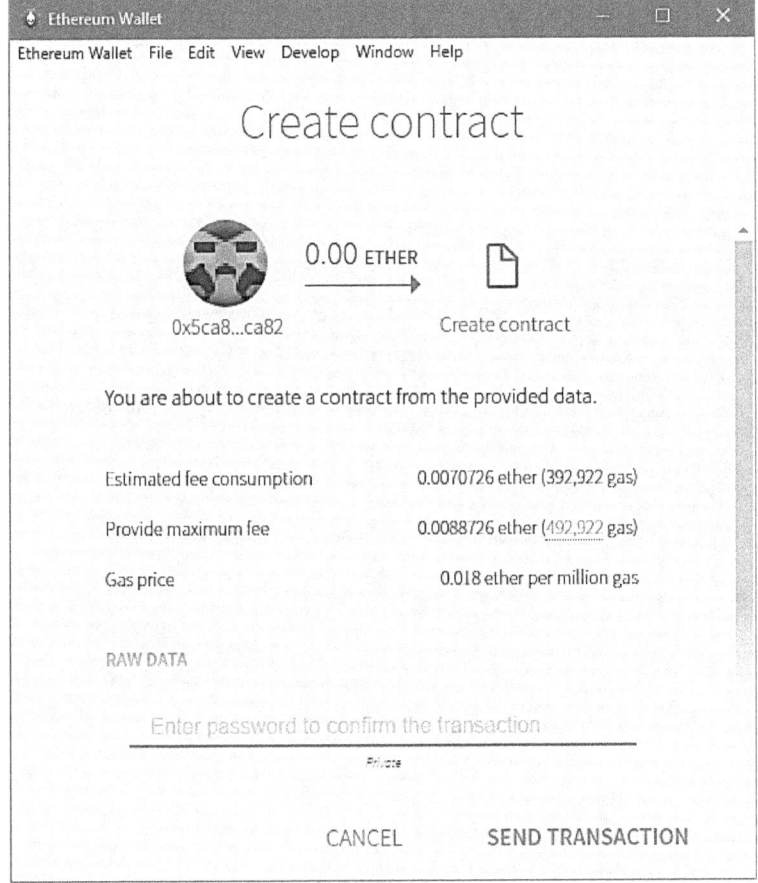

Figure 20.7

280

Upon entering the password for your account and click send transaction, the contract is successfully deployed, as shown in Figure 20.8

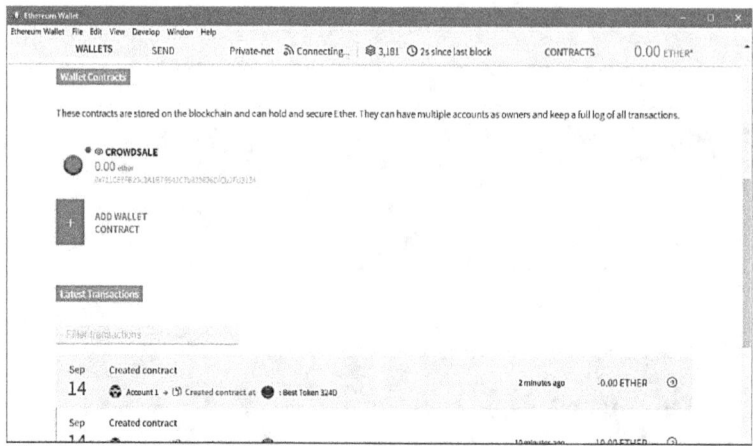

Figure 20.8

Now the new token Best Token is shown in your wallet, as shown in Figure 20.9

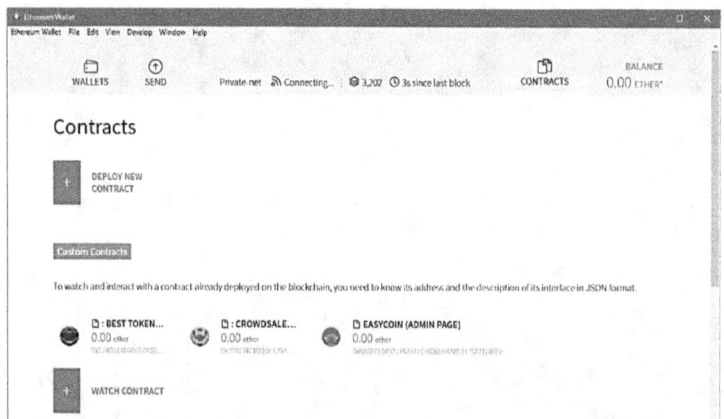

Figure 20.9

Tokens are currencies and other fungibles built on the Ethereum platform. For accounts to watch for tokens and send them, you must add their address to this list. Proceed to add BestCoin to the list, as shown in the following figure.

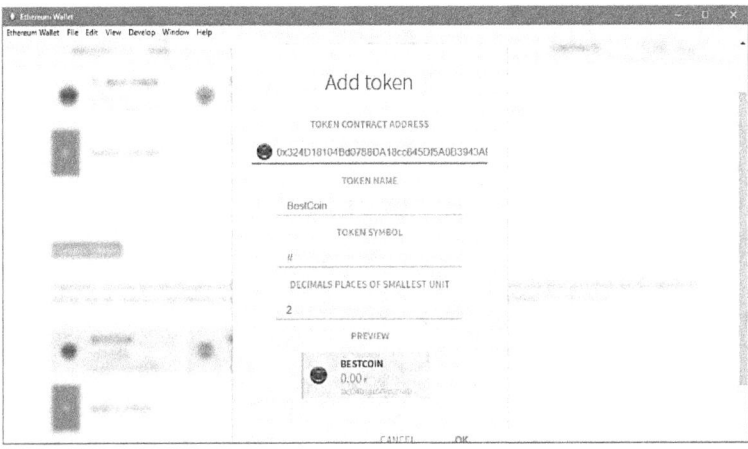

Figure 20.10

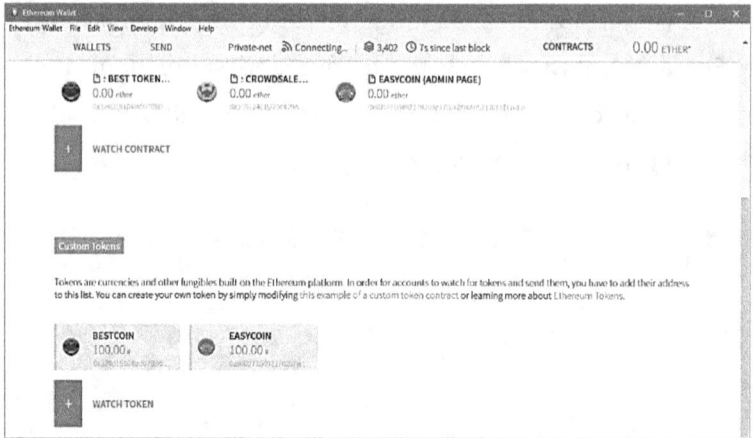

Figure 20.11

Now you can send some funds from BestCoin to a wallet, as shown in Figure 20.12.

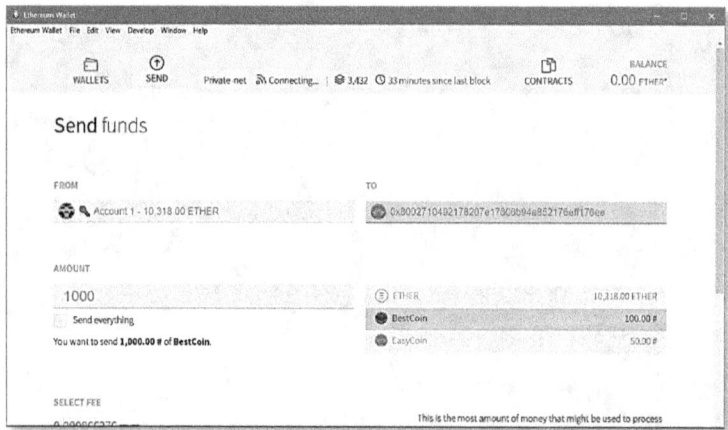

Figure 20.12

Chapter 21 Setting up a Private Ethereum Blockchain Network on Windows

Setting up a private Ethereum blockchain network is not an extremely difficult task for the coders. However, it may be a bit of a challenge for the beginners. I will skip some technical details and avoid using some jargon so that everyone can understand the basic concepts.

21.1 Prerequisites

Before setting up the network, you need to install the following software:

- Visual Studio Code
- git
- NodeJs
- Ethereum Wallet
- Geth

The **go-ethereum** client is commonly referred to as **geth**, which is the command line interface for running a full **Ethereum node** implemented in Go. By installing and running geth, you can run a private network or participate in the Ethereum main network. By running geth, you can perform the following tasks:

- mine real ether
- transfer funds between addresses.

- create smart contracts and send transactions.
- explore block history.
- and much more

21.2 Creating the Genesis Block

To set up the private network, we need to create the Genesis block, the first block of the blockchain in our network. The code for the genesis block is written in JSON format. JSON stores data as a name/value pair. For example:

"name": "John" ,
"age": 30

It uses JavaScript syntax, but the format is text only. Therefore, JSON can be read and used as a data format by any programming language. You can use any text editor to write the JSON code(JSON: JavaScript Object Notation), I use Notedpad++. The sample code for the genesis block is as follows

```
{

"config":{

 "chainId": 45,

 "homesteadBlock": 0,

 "eip155Block": 0,

 "eip158Block": 0,

 "byzantiumBlock": 12
```

```
    },

    "alloc" : {},

    "coinbase" : "0x0000000000000000000000000000000000000000",

    "difficulty" : "0x20000",

    "extraData" : "",

    "gasLimit" : "0x2fefd8",

   "nonce" : "0x0000000000000042",


    "mixhash"   :"0x0000000000000000000000000000000000000000000000000000000000000000",

    "parentHash" : "0x0000000000000000000000000000000000000000000000000000000000000000",

    "timestamp" : "0x00"

}
```

I will not discuss the contents of the genesis block here. Copy the code in a text editor and save the file as

myGenesis.json

Now run the following command in the command prompt to initialize the genesis block

```
geth init myGenesis.json
```

The output is as shown in Figure 21.1

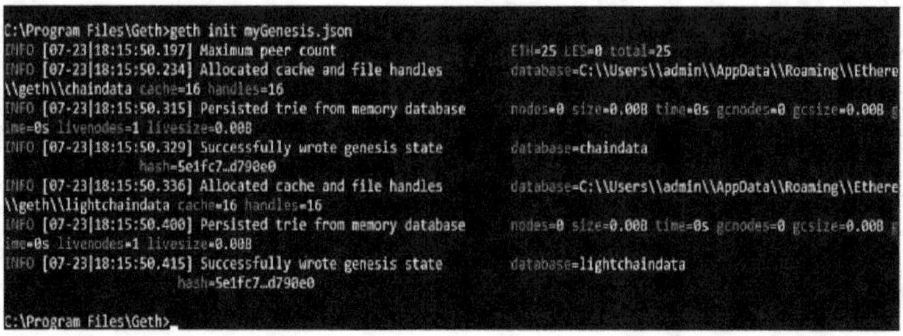

Figure 21.1

Once the genesis block is successfully created, a folder name 'Ethereum' will be created in the following path:

"C:\Users\admin\AppData\Roaming\Ethereum"

This folder contains the details of the Private Blockchain.

21.3 Starting the Private Network

Once the genesis block is created, run the following command to start the private network:

```
geth — networkid=5
```

*"networkid=1" stands for the main Ethereum network. So, any random number apart from 1 can be given as the network id. Also, "console" is appended to the command to enable us to write commands while the network is running.

The output is as shown in Figure 21.2

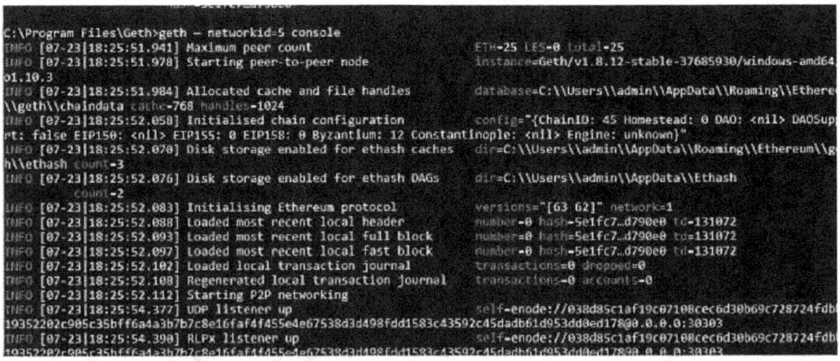

Figure 21.2

21.4 Launching the Ethereum Wallet

The output is as shown in Figure 16.3. Notice that the network name is Private net.

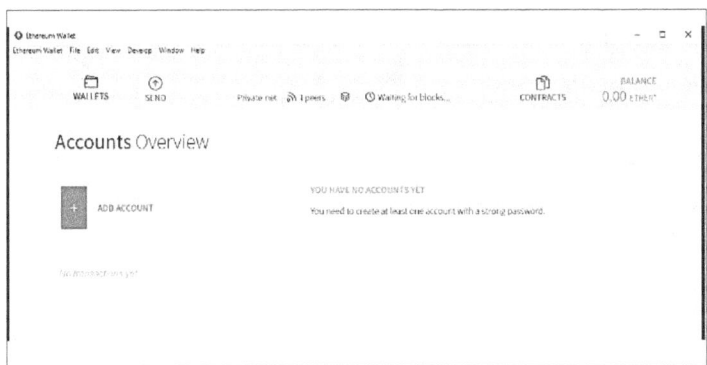

Figure 21.3

21.5 Creating a New Account Address

You can create an address in the Ethereum Wallet application. The address can be created on the Ethereum Wallet App. In the 'Wallets' section, click on 'Add Account' to create a new account address.

To create new account using the Geth Console, use the following command:

geth account new

The output is as shown in Figure 21.4.

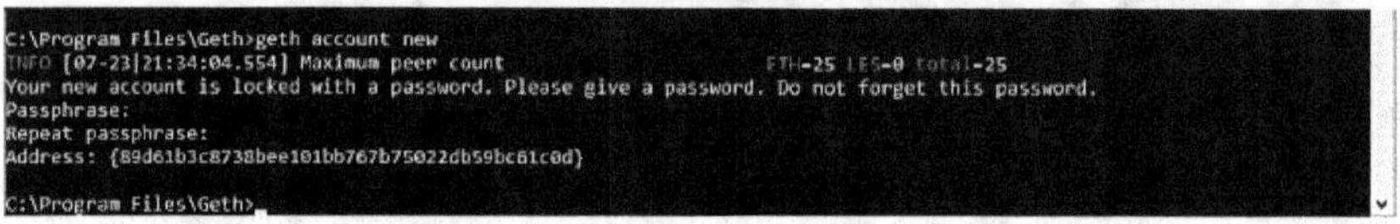

```
C:\Program Files\Geth>geth account new
INFO [07-23|21:34:04.554] Maximum peer count                       ETH=25 LES=0 total=25
Your new account is locked with a password. Please give a password. Do not forget this password.
Passphrase:
Repeat passphrase:
Address: {89d61b3c8738bee101bb767b75022db59bc61c0d}

C:\Program Files\Geth>
```

Figure 21.4

21.6 Start Mining

To start mining on the private network, Enter the geth console with the following command

Geth --rpc console

In the Geth Console type

miner.start()

The output is as shown in Figure 21.5

Figure 21.5

Now you can see that the mining process is generating Ethers, as shown Figure 21.6. Bear in mind that these are fake Ethers and can only be used for a private test net.

21.7 Stop Mining

Type Ctrl+C in the geth console and key in the following command:

```
miner.stop()
```

Type Exit to quit the geth console.

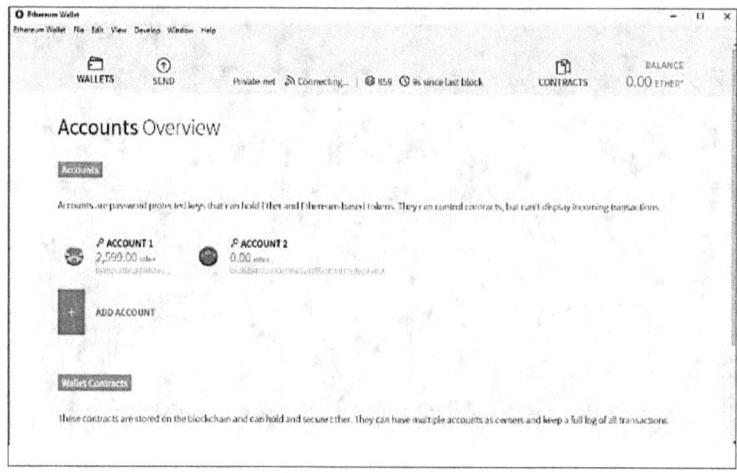

Figure 21.6

Chapter 22

Deploying Smart Contracts on Ropsten Testnet through Ethereum Remix

You have learned how to use the truffle framework in Visual Studio Code and node.js to deploy the smart contracts within a local test environment.

The next step is to try different test environments available to us. This chapter will guide you to deploy the same smart contract code on Ethereum remix IDE (IDE—Integrated Development Environment) on the Ropsten test net.

We need

- Metamask (Install as Google Extension)
- Remix-Solidity IDE (https://remix.ethereum.org)
- Ropsten Test Network

MetaMask is a bridge that allows you to access the decentralized and distributed web of blockchain in your browser today. It allows you to run Ethereum dApps in your browser without running a full Ethereum node. This make Ethereum as easy to use for as many people as possible.

Step 1

Install MetaMask Extension

Create an Account

Step 2

Copy your account address and request free Ether from **Ethereum Ropsten Faucet.**

(http://faucet.ropsten.be:3001/)

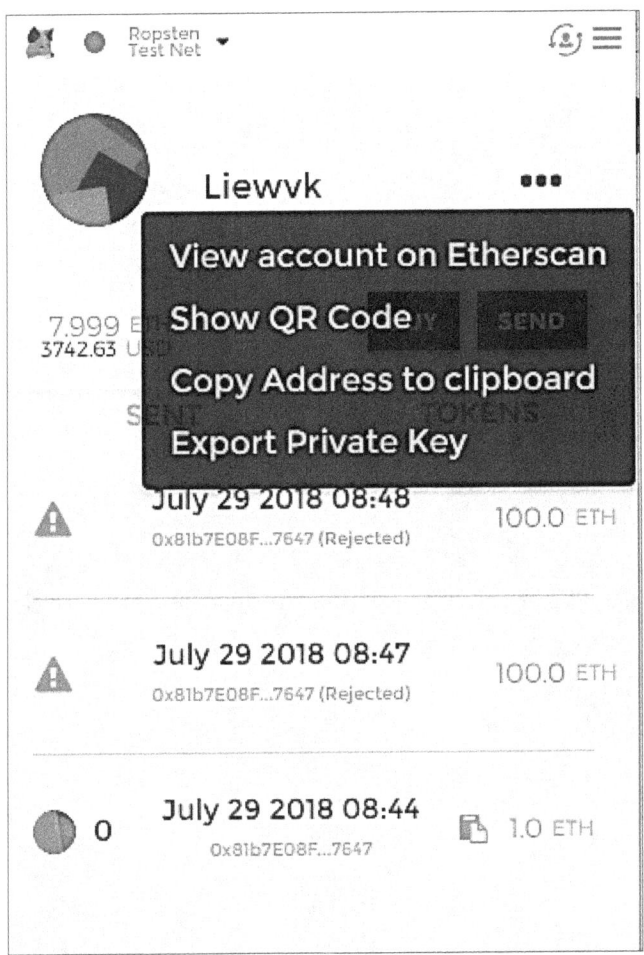

Figure 22.1

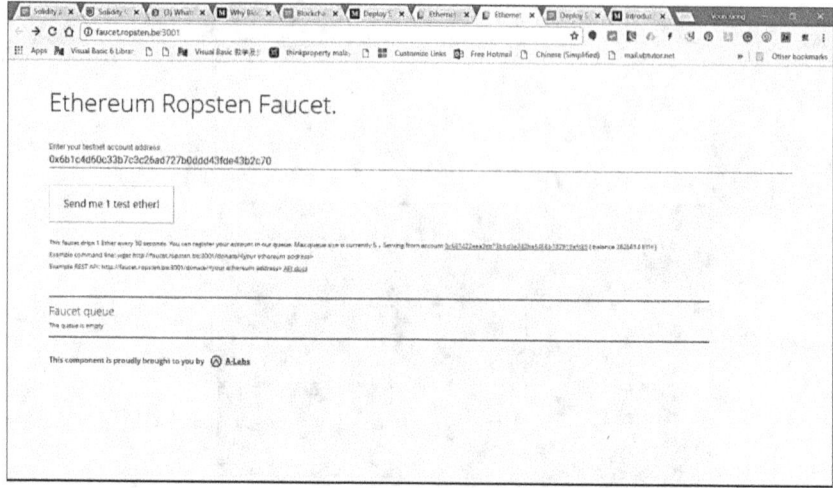

Figure 22.2

Launch Remix in the browser and paste any solidity smart contract file or write one your own, as shown in Figure 22.3.

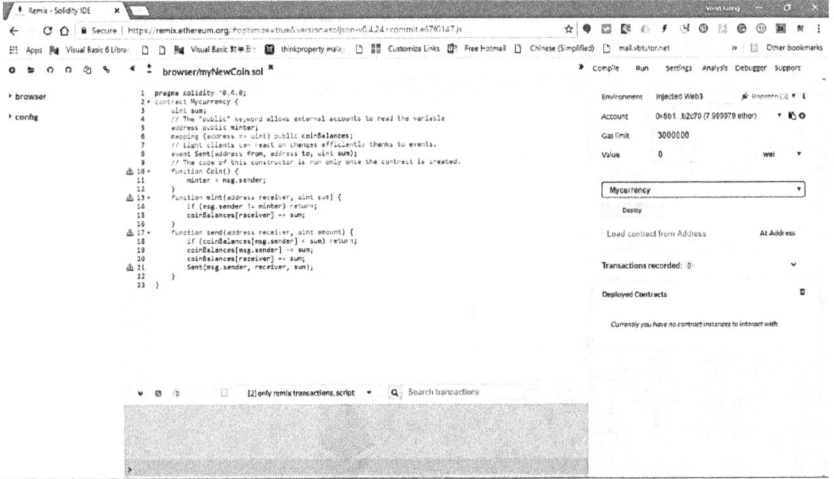

Figure 22.3

To deploy the contract, we need an account and with some ether on the Rospten test net.

- Meta mask!
- Select Rospten Test net

296

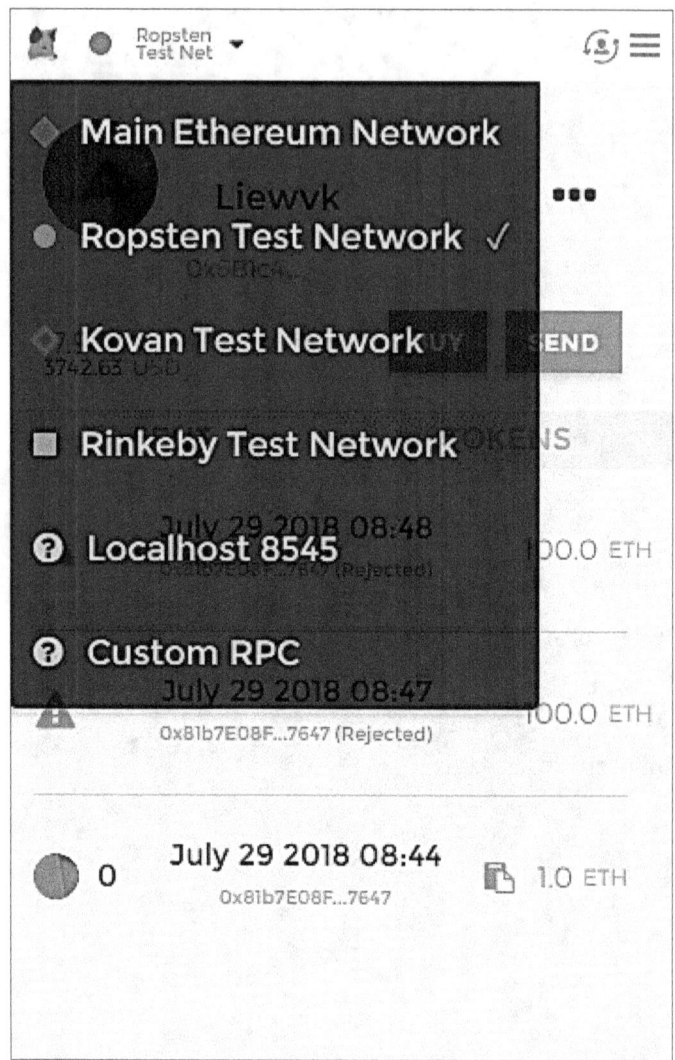

Figure 22.4

Step 3

Click to deploy the contract. Select **Injected Web 3 Ropsten** under environment and the account in Metamask is shown here under

Account with balance ether as well. If Web3 Ropsten not connected, reload the webpage.

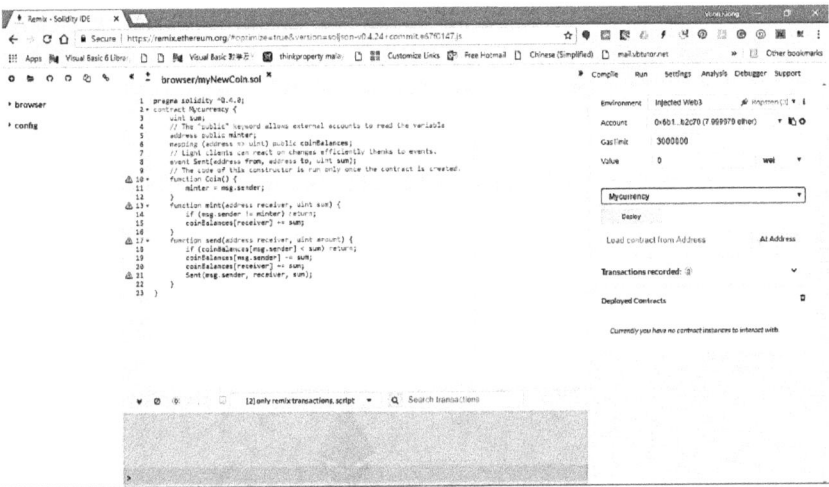

Figure 22.5

Now you can see that the transaction recorded. Next, launch Metamask and enter some gas price.

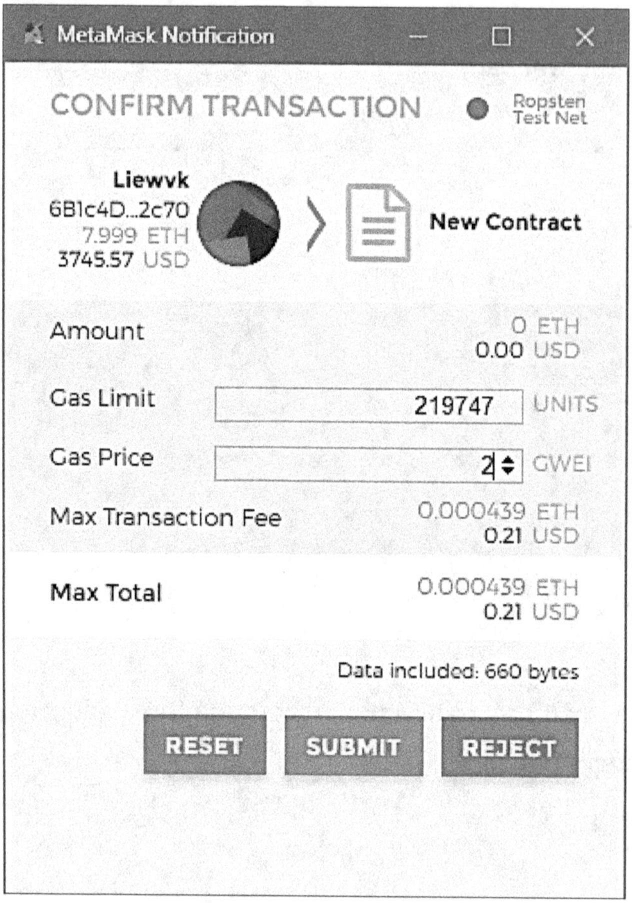
MetaMask Notification
CONFIRM TRANSACTION
Ropsten Test Net
Liewvk
6B1c4D...2c70
7.999 ETH
3745.57 USD
New Contract
Amount
0 ETH
0.00 USD
Gas Limit
219747
UNITS
Gas Price
2
GWEI
Max Transaction Fee
0.000439 ETH
0.21 USD
Max Total
0.000439 ETH
0.21 USD
Data included: 660 bytes
RESET
SUBMIT
REJECT

Figure 22.6

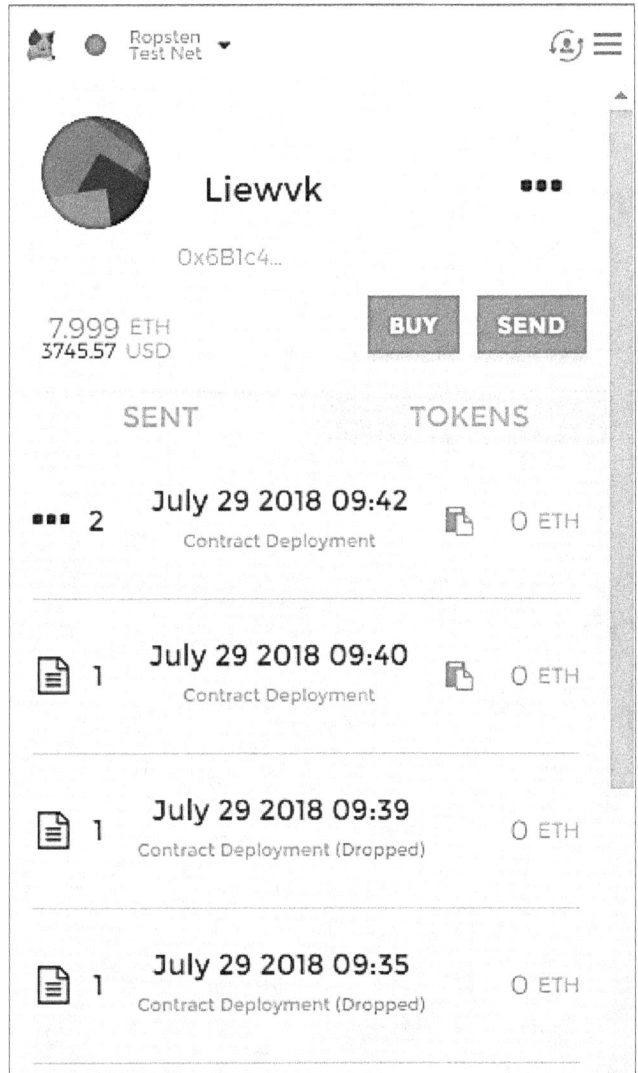

Figure 22.7

Click on the contract deployment—it should open the Etherscan page to look at our transaction details.

Figure 22.8

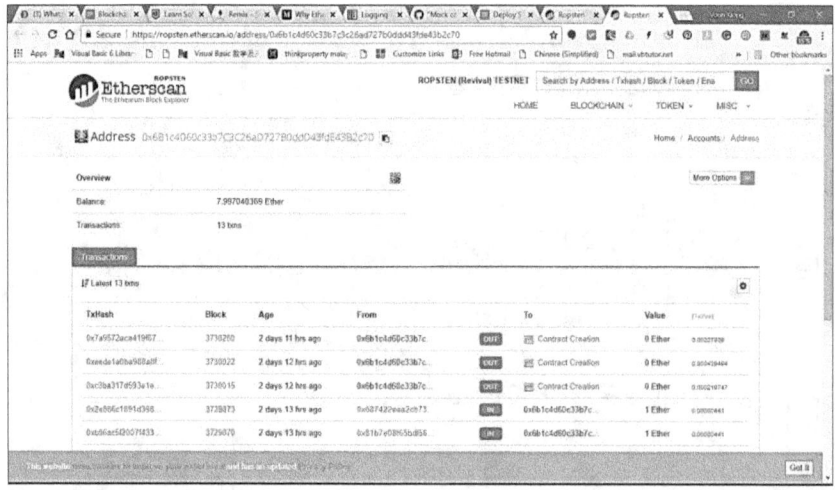

Figure 22.9

Chapter 23

Creating Multisig Wallet

Companies that are managing crypto assets for its investors need to keep their crypto assets in a safe and secure way. The best solution is to keep the crypto assets is to store them in a multisig wallet. Example of such companies are crypto exchanges, crypto custodian service companies, crypto index fund companies, crypto hedge fund companies and more.

The multisig wallet is one where you need control over multiple private keys to spend from that wallet. The address in the multisig wallet has multiple private keys behind it. The idea with multisig wallets is that multiple people can cooperatively control the funds in the wallet. With multisig, it allows users to have one bitcoin address with multiple key holders, thus ensuring funds from the address cannot be spent until all key holders sign off on it. It will add security and instill confidence in the investors.

The multisig wallet can be entrusted to a committee or council where members can comprise the management team and selected investors. Each member holds his or her private key for signing the wallet. Nobody can withdraw or spend the funds in the wallet unless all members agree to do so by using their private keys to sign the transaction.

23.1 Steps in Creating a Multisig Wallet

We will be using Electrum to create the multisig wallet. Electrum is a lightweight Bitcoin client, based on a client-server protocol. Electrum is known to be the safest Bitcoin wallet in the world.

Step 1 Installation of Electrum

First, you must install Electrum on your PC, laptop, or mobile phone. For PC and laptop, you can download Electrum from the following link :

https://electrum.org/#download

After downloaded the file, click, and install the Electrum based on your operating systems. For mobile phones, you can install it from Google Playstore. I prefer installing the mobile version because it is easier and has less issue. Our demos here will be based on the Mobile Version.

Step 2 Decide the number of co-signers

The different individuals or devices that are involved in signing the multisig wallet are called co-signers . You can create a multisig wallet with 3 cosigners of which at least 2 must sign spending transactions. The numbers can vary, for example, 5 co-signers of which at least 3 must sign. Also, ensure each of the co-signers for the multisig wallet must use electrum. Each co-signers' wallet will contain their own auto generated seed as well as the Master Public Keys (MPKs) of the other co-signers.

Step 3 Creating the multisig Wallet

When you start Electrum , you will be prompted to create the type of wallet you wish. Select Multi-signature as the wallet type, as shown in Figure 23.1. Next, choose the number of co-signers and how many signatures required. We chose 3 cosigners and 2 signatures required to approve the transactions, as shown in Figure 23.2.

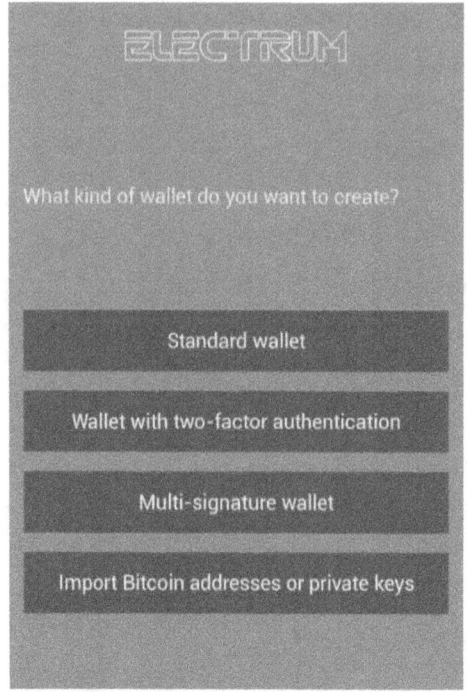

Figure 23.1

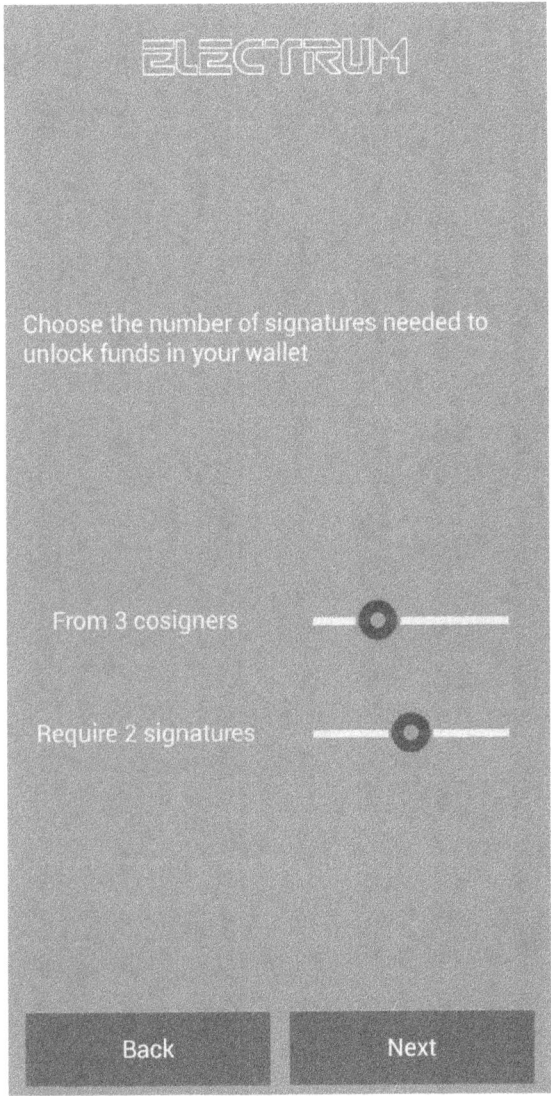

Figure 23.2

Touch Next and select create a new seed , as shown in Figure 23.3.

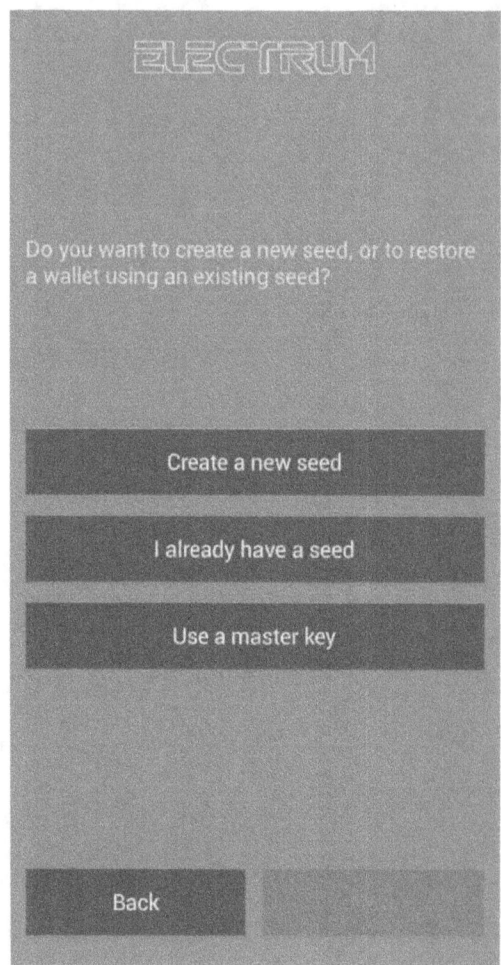

Figure 23.3

Now, select legacy as the seed type, as in Figure 23.4.

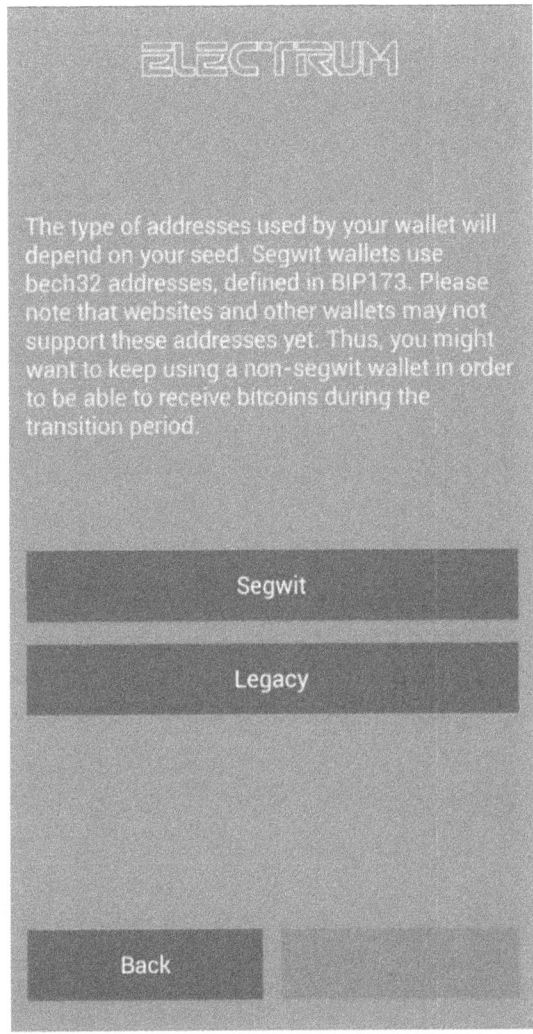

Figure 23.4

Electrum will now display a seed which you must write down in your notebook/paper, as shown in Figure 23.5. Keep the seed secret and never shared with anyone.

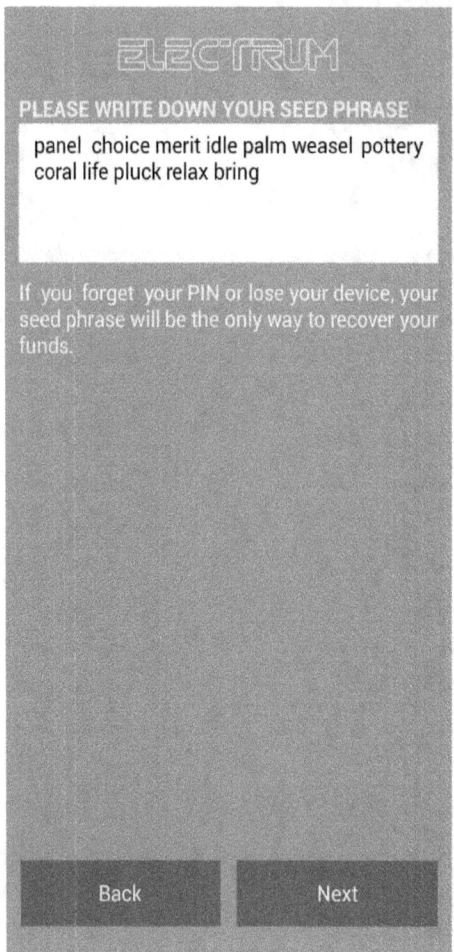

Figure 23.5

Electrum will now display your Master Public Key(MPK) which you can copy to the clipboard and email to your co-signers, as shown in Figure 23.6.

Figure 23.6

The subsequent step is to add Cosigners. You must have all the co-signers' MPKs before you start this step. For each subsequent cosigner, select "enter co-signer key" and then paste in their MPK in the next step. Electrum will ask you to paste your consigners MPK, or scan it using the camera button.

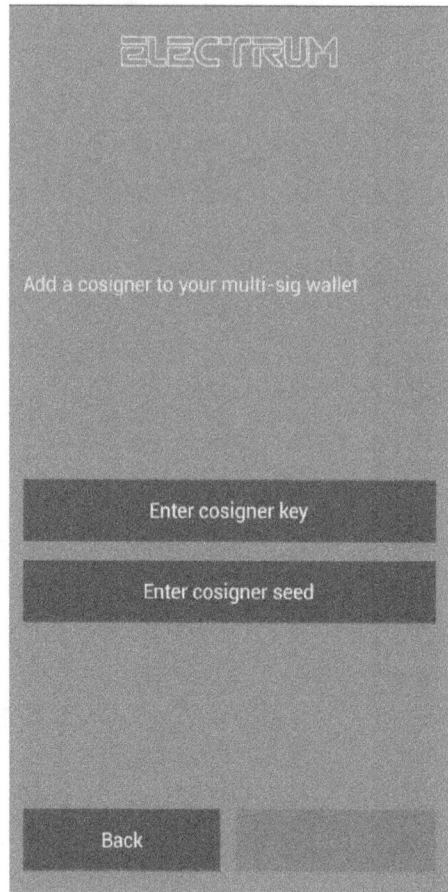

Figure 23.7

311

Figure 23.8

After registering all the consigners, you will be prompted to create a PIN , as shown in Figure 23.9.

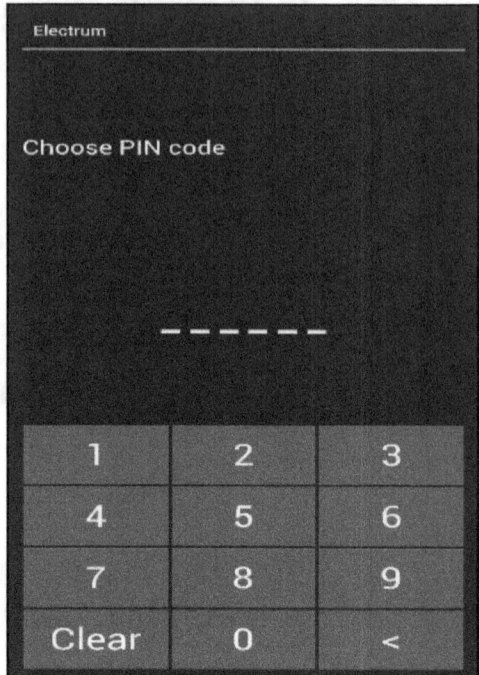

Figure 23.9

After entering the PIN, your multisig wallet will be created and ready to use, as shown in Figure 23.10. There are three main buttons, Send, Balance and Receive. When you touch the Balance button, it will show 0 BTC as you have not transferred any fund here.

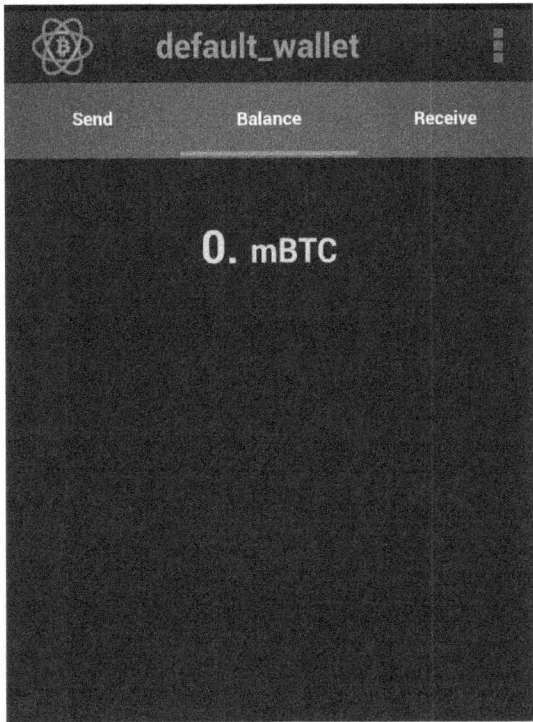

Figure 23.10

Touching the Send button will show the following screen, as shown in Figure 23.11. To send the fund, you need to paste the recipient BTC address, key in the amount and add any descriptions you want.

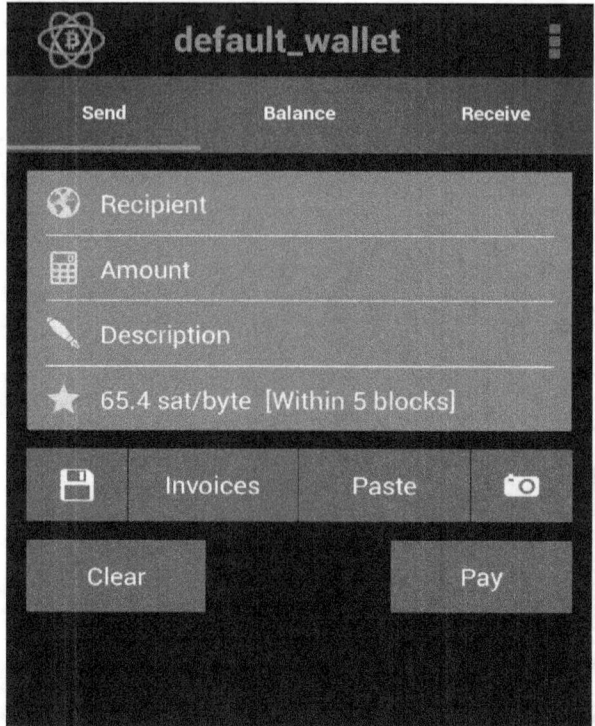

Figure 23.11

To receive the fund, you need to the sender scan your QR code or copy and key in your BTC address, as shown in Figure 23.12.

Figure 23.12

Chapter 24

Setting up Automotive Smart Supply Chain Management(SSCM) with Hyperledger Fabric

This Automotive Smart Supply Chain Management Application is built using Hyperledger Fabric developed by the Linux Foundation. Hyperledger Fabric is a permissioned private blockchain network that provides ledger services to application clients and administrators. It allows multiple organizations to collaborate as a consortium to form the network. The permissions to join the network are determined by a set of policies that are agreed to by the consortium when the network is configured.

24.1 Technical Requirements

The OS is 64-bit Ubuntu 16.04 VPS, other versions might not work.

Download Ubuntu 16.04.6 LTS (Xenial Xerus) from

http://cl.releases.ubuntu.com/16.04/

Select 64-bit PC (AMD64) desktop image

Choose this if you have a computer based on the AMD64 or EM64T architecture (e.g., Athlon64, Opteron, EM64T Xeon, Core 2). If you have a non-64-bit processor made by AMD, or if you need full support for 32-bit code, use the i386 images instead. Choose this if you are at all unsure.

You can install Ubuntu in a VM machine, I used Oracle Virtual Box. Download Oracle Virtual Box from

https://www.virtualbox.org/

To successfully install Hyperledger Fabric, you should be familiar with Go and Node.js programming languages, and have the following features installed on your computer: cURL, Node.js, npm package manager, Go language, Docker, and Docker Compose.

24.2 Installing cURL

Open a terminal window: **CTRL+ALT+T**.

Type the following command and enter your password:

```
$ sudo apt install curl
```

To check, run the following command in your terminal/command line:

```
$ curl -V
```

24.3 Installing Docker

To install Docker CE, you need the 64-bit version of one of these Ubuntu versions:

- Cosmic 18.10
- Bionic 18.04 (LTS)
- Xenial 16.04 (LTS)

Docker CE is supported on x86_64 (or amd64), armhf, arm64, s390x (IBM Z), and ppc64le (IBM Power) architectures.

24.4 Uninstall old versions

Older versions of Docker were called docker, docker.io , or docker-engine. If these are installed, uninstall them:

```
$ sudo apt-get remove docker docker-engine docker.io containerd runc
```

For Ubuntu, you have the choice between the Community Edition (CE) or the Enterprise Edition (EE). We recommend CE, since it is ideal for developers and small teams looking to experiment with Docker.

24.5 Install using the repository

Before you install Docker CE for the first time on a new host machine, you need to set up the Docker repository. Afterward, you can install and update Docker from the repository.

24.6 Set Up the Repository

Update the apt package index:

```
$ sudo apt-get update
```

Install packages to allow apt to use a repository over HTTPS:

```
$ sudo apt-get install apt-transport-https ca-certificates curl gnupg-agent \ software-properties-common
```

Add Docker's official GPG key:

```
$ curl -fsSL https://download.docker.com/linux/ubuntu/gpg | sudo apt-key add -
```

Verify that you now have the key with the fingerprint 9DC8 5822 9FC7 DD38 854A E2D8 8D81 803C 0EBF CD88, by searching for the last 8 characters of the fingerprint.

```
$ sudo apt-key fingerprint 0EBFCD88

  pub   rsa4096 2017-02-22 [SCEA]
        9DC8 5822 9FC7 DD38 854A  E2D8 8D81 803C 0EBF CD88
uid              [ unknown] Docker Release (CE deb) <docker@docker.com>
sub   rsa4096 2017-02-22 [S]
```

Use the following command to set up the stable repository.

```
$ sudo add-apt-repository \
   "deb                         [arch=amd64] https://download.docker.com/linux/ubuntu \
   $(lsb_release -cs) stable"
```

24.7 Install Docker Ce

Update the apt package index.

```
$ sudo apt-get update
```

Install the latest version of Docker CE and containerd, or go to the next step to install a specific version:

```
$ sudo apt-get install docker-ce docker-ce-cli containerd.io
```

Verify that Docker CE is installed correctly by running the `hello-world` image.

```
$ sudo docker run hello-world
```

If you do not want to use `sudo` when you use the `docker` command, create a Unix group called `docker` and add users to it. When the `docker` daemon starts, it makes the ownership of the Unix socket read/writable by the `docker` group.

To create the `docker` group and add your user:

1. Create the docker group:

```
$ sudo groupadd docker
```

2. Add your user to the `docker` group:

```
$ sudo usermod -aG docker $USER
```

3. Log out and log back in, so that your group membership is re-evaluated.

4. On a desktop Linux environment such as X Windows, log out of your session completely and then log back in.

5. Verify that you can run Docker commands without **sudo**.

```
$ docker run hello-world
```

6. This command downloads a test image and runs it in a container. When the container runs, it prints an informational message and exits.

24.8 Install Docker Compose

To install Docker Compose, run the following commands in your terminal/command line:

```
$ sudo apt update
```

```
$ sudo apt install docker-compose
```

Check to make sure that you have Docker version 17.03.1-ce or greater, and Docker Compose version 1.9.0 or greater:

```
$ docker --version && docker-compose --version
```

To install **Node.js** and **npm**, run the following commands in your terminal/command line:

```
$ sudo bash -c "cat >/etc/apt/sources.list.d/nodesource.list" <<EOL
deb https://deb.nodesource.com/node_6.x xenial main
deb-src https://deb.nodesource.com/node_6.x xenial main
EOL

$ curl -s https://deb.nodesource.com/gpgkey/nodesource.gpg.key | sudo apt-key add -

$ sudo apt update

$ sudo apt install nodejs

$ sudo apt install npm
```

Verify the installation, as well as the versions of both **Node.js** and npm, and make sure the **Node.js** version you are installing is v8.x and the **npm** version is greater than 4.x

Suggest you install the **LTS** release, use this PPA

```
curl -sL https://deb.nodesource.com/setup_8.x | sudo bash -
```

You can check the versions of nodejs and npm

```
$ node --version && npm --version
```

24.9 Installing Go Language

Visit https://golang.org/dl/ and make a note of the latest stable release (**v1.8 or later**).

To install Go language, run the following commands in your terminal/command line:

```
$ sudo apt update

$ sudo curl -O https://storage.googleapis.com/golang/go1.9.2.linux-amd64.tar.gz
```

Note: Switch out the black portion of the URL with the correct filename.

```
$ sudo tar -xvf go1.9.2.linux-amd64.tar.gz

$ sudo mv go /usr/local

$ echo 'export PATH=$PATH:/usr/local/go/bin' >> ~/.profile

$ source ~/.profile
```

Check that the Go version is v1.8 or later:

```
$ go version
```

24.10 Installing Hyperledger Fabric Docker Images and Binaries

Next, we will download the latest released Docker images for Hyperledger Fabric and tag them with the `latest` tag. Execute the command from within the directory into which you will extract the platform-specific binaries:

```
$ curl -sSL https://goo.gl/6wtTN5 | bash -s 1.1.0
```

NOTE: Check http://hyperledger-fabric.readthedocs.io/en/release-1.1/samples.html#binaries for the latest URL (the blue portion in the above curl command) to pull in binaries.

This command downloads binaries for `cryptogen`, `configtxgen`, `configxlator`, `peer` and downloads the Hyperledger Fabric Docker images. These assets are placed in a `bin` subdirectory of the current working directory.

To confirm and see the list of Docker images you have just downloaded, run:

```
$ docker images
```

The expected response is:

```
REPOSITORY                      TAG            IMAGE ID        CREATED          SIZE
hyperledger/fabric-orderer      x86_64-1.0.3   fd1055ee597a    37 hours ago     151MB
hyperledger/fabric-peer         x86_64-1.0.3   b7f253e87c0c    37 hours ago     154MB
hyperledger/fabric-ccenv        x86_64-1.0.3   2e5898d8b21b    38 hours ago     1.28GB
hyperledger/fabric-tools        latest         ba9750b2565d    4 weeks ago      1.33GB
hyperledger/fabric-tools        x86_64-1.0.2   ba9750b2565d    4 weeks ago      1.33GB
hyperledger/fabric-couchdb      latest         3f922f54bd68    4 weeks ago      1.47GB
hyperledger/fabric-couchdb      x86_64-1.0.2   3f922f54bd68    4 weeks ago      1.47GB
hyperledger/fabric-kafka        latest         0b4b1d249e65    4 weeks ago      1.29GB
hyperledger/fabric-kafka        x86_64-1.0.2   0b4b1d249e65    4 weeks ago      1.29GB
hyperledger/fabric-zookeeper    latest         1efb063147d3    4 weeks ago      1.3GB
hyperledger/fabric-zookeeper    x86_64-1.0.2   1efb063147d3    4 weeks ago      1.3GB
hyperledger/fabric-orderer      latest         6efd17e86e65    4 weeks ago      151MB
hyperledger/fabric-orderer      x86_64-1.0.2   6efd17e86e65    4 weeks ago      151MB
hyperledger/fabric-peer         latest         0e2ed51971c9    4 weeks ago      154MB
hyperledger/fabric-peer         x86_64-1.0.2   0e2ed51971c9    4 weeks ago      154MB
hyperledger/fabric-javaenv      latest         0be45dbd7ff4    4 weeks ago      1.41GB
hyperledger/fabric-javaenv      x86_64-1.0.2   0be45dbd7ff4    4 weeks ago      1.41GB
hyperledger/fabric-ccenv        latest         d0f166e1a89e    4 weeks ago      1.28GB
hyperledger/fabric-ccenv        x86_64-1.0.2   d0f166e1a89e    4 weeks ago      1.28GB
hyperledger/fabric-baseos       x86_64-0.3.2   bbcbb9da2d83    5 weeks ago      129MB
```

Figure 24.1

Note the tags for each of the repositories above boxed in red. If the Docker images are not already tagged with the `latest` tag, perform the following command for each of the Docker images:

```
$ docker tag hyperledger/fabric-tools:x86_64-1.0.2 hyperledger/fabric-tools:latest
```

Swap out the blue portion with the tags you see in your list of repositories. Also, swap out the red portion with the name of the Docker image you are switching the tag for (e.g.: fabric-tools, fabric-ccenv, fabric-orderer, etc.). Repeat this step for all Docker images you see in the list.

24.11 Installing the Automotive Supply Chain Sample

Follow the below directions in your terminal window:

```
$ git clone https://github.com/hyperledger/education.git
```

```
$ cd education/LFS171x/fabric-material/autopart-app
```

Make sure you have Docker running on your machine before you run the next command.

Also, make sure that you have completed the Installing Hyperledger Fabric section in this chapter before moving on to this application section, as you will likely experience errors.

First, remove any pre-existing containers, as it may conflict with commands in this tutorial:

```
$ docker rm -f $(docker ps -aq)
```

Then, let us start the Hyperledger Fabric network with the following command:

```
$ ./startFabric.sh
```

Install the required libraries from the **package.json** file, register the **Admin** and **User** components of our network, and start the client application with the following commands:

```
$ npm install

$ node registerAdmin.js

$ node registerUser.js

$ node server.js
```

Load the client simply by opening `localhost:8000` in any browser window of your choice, and you should see the user interface for our simple application at this URL.

24.12 Query All Part Recorded

```
// queryAllPart - requires no arguments
const request = {
    chaincodeId:'part-app',
    txId: tx_id,
    fcn: 'queryAllPart',
    args: ['']
};
return channel.queryByChaincode(request);
```

24.13 Query a Specific Part Recorded

```
// queryTuna - requires 1 argument
const request = {
    chaincodeId:'part-app',
    txId: tx_id,
    fcn: 'queryPart',
```

```
        args: ['1']
    };
    return channel.queryByChaincode(request);
```

24.14 Change Part Holder

```
// changePartHolder - requires 2 argument
    var request = {
        chaincodeId:'part-app',
        fcn: 'changePartHolder',
        args: ['1', 'Alex'],
        chainId: 'mychannel',
        txId: tx_id
    };
    return channel.sendTransactionProposal(request);
```

24.15 Record a Part

```
// recordPart - requires 5 argument
    var request = {
        chaincodeId:'part-app',
        fcn: 'recordPart',
```

```
        args: ['11', '239482392', '28.012, 150.225',
'0923T', "Hansel"],

        chainId: 'mychannel',

        txId: tx_id

    };

    return channel.sendTransactionProposal(request);
```

To close the app, remove all Docker containers and images with the following command :

```
$ docker rm -f $(docker ps -aq)

$ docker rmi -f $(docker images -a -q)
```

Appendix

White Paper#1 Blockchain Based School Ecosystem

Abstract

The current school system is too structured, rigid, and inhibits creativity. The current school curriculum inadequately prepares the students to survive the fast-changing world of the 21st century. While schools need to comply with the national education policy to teach designated subjects, schools should include other programs that could help to resolve the issue. Therefore, our school proposes building an ecosystem using blockchain technology where students can freely create and share their contents. We believe that the blockchain ecosystem will nurture young children in developing creative minds and entrepreneurial skills.

I have written this white paper for a hypothetical blockchain project. This blockchain project is to build a private blockchain ecosystem for an international school.

First, we need to conduct a feasibility study before we start planning any blockchain project. Here, I am using a methodology called the CATWOE analysis. It can be applied to any new project.

CATWOE Analysis of Building a Blockchain School

CATWOE is an acronym that stands for Customers – Actors – Transformation process – Worldview – Owners – Environmental constraints. It is a simple analytical approach to find solutions to problems. The CATWOE Analysis makes it possible to identify problem areas, look at what an organization wants to achieve, and which solutions can influence the stakeholders. The analysis uses thought methodology from multiple perspectives. It is especially useful for an organization that wants to implement a new project that involves a drastic transformation process. The implementation of the blockchain technologies in a school curriculum qualifies for such transformation. Therefore, there is a need to understand the problems and try to find solutions before we proceed with the project implementation

C – Clients

They are the users and stakeholders of a system. In this case, they are the students, teachers, parents, the management staff, the education department, and others. They will benefit if the change is positive and the problems are solved. However, they may stand to lose or suffer if the change is negative and new problems are created. Therefore, we need to find out whether the blockchain technologies can solve current problems and bring positive changes in the school system. If the outcome could be negative or even damaging, we need to abort the project.

A-Actors

They are usually the employees within an organization, in this case, teachers and support staff. They are responsible for carrying out work and involved with the implementation of the blockchain system. Therefore, we need to conduct an inventory analysis to know their qualities, capabilities, and interests to get a clear picture of their impact on the organization. We may need to hire new employees or retrain the current ones to ensure competency with respect to blockchain implementation. We also need to conduct training for the employees.

T – Transformation Process

Transformation is the change that a system or process leads to. It is the process in which input (including raw materials, man-hours, knowledge) is transformed by an organization into output (such as a final product or solution to a problem).

To implement the blockchain system, we need to know in advance what kinds of input requires and forecast what the result (output) will be. Besides that, we must carefully consider the intermediate steps. In this case, the input is the blockchain technologies and the output could be a system that churns out an intelligent pool of young entrepreneurs that thrive on co-creating and co-sharing.

W – Worldview

Stakeholders often have different ideas and approaches to the same issue, with other conflicting interests. The goal of the CATWOE analysis is to make their different viewpoint explicit and try to achieve a methodology stand. In this project, we need to achieve consensus among the stakeholders that involve the students themselves, we do not want to force the ideas on them. Besides that, some teachers might be afraid in carrying out the transformation as they must learn new technologies. Parents would be overly concern about the implementation of the blockchain technologies because it will bring profound impacts on their children, either positively or negatively.

In addition, the government might want to regulate the project to ensure it complies with the national education policies and philosophies. On the other hand, business leaders may want to look for financial gains by sponsoring the project or they may refuse to support the project at all. Therefore, there is an urgent need to conduct surveys and research to figure out how to secure agreement from most stakeholders to implement the project.

O – Owners

This usually refers to the owner, entrepreneur, or investor of an organization, who wants to make changes and who decides whether a project should start or stop. As decision makers, they have the highest authorities. Commitment and support from the parties are important to ensure successful implementation of the blockchain project and long-term sustainability of the project.

E – Environmental Constraints

This is the actual environmental elements that may influence the organization and can limit or restrict the implementation of the blockchain technologies in the school system. Examples include political influence, ethical boundaries, regulations from the government, financial constraints, and social factors. There is a need to work closely to overcome the constraints via negotiations and other means with the regulators and other parties

After conducted the CATWOE analysis, I have identified the following problems where most schools are facing.

Problems

- The Current school system is too structured and too rigid, inhibiting creativity
- The Curriculum methodology too centered on academics and examinations
- Teacher-centered, lack of peer learning
- The Administration is centralized and autocratic
- Does not prepare children for the future
- Lack of participation from stakeholders

The proposed solution

- Create a self-perpetuating and self-sustaining ecosystem where students can create and share digital content. It can also include tangible things like arts and craft, scientific inventions, or intangible things like music, song, new

- ideas, games, and so on. These tangible assets can be digitized and shared among the students.
- Not only they can share digital content, but they can also buy and sell them. It is akin to an autonomous economic system where students can self-fund their projects by trading their digital assets.
- The latest technology that can power this system is blockchain, a subset of decentralized ledger technologies.
- The ecosystem should be enlarged to include the actors of the system – the teachers, coaches, supporting staff and the administrators.
- The ecosystem must also be connected to stakeholders, including the business owners (who can provide financial support and sponsorship), the government (who may want to regulate the activities in the system), parents (who are concerned with their children development), etc.
- The ecosystem can be extended to include students from around the world in the future.

The Architecture

- Create a permissioned private blockchain platform for the students. The students can interact freely in their own close loop decentralized and distributed ecosystem.
- Content or assets can be created and tokenized and shared among the students. They can trade their assets using the tokens, creating a token economic system.

- Develop APIs so that the stakeholders can interact with the blockchain. Administrators and teachers should be allowed to monitor and delete certain contents that are inappropriate like pornographic materials etc via the API. On the other hand, parents can monitor their children progress but may not be allowed to delete the contents or add comments. In addition, business owners and investors can monitor the progress of the project and provide support and advice if necessary (for example if the system crashed or stalled). In addition, regulators might want to monitor the blockchain for compliance.
- Proposed using Ethereum Proof of Authority(PoA) protocol known as Clique. The benefits of using PoA are as follows:
- Saves electricity power
- Eliminates the need to invest into large numbers of 'Miners' servers
- Increase the transaction speed tremendous compared to Proof-of-Work(PoW)
- Better security since only members can access the network
- The ecosystem can be hosted on a cloud server like AWS and Microsoft Azure, but you can set up your own servers. The conceptual model is illustrated in the figure below:

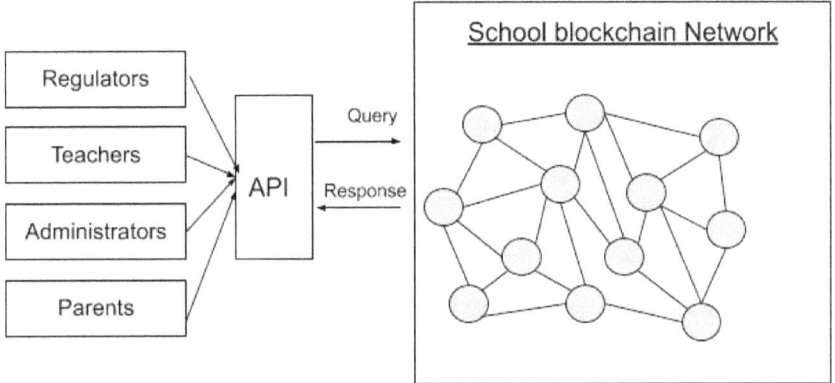

The Blockchain School

The Legal Framework

Obviously transforming a school into a blockchain school needs to obtain approval from the Ministry of Education. It must comply with national education policies. Therefore, we need to design the blockchain platform as a new approach in teaching and learning, keeping content within the requirements of the curriculum imposed by the Ministry of Education.

Council Members

Name	Designation
Abraham	Chairman
Bedene	Advisor
George	Principal
Franklin	Project Director
Lin	CTO
Chan	Blockchain Architect

Project Roadmap

Initial Research and Development

October 2020

Preparation of whitepaper

January 2021

Blockchain and Smart Contract Development

January 2021

Test run

February 2021

Launching of School Blockchain Network

April 2021

White Paper#2 Chi Crypto Index fund

Abstract

Chi has been designed to be a decentralized digital economy platform that offers blockchain-based financial services, business applications, education, and training services and more. One of the core services is the Chi Index Fund, a cryptocurrency-only fund investment vehicle utilizing the AI trading strategy. It provides an opportunity for investors to build their own portfolio or track an index and reap profits from the crypto asset class.

Chi fund management team shall employ a hedging strategy to maximize profit and minimize risks for the investors. The funds raised will be kept in a secure multisig custodian wallet to hedge against the risk of cyberattacks. A large proportion of the funds shall be invested in Chi Index Fund comprising a basket of cryptocurrencies that will generate returns for the investors using smart AI algorithmic trading. The remaining balance shall be utilised for marketing activities. The Chi trading platform offers significantly lower fees compared to traditional stock market trading.

In addition, Chi shall create a utility token known as the Chi Token that will power the Chi Blockchain platform. Chi token will be an ERC-20 token minted using a smart contract deployed on the Chi Ethereum blockchain network based on the Proof of Authority (POA) consensus protocol. The Chi Token will be utilized as an internal cryptocurrency within the Chi digital economy platform. Besides that, Chi tokens will be utilized as the gas fee for token transactions and for developing decentralized applications (dApps) like P2P lending, supply chain management, health care, decentralized marketplaces, identity management, proof of provenance, smart cities and more.

1 Introduction

In the last decade, cryptocurrency has become a new asset class. Its phenomenal growth in recent years has attracted many investors who used to invest in traditional financial products to start investing in crypto assets. Reports have shown that there is a significant amount of capital flowing into the crypto market. This capital flow has created an increasing demand for new financial products that cater to the needs of the crypto market.

Indeed, cryptocurrencies are rapidly gaining traction with the public. According to CoinMarketCap, the total market cap for all cryptocurrencies reached an amazing $739 billion in January 2018. Though the market cap dropped to a low $113 billion in December 2018 due to the bear market, it rebounded strongly in 2019 to a figure between $250 billion to $350 billion. Though much of this value has been generated by individual traders, it is also largely the result of large investment funds.

To capitalize on the immense growth potential of the blockchain driven economy, Chi has created the decentralized digital economy platform with the aim to improve the socio-economic status of individuals by making innovative and affordable blockchain based products and services easily accessible. Two core services that will be developed on the Chi Blockchain Platform are the Chi Index Fund and the Chi Token. More products and services will be developed in the future.

2 Chi Index Fund

2.1 What is Chi Index Fund?

Chi Index Fund is a cryptocurrency-only fund investment vehicle utilizing quantitative trading strategy. Quantitative trading consists of trading strategies based on quantitative analysis, which rely on mathematical computations and number crunching to identify trading opportunities. Price and volume are two of the more common data inputs used in quantitative analysis as the main inputs to mathematical models. The advantage of quantitative trading is that it allows for optimal use of back-tested data and eliminates emotional decision-making during trading.

Chi Index Fund was created and designed to mitigate the problems in cryptocurrencies trading. The problems include technical difficulties and volatility of cryptocurrencies. Chi Index is among the world's first cryptocurrency-only tokenized index fund that aims to ease trading in the crypto market. Chi Index Fund will maintain a diverse portfolio of selected cryptocurrencies, comprising the top twenty coins in terms of market capitalisation. To continuously track the index, the portfolio will be adjusted periodically using an AI powered rebalancing technique.

The benefits of Chi Index Fund are many: convenience, minimal broker fees, minimal exit fees, full transparency, full control, and a lower price bound. Automation allows Chi Index Fund to operate with fees of only 0.5% p/a as opposed to the market average of 3% p/a.

Chi Index Fund will be incorporated into Chi hedging strategies with the aim to maximize profit and minimize risks in crypto fund investment. Chi financial service team will employ a hedging strategy to maximise profit and minimise risks for the investors. Half of the funds raised will be used to purchase Bitcoins (BTC) at the current market value and deposit them in a secure multisig custodian wallet to hedge against the risk and volatility of the crypto market. A portion of the other half of the funds shall be invested in Chi Index Fund comprising a basket of cryptocurrencies that will generate returns for the investors using smart AI algorithmic trading. The remaining balance shall be utilised for marketing activities. The Chi trading platform offers significantly lower fees compared to traditional stock market trading.

2.2 Trading Strategy

Chi Index Fund will employ trading strategy like that of traditional index funds such as the S&P 500 index fund. In crypto trading, any front runners would need to anticipate coins entering the top 20 in Coinmarketcap ranking and must have enough liquid capital on exchange to move market rates. Chi Index Fund shall employ several strategies to mitigate this risk:

- Cryptocurrencies will be sent to the exchange 12 hrs in advance of the trade so that traders cannot follow the hot wallet to know exactly when a purchase or sale will be made. A weekly rebalancing window affords sufficient time to do this.
- Trades will be executed over multiple exchanges.
- Trades will be executed at varying times within the rebalancing window to prevent predictability.
-

3 The Chi Token

3.1 What is Chi Token?

Chi is a utility token that will power the Chi Blockchain Platform. Chi is an ERC-20 token minted using a smart contract deployed on the Chi POA Ethereum blockchain network. POA means Proof of Authority, a consensus protocol employed by the Chi blockchain network to validate Chi transactions. The Chi blockchain network is a private blockchain that allows global accessibility by members of the Chi platform and enables them to conduct 24/7 trading and transaction of Chi Tokens without having to pay expensive intermediary fees.

Chi Blockchain Network will be built using Parity Ethereum Client based on the Proof of Authority (POA) consensus protocol. The Chi Blockchain Network will be hosted on a virtual private cloud server.

Chi Token is an ERC20 token minted using a smart contract written in the Solidity programming language. The token smart contract will be deployed on the Chi blockchain network.

Chi Token will be utilized as an internal cryptocurrency within the Chi ecosystem and as gas fee for token transactions and for developing decentralized applications (dApps) such as P2P lending, supply chain management, health care, decentralized marketplace, identity management, proof of provenance, smart city and more. Besides that, it can be used as an incentive for the registration of new users.

Chi Token distribution is shown in the following chart:

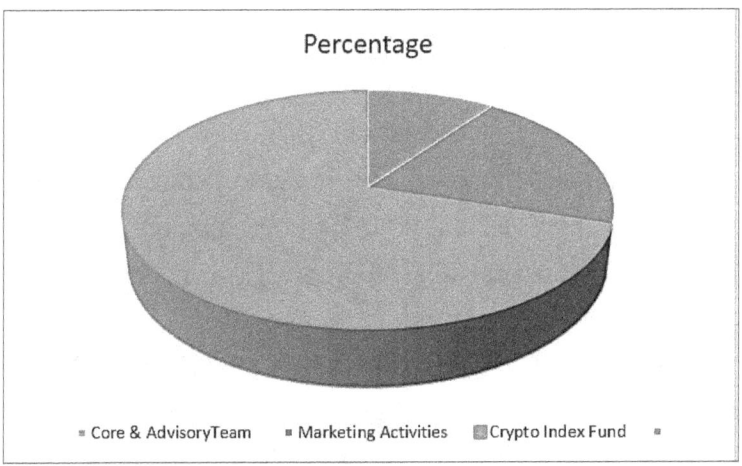

Token Type: ERC20

Maximum Supply (Hard Cap): 30,000 000 000 (3 billion Chi) Token

	Percentage	Volume
Core & AdvisoryTeam	10%	300000000
Marketing Activities	20%	600,000,000
Crypto Index Fund	70%	2,100,000,000
	Total	3,000,000,000

3.2 What is Proof of Authority (POA) Consensus Protocol?

According to Binance, Proof of Authority (PoA) is a reputation-based consensus algorithm that employs a practical and efficient solution for blockchain networks, particularly the private blockchain networks. The term was proposed in 2017 by Ethereum co-founder and former CTO Gavin Wood.

The POA consensus algorithm leverages the value of identities, which means that block validators are not staking coins but their own reputation instead. Therefore, POA blockchains are secured by validator nodes that are preselected as trustworthy entities.

The Chi POA blockchain network employs a limited number of validators and this makes it highly scalable. Blocks and transactions are verified by pre-approved validators, who act as moderators of the system. In contrast to POW, POA does not require nodes to spend a huge amount of computational resources and electricity to maintain the blockchain network.

The Chi POA blockchain network has much higher transaction rate, low latency and higher tolerance for compromised and malicious nodes compared to blockchain networks that are powered by POW or POS consensus algorithms. The highly efficient and secure POA system will ensure the safety of crypto funds and financial data. It is also flexible enough to develop innovative business applications on Chi POA blockchain platform.

3.2 The Chi Blockchain Platform

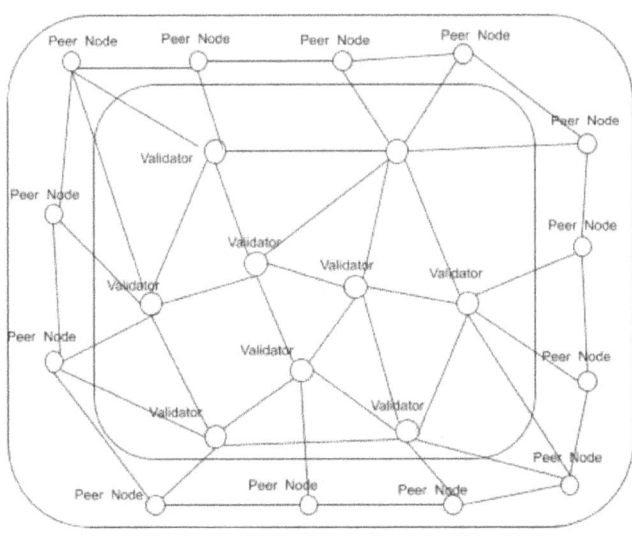

The Chi Blockchain Network

The Chi blockchain network consists of validator nodes and peer nodes. Only validator nodes have the authority to verify transactions and to elect new validators or dismiss misbehaved validators. Peer nodes are required to help maintain the network.

Some of the nodes can be assigned the status of a Master node if they agreed to host the Chi Blockchain Network 24/7 and carry out additional duties. The role of Master nodes is to ensure the blockchain security and reliability of Chi Blockchain Network. In addition, all the nodes will be incentivized with Chi Tokens.

All nodes are subjected to yearly re-election using smart contracts to ensure democracy and transparency. Malicious nodes will be voted out while the nodes who performed well will be re-elected to protect the integrity of the Chi POA Blockchain network.

The Chi blockchain network will be hosted on a secure enterprise cloud server such as AWS. We rely on public-key cryptography, multiple factor authentication and system isolation of private keys to ensure topmost security and reliability.

3.4 Setting Up Chi Blockchain Network Using Parity Ethereum

The Chi blockchain network will be set up using Parity Ethereum. Parity Ethereum is the fastest and most Advanced Ethereum Client.

Parity Ethereum is built for mission-critical use: Miners, service providers, and exchanges need fast synchronization and maximum uptime. Parity Ethereum provides the core infrastructure essential for speedy and reliable services.

- Clean, modular codebase for easy customization
- Advanced CLI-based client
- Minimal memory and storage footprint
- Synchronize in hours, not days with Warp Sync
- Modular for light integration into your service or product

Parity Ethereum was developed using the sophisticated and cutting-edge Rust programming language. Parity Ethereum is licensed under GPLv3 and can be used for all your Ethereum needs.

For the complete guide to install Parity Ethereum and to set up the Chi POA blockchain network, please refer to the Chi technical whitepaper.

3.5 Chi Token Smart Contract

The Chi Token is an ERC20 token minted using a smart contract based on the Solidity programming language. The code shown here is the intellectual property of Chi Management Ltd. Prior consent is required to adapt the code.

```
pragma solidity ^0.5.0;
contract ChiToken {
    /* This creates an array with all balances */
    mapping (address => uint256) public balanceOf;
    string public name;
    string public symbol;
    uint8 public decimals;

    /* Initializes contract with initial supply tokens
to the creator of the contract */
```

```
constructor(
    uint256 initialSupply,
    string tokenName,
    string tokenSymbol,
    uint8 decimalUnits
    ) public {
    balanceOf[msg.sender] = initialSupply;   // Give the creator all initial tokens
    name = tokenName;                        // Set the name for display purposes
    symbol = tokenSymbol;                    // Set the symbol for display purposes
    decimals = decimalUnits;                 // Amount of decimals for display purposes
}

/* Send coins */
function transfer (address _to, uint256 _value) public returns (bool success) {
    require(balanceOf[msg.sender] >= _value);   // Check if the sender has enough
    require(balanceOf[_to] + _value >= balanceOf[_to]);   // Check for overflows
    balanceOf[msg.sender] -= _value;            // Subtract from the sender
    balanceOf[_to] += _value;                   // Add the same to the recipient
    return true;
}
}
```

3.6 Chi Token Listing

The Chi Token will be listed on multiple exchanges. The full list of exchanges will be available on our website when trading begins. Additional exchanges will be added over time. Trading will be automated via API integration with the exchanges.

The liquidation price of the Chi Tokens will be determined through the use of an exchange service developed by Chi. Automation of liquidation price updates are an essential part of smooth business operation; however, automation can also expose security risks due to the necessity of online private key storage. We circumvent this risk by implementing a two-tier permissions system, with multiple addresses allocating only the necessary permissions to fulfill a particular task, such as updating the liquidation price. This strategy enables risk-mitigating automation without having to store crucial private keys online.

4. Security

4.1 Safe Storage of Crypto Assets

Chi will implement security industry best practices for defense against cyberattacks and bad actors. Strong identity verification and authentication procedures are in place to ensure secure operations. Besides that, the vast majority of Chi cryptoassets will be stored offline in cold wallets.

Chi will at any stage hold varying amounts of the 20 coins that form the index it tracks. The majority of each of these cryptocurrencies will be stored in cold wallets with a small percentage of each currency stored in a wallet on our servers to facilitate automatic rebalancing. If rebalancing necessitates moving more of the cryptocurrency to these hot wallets this will be done manually via interfacing with various cold wallets – Chi's portfolio managers will be notified ahead of time to accommodate this. The weekly rebalancing period affords more than sufficient time for this purpose.

Ledger Nano S will be used for the storage of all cryptocurrencies it supports. For all cryptocurrencies that are not supported, encrypted USB drives will be utilized. These storage devices will be held in secure safe deposit boxes with back-up paper wallets stored at separate secure locations. Locations are undisclosed due to security considerations. A public audit will confirm the presence and safe storage of the USB drives and paper wallets, to be accessible for all members. Wallet interactions with Chi will be facilitated through light clients running within their own containerized services.

4.2. Multisig Wallet

To further improve security and increase trust among the investors, the best solution is to store the crypto assets in a multisig wallet.

The multisig wallet is one where you need control over multiple private keys to spend from that wallet. The address in the multisig wallet has multiple private keys behind it. The idea with multisig wallets is that multiple people can cooperatively control the funds in the wallet. With multisig, it allows users to have one Bitcoin address with multiple key holders, so funds from the address cannot be spent until all key holders sign off on it

In the case of Chi, the multisig wallet will be entrusted to a council comprising the management team and selected investors. Each member holds his or her private key for signing the wallet. Nobody can withdraw or spend the funds in the wallet unless all members agree to do so by using their private keys to sign the transaction.

For steps on creating a multisig wallet, please refer our technical guide on multisig wallet creation.

5. Funds Allocation

To maximize profit and minimize risk for our investors, 50% of the funds raised will be used to purchase Bitcoins (BTC) at the current market value and deposit them in a secure multisig custodian wallet to hedge against the risk and volatility of the crypto market. Another 25% of the funds will be used to invest in Chi Index Fund. The balance 25% will be spent on marketing activities.

Bitcoin might be a volatile product on the current market, but Bitcoin had shown a consistent increment on a yearly basis, from the average of USD 144 back in 2013 up to the current average of USD 8000. In the current volatility of the market which involves USD value, gold value and Bitcoin value, the prices have gone up and down constantly, but Bitcoin has shown an upwards trend since its creation back in 2008 (as shown in Figure).

The value of Bitcoin may fluctuate from time to time, but in the long run, Bitcoin price will increase in value. Hence, if Bitcoin is held, users will earn substantial profit in the future, as shown in the figure below.

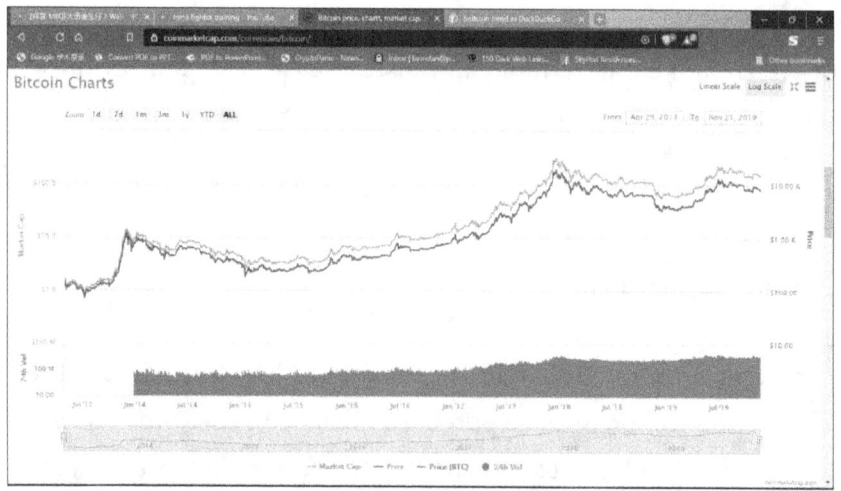

6 Project Roadmap

Research and Development

October 2020

Chi Blockchain Platform Development

November 2020

Smart Contract and AI Trading System Development

December 2020

Launching of Chi Project

February 2021

Listing of Chi Token

March 2021

7. The Future

Upon the maturity of our index fund, we will eventually expand our blockchain use into other areas such as payment systems. Our blockchain solution provides a new way for consumers, businesses, and banks to transact and is key to the company's strategy to provide payment solutions that meet every need of financial institutions and their end-customers.

We plan to implement the technology initially in the realm of business-to-business (B2B) transactions. We believe that blockchain technology will help to address challenges involving speed, transparency and costs associated with cross-border payments.

Blockchain is the technology behind cryptocurrencies like Bitcoin and Ethereum. Through blockchain technology companies can create an irrevocable digital ledger of transactions. The technology can be integrated into many business processes today to improve security, transparency, trust and more. Besides that, smart contracts can be created for literally any task, such as smart homes and property insurance, payment cards, logistics, healthcare, insurance, and many other industries. Additionally, blockchain technology removes the need for a central authority to manage transactions, making these transactions highly secure and impenetrable for hackers.

Although the blockchain technology has yet to be widely adopted, it has already proven critical for businesses and even more so for the B2B realm since it often deals with large transactions that involve multiple trustless parties across the supply chain.

8. The Chi Blockchain Council

The Chi Blockchain Council is a volunteer group comprises subject experts and enthusiasts who are evangelizing the blockchain research and development, cryptocurrency investment, use cases and product knowledge for a better world. The Chi council focuses on creating an environment and raise awareness among businesses, enterprises, developers, and society by educating them in the blockchain and cryptocurrency space. We are a private de-facto organization working individually and proliferating blockchain technology globally. We aim at providing easily accessible expertise on blockchain and cryptocurrency investment on a global platform.

The Chi Blockchain Council has introduced an exclusive Membership offer for all the enthusiasts and experts who are passionate to learn this remarkable Blockchain and Cryptocurrency investment technology. This membership program aims to solve all the issues of lacking content on Blockchain and Cryptocurrency Investment technology. We provide various training sessions, podcasts, eBook, webinars, premium cryptocurrency investment content, workshop and a lot more give you a competitive edge over others. Public can join individually, companies or community basis.

8.1 The Chi Blockchain Council

Council Members

Name	Designation
Abraham	Chairman
Bedene	Advisor
George	CEO
Franklin	COO
Lin	CTO
Danny	CMO
Chan	Blockchain Architect

INDEX

'child blockchains', 203

Aave, 181, 184, 185

AAVE, 185

Advanced Message Queuing Protocol, 128

altcoins, 26, 28, 51, 60, 61, 71, 82, 192

alternative coins, 51

AMQP., 127

asset management, 180

Asymmetric cryptography, 47

Auditable, 30

audited token, 91

AWS, 157, 195, 196, 197, 341, 353

Binance, 75, 86, 351

Biometric Data, 170

Bit Gold, 27, 44

Bitcoin, 26, 27, 28, 33, 35, 36, 37, 43, 44, 46, 47, 48, 51, 52, 53, 54, 57, 60, 61, 66, 74, 77, 82, 83, 84, 96, 100, 107, 108, 113,

135, 141, 143, 164, 176, 189, 192, 198, 202, 306, 357, 358, 359, 360

BitTicket, 224

bitWage, 176, 177

Bitwise 10 Private Index Fund, 141

Block Height, 35, 36

blockchain, 2, 26, 27, 28, 29, 30, 33, 34, 35, 36, 38, 40, 41, 42, 48, 50, 51, 52, 53, 54, 61, 62, 65, 66, 68, 69, 70, 72, 73, 74, 87, 89, 90, 91, 92, 93, 94, 95, 96, 97, 98, 99, 100, 101, 103, 104, 107, 108, 110, 113, 115, 116, 125, 126, 129, 130, 131, 133, 134, 135, 139, 145, 146, 147, 148, 150, 151, 152, 153, 154, 155, 156, 157, 158, 162, 164, 166, 168, 170, 172, 173, 174, 175, 176, 178, 182, 183, 189, 190, 191, 192, 193, 194, 195, 197, 198, 199, 200, 202, 203, 204, 205, 206, 208, 210, 219, 220, 222, 223, 224, 225, 226, 227, 228, 230, 233, 234, 235, 236, 237, 238, 239, 240, 242, 244, 256, 258, 260, 263, 269, 272, 287, 288, 295, 320, 335, 336, 337, 338, 339, 340, 341, 342, 345, 346, 349, 350, 351, 352, 353, 354, 360, 361

Blockchain Network, 30, 34, 162, 287, 344, 349, 352, 353

Blockchain Platform, 65, 347, 349, 352, 359

B-Money, 27

borrowing, 182, 185, 187

browser-based IDE, 67, 209, 212

by machine to machine, 113

Byzantine fault tolerant, 102

candidate block, 52, 54, 55

CDP, 183, 184

centralized model, 133

centralized network, 32

CFT, 102

Chaincode, 66, 103

Channels, 101, 103, 108, 109, 205

Chocolatey, 252, 253

ChronoBan, 175

client-server protocol, 199, 306

Coinbase, 56, 57, 75, 143

Coinbase transaction, 56

Coinmarketcap, 61, 84, 92, 348

Cold Wallet, 75

collateral, 181, 185, 186

collateral., 181, 185, 186

collateralization ratio, 184

committing peers, 104, 107, 108

COMP, 186, 187

Compound, 181, 186, 187

Consensus, 30, 102, 166, 167, 351

consensus mechanism, 29, 33

consensus protocol, 100, 102, 167, 202, 345, 349

Corda, 66, 125, 126, 127, 128, 196

Corda networ, 126

CorDapps, 126

Cosigners, 313

crash fault tolerant, 102, 108

Cross-border money transfer, 129

Cross-border payment, 132, 145

crowdfunding, 67, 82, 84, 138, 209

crowdsale, 60

crypto assets, 71, 134, 137, 139, 140, 141, 142, 143, 192, 305, 346, 357

crypto crowdfunding, 28, 61, 85

crypto funds, 140, 352

crypto hedge fund, 2, 140, 305

crypto index funds, 140, 143

crypto money, 51

crypto token, 93

crypto wallet, 72, 73, 74, 93

Crypto wallet, 72

Crypto20, 142

cryptoassets, 71, 181, 182, 185, 356

cryptocurrency, 2, 26, 27, 28, 44, 51, 61, 71, 72, 75, 83, 84, 85, 86, 88, 93, 96, 102, 114, 115, 129, 133, 134, 135, 136, 137, 139, 143, 174, 175, 185, 189, 210, 217, 220, 224, 251, 256, 266, 345, 346, 347, 350, 356, 361, 362

cryptographic authentication technology, 29

cryptographic function, 57

cryptographic hashes, 38

Cryptokitties, 65, 194, 198, 202, 206

cTokens, 186

current target, 37, 58, 59

custodian services, 140

cyberattack, 79, 80

cybersecurity, 173, 174

DAG, 115, 116

Dai, 44, 45, 183, 184

DAI, 186, 187, 188

DApps, 2, 60, 62, 70, 83, 96, 222

Data Authentication, 191

data protection, 173, 174

decentralized applications, 61, 67, 83, 96, 346, 350

decentralized digital ledger, 28

Decentralized exchanges, 181

Decentralized finance, 178

decentralized network, 29, 30, 33, 52, 164

decentralized platform, 61, 71, 102, 178

decrypt, 40, 47, 49

DeFi, 178, 179, 180, 181, 183, 186

Dharma, 181

Diamond Time-Lapse, 146, 191

Difficulty, 35, 37, 58, 59, 149

Digital Asset, 100, 192

digital assets, 65, 178, 183, 185, 192, 193, 340

Digital government, 164

digital signature, 47, 48

Digital Signature, 47, 49

Directed Acyclic Graph, 115, 116

distributed DNS, 200

distributed ledger technologies, 29, 113

DLT, 29, 98, 100, 101, 102, 103, 113, 125, 127, 222

Docker CE, 322, 323, 324

doorman service, 128

double spending, 43, 46

dYdX, 181, 187, 188

Electrum, 74, 306, 307, 311, 312, 313

Elix, 138

endorsers, 104, 106

EOS, 28, 142

ERC20 token, 91, 137, 185, 227, 229, 350, 354

ERC20 tokens, 185

ETH, 60, 62, 63, 64, 83, 84, 135, 136, 137, 138, 141, 181, 183, 187, 188, 205

Ether, 28, 60, 61, 62, 63, 64, 65, 96, 135, 137, 237, 242, 243, 245, 266, 267, 269, 282, 296

Ethereum, 2, 26, 28, 33, 48, 60, 61, 62, 65, 66, 67, 68, 69, 70, 71, 73, 74, 78, 83, 84, 91, 96, 100, 101, 107, 108, 113, 125, 135, 137, 138, 141, 143, 166, 181, 182, 183, 185, 186, 189, 192, 196, 198, 201, 202, 203, 204, 205, 206, 209, 210, 217, 222, 224, 227, 230, 235, 236, 240, 242, 251, 254, 255, 256, 257, 260, 263, 265, 272, 277, 285, 287, 290, 291, 295, 296, 341, 345, 349, 351, 353, 354, 360

Ethereum Classic, 28, 143, 224

Ethereum Mainnet, 60, 70, 91

Ethereum Virtual Machine, 61, 66, 84, 209, 230, 235, 251, 257

Ethereum Wallet, 73, 277, 287, 291

Etherscan, 63, 216, 303

ETHLend, 137

event management and ticketing, 222, 228

EventChain, 223, 227

Everledger, 146, 191

EVM, 61, 66, 209, 230, 235, 251, 257

exchange, 2, 65, 71, 75, 79, 80, 84, 86, 87, 92, 131, 165, 175, 348, 349, 356

Exchange Wallet, 75

financial transactions, 29, 67, 131, 173, 174, 209

Fog' and 'Mist' computing, 114

fork, 115, 116, 176

Fraud prevention, 173, 174

full-node wallet, 73

Ganache, 230, 231, 236, 237, 241, 243, 244, 245, 249, 272, 273

Gas, 62, 63, 64

gas fees, 63, 64

gas limit, 62, 64, 166

Gas Price, 62, 64

genesis block, 33, 53, 54, 288, 289, 290

Geth, 287, 292

git, 253, 287, 330

Go, 101, 287, 321, 327, 328

go-ethereum, 287

GUTS, 225

Gwei, 62, 63, 64

hacking, 71, 79, 80, 102, 178

hardware wallets, 75, 76, 140

Hardware wallets, 76

Hash, 35, 39

hash algorithm, 52, 57

hash function, 39, 40, 57, 58

hashing algorithm, 33, 40, 41

hexadecimal characters, 39

HodlBot, 143

hot wallet, 73, 74, 79, 80, 349

HR, 172, 173, 174, 175, 176

HTTP, 199, 200, 201

Huobi, 75

Hyperledger Fabric, 66, 100, 101, 102, 103, 104, 107, 109, 110, 111, 156, 162, 196, 320, 321, 328, 330

Hyperledger Greenhouse, 98

Hyperledger Sawtooth, 66

ICO, 28, 61, 62, 64, 82, 83, 84, 85, 86, 92, 94, 185, 189, 195, 277

IEO, 2, 85, 86, 87, 88, 89, 90, 91, 92, 94

IEO launchpads, 86

immutability, 40, 116, 151

immutable, 38, 93, 133, 153, 174, 175, 191, 224

Immutable, 30

Injected Web 3 Ropsten, 300

interest rate, 185

Internet of Things, 113, 115

Interplanetary File System, 199

IoT, 65, 67, 97, 113, 114, 115, 209

IoT technologies, 113

IOTA, 113, 114, 115, 116, 117, 118, 121, 122, 123, 124, 125, 126

IPFS, 70, 199, 200, 222

IPO, 82, 83, 89, 93, 94

Java, 101, 126, 195

JSON, 170, 288

JVM runtime environment, 126

Kafka, 107

Kickstarter, 82, 84

KYC, 87, 88, 94, 128, 192

KYC/AML, 87, 88

LaborX, 175

LAVA, 226

Lazy Tips, 121, 122

ledger, 27, 29, 33, 51, 97, 98, 100, 103, 104, 106, 108, 110, 113, 115, 123, 125, 126, 133, 146, 153, 156, 157, 163, 172, 223, 320, 340, 360

Ledger, 76, 103, 113, 115, 357

Ledger Nano S, 76, 357

LEND token, 185

Lending, 184, 187

light wallet,, 73

Lightning network, 202, 204

Linux Foundation, 97, 100, 320

liquidators, 186

liquidity, 181, 184, 186

Litecoin, 28, 135, 142, 143

Luno, 75

LuxTag, 147

M2M, 113, 114, 115, 155

Maker Governance, 183

Maker Protocol, 183

MakerDao, 184

MakerDAO, 181, 182, 183

mapping, 218, 219, 279, 354

margin trading, 187

Master Public Key, 312

Mastercoin, 84

Membership service provider, 103

memory pool, 55

Merkle root, 42

Merkle tree, 40, 41

Merkle trees, 27

metadata, 35, 40

MetaMask,, 74, 243

miner, 37, 53, 54, 57, 58, 63, 292, 293

mining, 28, 30, 33, 36, 37, 41, 46, 51, 52, 53, 54, 55, 56, 57, 58, 102, 107, 138, 292, 293

mining algorithm, 51, 57

MKR, 183, 184

MPK), 312

MSD, 183

MSP, 110, 111

Multi collateral Dai, 183

multisig wallet, 74, 305, 306, 317, 357, 358

National Digital ID Blockchain Net, 166, 167, 168, 169, 170

Nebulis., 200

NEXO, 94, 135, 136, 137

NextCoin, 84

Nick Szabo, 28, 43, 66

node, 33, 34, 41, 42, 55, 56, 58, 61, 72, 73, 74, 117, 119, 126, 128, 141, 167, 168, 169, 198, 199, 200, 255, 275, 287, 295, 326, 327, 331, 353

Node.js, 101, 231, 254, 321, 326, 327

NodeJs, 287

Nonce, 35, 36

Oasis, 184

offline wallet, 75

Okcoin, 131

Oklink, 131

Omni Layer, 84

on-chain governance, 169

Online wallet, 75

open governance, 99

open source, 97, 99, 115, 125, 131

Oracle Virtual Box., 321

Ordering service, 103, 110, 156

P2P lending, 132, 133, 134, 138, 346, 350

paper wallet, 77, 78

parent chain, 203

PAX, 134, 135

PeaCounts, 176

Peers, 103, 104, 110

peer-to-peer network, 28, 30, 45, 70, 126, 223, 227

PKI, 47

Plasma, 202, 203, 204, 205, 206

Plasma Chain, 206

PoA, 100, 166, 167, 341, 351

Poisson Point Process, 118

Polymath, 94, 193

PouchNATION, 226

PoW, 52, 166, 167, 202, 341

PowerShell, 252, 253, 254, 256

private key, 47, 48, 49, 73, 74, 75, 77, 80, 191, 305, 356, 358

private network., 91

programmable blockchain, 61

proof of authority, 100

proof of work, 37, 46, 57

Proof of Work, 52, 55, 56, 57

provenance tracking, 146

public key, 47, 48, 49, 77

public key cryptography, 47

QR code, 75

R3, 125, 131, 196

remittances, 129, 130, 131

Remix, 67, 68, 209, 212, 213, 214, 215, 295, 298

Remix IDE, 68, 212, 213, 214, 215

reputation-based consensus algorithm, 166, 351

reward, 52, 56, 57, 138

Ripple, 28, 131, 141

Ropsten Faucet, 296

Ropsten test network, 166

Rospten test net, 299

RW Sets, 106

SALT, 134, 135, 136, 137

Satoshi Nakamoto, 27, 43, 44, 66, 71, 82

SBFT, 107

scalability, 96, 115, 132, 198, 202, 205

Security Token Offering, 85, 92

SHA256, 57

Signature Verification Algorithm, 111, 112

signed integer, 211

Simplified Byzantine Fault Tolerance, 107

simplified payment verification, 72, 74

Single Collateral Dai, 183

smart contract, 62, 63, 64, 65, 66, 68, 91, 93, 98, 102, 103, 110, 134, 137, 138, 156, 175, 176, 193, 194, 195, 198, 205, 206, 210, 212, 213, 217, 222, 227, 228, 231, 233, 234, 235, 238, 239, 240, 241, 242, 243, 256, 258, 263, 279, 283, 295, 298, 345, 349, 350, 354

smart contracts, 181, 185, 188

Solidity, 2, 67, 68, 69, 101, 126, 195, 209, 210, 211, 212, 217, 222, 228, 229, 233, 235, 238, 252, 256, 257, 279, 295, 350, 354

Solidity Plugin, 67, 209, 212

SOLO, 107

spot trading, 187

SPV wallet, 74

stablecoin, 183

state channel, 205

state variable, 69, 219

STO, 85, 92, 93, 94, 189

supply chain management, 2, 67, 97, 148, 164, 194, 209, 346, 350

Swift, 130

Tangle, 115, 116, 117, 118, 120, 121, 122, 124, 125, 126

Timestamp, 35, 37, 63

TLS-encrypted messages, 127

tokenise, 176

tokenization, 93, 95

tokenized physical assets, 180

tokenomics, 90

transaction fees, 35, 51, 52, 56, 227

transaction pool, 55

Transaction Tracking, 145

transaction workflow, 105

Transparent, 29

Trezor, 76, 77

Tron, 66

Truffle, 230, 231, 232, 233, 234, 238, 239, 240, 241, 246, 251, 252, 254, 256, 257, 258, 260, 261, 263, 269, 270, 272

Truffle Box, 231, 232, 240, 246

TUSD, 134, 135, 138

two factor encryption, 80

Ubuntu, 320, 321, 322

uint, 68, 69, 211, 212, 213, 214, 218, 219, 234

undercollateralized, 184, 186

UNI, 187

unsigned integer, 69, 211, 213, 215

unweighted random walk, 120, 121, 122, 124

URW, 121

USDC, 134, 135, 187

USDT, 187

validator, 162, 168, 206, 351, 352

Visual Studio Code, 67, 209, 212, 253, 256, 287, 295

Vitalik Buterin, 28, 60, 66, 83, 84, 202

VS Code, 236, 248, 252, 255, 256

Wal-Mart, 145

WBTC, 187

Web3 is, 263

Wei Dai, 27, 43, 44

weighted random walk, 121, 123, 124

whitepaper, 46, 47, 51, 85, 90, 142, 164, 343, 354

WRW, 121, 123

X-Road, 164, 165

XRP, 28, 136, 141

zk-Snarks protocol, 176

ZRX, 187

References

Aitken, R. (2019, March). *Kickstarter Versus 'Crypto' ICOs: Are Traditional Platforms Having The Last Laugh?* Retrieved from Forbes: https://www.forbes.com/sites/rogeraitken/2019/03/19/kickstarter-versus-crypto-icos-are-traditional-platforms-having-the-last-laugh/#4c781ba26a2c

Bahrynovska, T. (2019, March 13). *How Smart Contract Can Boost the Ticketing Industry.* Retrieved from https://applicature.com/blog/blockchain-technology/smart-contracts-in-the-ticketing-industry

Ball, C. (2018). *Blockchain and Ethereum -- How Can They Be Used for Events?* Retrieved from Corbin Ball & Co.: https://www.corbinball.com/article/42-technology-how-to-use-it-better/224-blockchain-and-ethereum-how-can-they-be-used-for-events

Bitcoin Electrum. (n.d.). *Creating a multisig wallet.* Retrieved from https://bitcoinelectrum.com/creating-a-multisig-wallet/

Bitcoin Wiki. (n.d.). *Wei Dai.* Retrieved from https://en.bitcoin.it/wiki/Wei_Dai

Bitwise . (n.d.). *The Bitwise 10 Crypto Index Fund.* Retrieved from https://www.bitwiseinvestments.com/funds/Bitwise-10

Brant Carson, G. R. (n.d.). *Blockchain beyond the hype: What is the strategic business value?* Retrieved from McKinsey Digital: https://www.mckinsey.com/business-functions/mckinsey-digital/our-insights/blockchain-beyond-the-hype-what-is-the-strategic-business-value

Brooke, S. (2018, July). *How Will Blockchain Make Predictive Analytics Accessible?* Retrieved from https://towardsdatascience.com/how-will-blockchain-make-predictive-analytics-accessible-d256d543081d

Day, N. (2018). *What Are Smart Contracts and How Will They Affect Payroll and HR? Blockchain Article 4/10.* Retrieved from Recruitment Group: https://jgarecruitment.com/what-are-smart-contracts-and-how-will-they-affect-payroll-and-hr-blockchain-article-410/

DevTeam.Space. (n.d.). *Private Blockchain: Implementation Guide.* Retrieved from https://www.devteam.space/blog/private-blockchain-implementation-guide/

Don Tapscott, A. T. (2017). Blockchain Revolution: How the Technology Behind Bitcoin and Other Cryptocurrencies Is Changing the World. Portfolio.

Ethereum Papaer Wallet Generator. (n.d.). Retrieved from https://generatepaperwallet.com/ethereum/index.html

Gale, S. F. (2018). *Blockchain: The Future of HR?* Retrieved from Workforce: https://www.workforce.com/news/blockchain-future-hr

GBT. (2019, August 20). *[Crypto wallet]Private wallet VS Exchange wallet (feat. Planet Wallet).* Retrieved from https://medium.com/grabityio/crypto-wallet-private-wallet-vs-exchange-wallet-feat-planet-wallet-61b29942439c

Hot wallet. (n.d.). Retrieved from https://en.bitcoin.it/wiki/Hot_wallet

Leewayhertz. (n.d.). *Peer to Peer Lending Blockchain Platform.* Retrieved from https://www.leewayhertz.com/blockchain-p2p-lending-platform/

Maltseva, D. (2018, May 17). *10 most popular & promising Blockchain platforms.* Retrieved from https://dev.to/dianamaltseva8/10-most-popular--promising-blockchain-platforms-djo

Marx, L. (2018, July 5). Storing Data on the Blockchain: The Developers Guide.

Mearian, L. (2019, April 17). *What's a crypto wallet (and how does it manage digital currency)?* Retrieved from https://www.computerworld.com/article/3389678/whats-a-crypto-wallet-and-does-it-manage-digital-currency.html

Mitchell, S. (2018, 12 28). *Top 5 Paper Wallets*. Retrieved from https://coinrevolution.com/top-5-paper-wallets/

Mogan Creek Digital Assets with Bitwise. (2019). *An index fund built for the world's leading institutions*. Retrieved from https://www.digitalassetindexfund.com/

Nakamoto, S. (2009, January 3). *Bitcoin: A Peer-to-Peer Electronic Cash System*. Retrieved from https://bitcoin.org/bitcoin.pdf

Passion, S. (2019, February 7). *Create Your Own Cryptocurrency in Private Consortium Network Ethereum Azure Blockchain*. Retrieved from https://www.codeproject.com/Articles/1276651/Create-Your-Own-Cryptocurrency-in-Private-Consorti

PWC UK. (2017). *How blockchain technology could impact HR and the world of work*. Retrieved from PWC : https://www.pwc.co.uk/issues/futuretax/how-blockchain-can-impact-hr-and-the-world-of-work.html#cta-1

Rosic, A. (2017). *Paper Wallet Guide: How to Protect Your Cryptocurrenc*. Retrieved from https://blockgeeks.com/guides/paper-wallet-guide/

SALT. (n.d.). https://www.saltlending.com/.

Solidity. (n.d.). Retrieved from https://solidity.readthedocs.io/en/v0.4.24/types.html

TRUFFLE SUITE. (n.d.). *TRUFFLE- Smart Contracts Made Sweeter.* Retrieved from https://www.trufflesuite.com/

Verlinden, N. (2018). *Back to Basics: What is Digital HR?* Retrieved from AIHR Digital: https://www.digitalhrtech.com/back-to-basics-what-is-digital-hr/

Verlinden, N. (2018). *HR Digital Transformation: The 6 Stages of Successful HR Transformation.* Retrieved from AIHR Digital: https://www.digitalhrtech.com/guide-hr-digital-transformation-hr-transformation/

Verlinden, N. (2018). *https://www.digitalhrtech.com/ai-in-hr-whats-all-the-fuss-about/.* Retrieved from AIHR Digital: https://www.digitalhrtech.com/ai-in-hr-whats-all-the-fuss-about/

Verlinden, N. (2018). *Top 15 Digital HR Tech Trends for 2018.* Retrieved from AIHR Digital: https://www.digitalhrtech.com/digital-hr-trends-hr-tech-trends-2018/

Wachal, M. (2018, August 16). *What is a blockchain wallet?* Retrieved from https://blog.softwaremill.com/what-is-a-blockchain-wallet-bbb30fbf97f8

www.ingramcontent.com/pod-product-compliance
Lightning Source LLC
Chambersburg PA
CBHW071348210526
45465CB00001B/13